THE IRISH RAJ

Illustrated Stories about Irish in India and Indians in Ireland

The Irish Raj

Illustrated Stories about Irish in India and Indians in Ireland

Narinder Kapur

Greystone Press
Antrim, N Ireland

Published in 1997 by
Greystone Press
Caulside Drive
Antrim
Northern Ireland
BT41 2RS

ISBN 1 870157 24 9

Printed by W & G Baird Limited, Northern Ireland

Dedication

This work is dedicated to those in this book who settled in Ireland and in India, and who are sadly no longer with us. I pay tribute to their determination, to their self-sacrifice and to their generosity.

My personal dedication is to the memory of my cousin, Sat Pal Kapur (1920–1977), who came to Ireland in 1947.

Acknowledgements

Many people and organizations have contributed directly or indirectly to this book.

I thank the Community Relations Unit, Northern Ireland, and in particular Dr Tom Gardner and Mrs Marguerite Egan, for providing me with funding that helped defray many of my research costs, and also for many helpful suggestions. The views in this book are of course my own, and do not represent those of the Community Relations Unit.

I thank those who have kindly provided financial sponsorship to help with the printing of the book. At the time of printing, these included Shanti Treon, Steven Kher, Suman Kher, Suneil Kher, Raj Kapur, Davinder Kapur, Joginder Kapur, Jagesh Kapur and Raman Kapur.

I am grateful to Mr Bagwan Das Dhand who, in the 1960s, prepared some notes towards a possible book of this type. These notes, together with his helpful discussions with me, have been invaluable.

Numerous people in Northern Ireland, the Irish Republic and England have been of help. It is not possible to name them all, but they have included – Mr A S Anand, Mr C L Treon, Shanti Treon, Mr P Gupta, Mrs F Sumra, Dr Jeawon, Mr S Sumra, Dr R Powell, Mrs P Abbott, Mr K Sumra, Mr M Singh, Mr B Negi, Mr H Bedi, Mr R P Mehan, Mr R Dean, Tohani family, Mr N L Abroal, Mr D Rana, Mr K Panesar, Ms Lynn Hoggarth, Mr L Chada, Mr B Tandon, Mr S Kher, Mrs A Kapur, Miss Charlotte Vij, Mr Lal Dingliana, Dr Prabhu Kulkarni, Mrs Sunita Sharma, Mr Balwant Negi, Mr Michael Coleman, Dr Davinder Kapur and Dr Raj Kapur.

I conducted many interviews with individuals both in Northern Ireland and the Irish Republic. Those interviews gave me much pleasure, and also a vast amount of information. It was not possible to include all such interview material in this book, but I am nevertheless grateful to every person I interviewed. I hope that I have accurately reflected the facts and the stories that I gathered in my field work. There are bound to be a few errors in historical material with an autobiographical component, especially where it is in part based on retrospective material. Any inaccuracies or errors in this work are my responsibility. My apologies for any errors that have crept in and to any individuals I may have omitted to thank in these Acknowledgements.

I thank my wife Ritu, my two daughters, Sarina and Soniya, and my son Shashi, for putting up with my many absences from home while I have been working on this book.

As in the case of my previous books, the royalties from this book will go to charitable causes in India and Northern Ireland.

Preface

This book is mainly about the journeys that took Irishmen to India and, more particularly, about the journeys that took Indians from their mother country to the island of Ireland. For practical reasons, I have concentrated on those who came from India to settle in Northern Ireland – the major flow of settlers was in fact in this particular direction. Many Indians who settled in Ireland lived in that area of west India, in Punjab, that later became part of Pakistan, so many of the stories in the book would also apply to those from the rest of the subcontinent.

The Roman writer, Pliny the Younger, is reported to have said –

> I hold it a noble task to rescue from oblivion those who deserve to be remembered.

Books about the lives of people, many of whom may have long since died, enable them to 'live on'. Such books can be one of our few links with the past. Without them, precious memories and knowledge may be lost for ever. This book is not intended to be an academic treatise. I would prefer it to be seen as a story book, stories with lessons. The only good reason for looking to the past is so that we can learn lessons for the future. The many stories in this book provide ample lessons for the challenges of today and tomorrow.

Narinder Kapur
Southampton, February 1997

Map Of Ireland

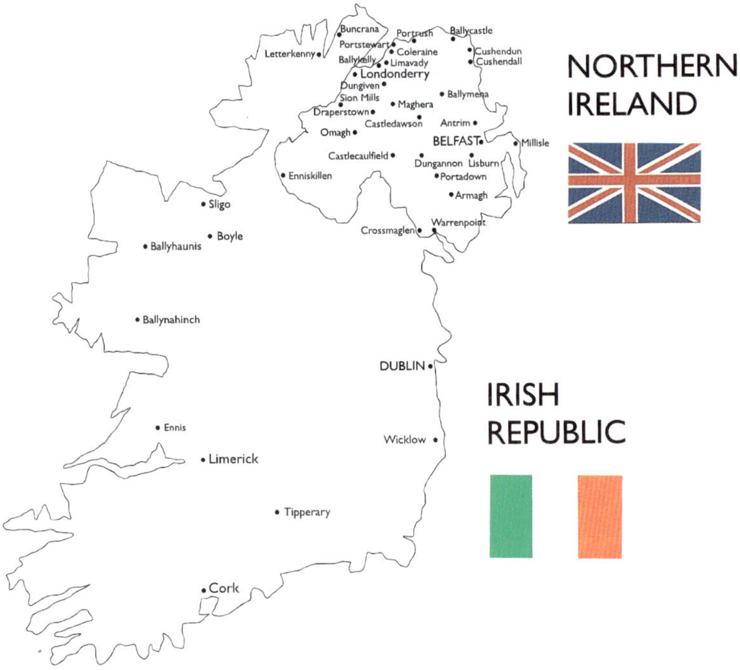

Ireland is the 20th largest island in the world. It is approximately 250 miles long and 150 miles wide. It contains the largest lake in the British Isles (Lough Neagh in Northern Ireland), and it also has the longest river in the British Isles – the Shannon in the Irish Republic. The population of the Irish Republic is around 3.5 million, while the population of Northern Ireland is around 1.5 million. Many Irish men and women emigrated to other parts of the world in the 19th and 20th centuries – it is thought that there are around 60 million people world-wide who claim some form of Irish ancestry. Ireland has one native language, Celtic. It is estimated that around one third of the population in the Irish Republic can speak some Celtic, though relatively few speak it as fluently as English. Everyone in both parts of Ireland would be conversant with English. Both India and Ireland have adopted English as their effective first language.

As in the case of the Indian flag, the major colours of the flag of the Irish Republic are green, white and orange. The Irish Republic flag is thought to have been inspired by the French flag, which is blue, white and red. The green of the Irish Republic flag is said to refer to the emerald green of Ireland, the orange to refer to the Protestant tradition, and the white to stand for peace. The current Irish Republic flag came into use in 1921, and was officially adopted as the national flag in 1937.

The official flag of Northern Ireland is the Union Jack, which is the flag of the United Kingdom. The similarities between the flag of India and the flag of the Irish Republic once led to a delicate encounter in Northern Ireland, where flags can sometimes generate strong emotions. In the 1960s, during a visit of the Indian High Commissioner to the Indian community in Northern Ireland, a few Indians decided to fly the Indian flag above the building where a reception for the High Commissioner was taking place. When the flag was seen by some locals, it was mistaken for the flag of the Irish Republic. A small crowd then gathered, demanding that the flag be taken down. It was only after the crowd was reassured that the flag was the flag of India, and not the flag of the Irish Republic, that calm was restored!

Map Of India

India is the seventh largest country in the world. From north to south, it measures almost 2000 miles, and from east to west it is around 1200 miles. India's population is close to 900 million. It is the second most populous country in the world, after China, and its population is almost that of Africa and South America combined. It has around 16 main languages, together with many variations of these – a recent survey found 322 separate languages and dialects, together with 24 different scripts. The sixteen languages are - Assamese, Bengali, English, Gujarati, Hindi, Kannada, Kashmiri, Malayali, Marathi, Oriya, Punjabi, Sanskrit, Sindhi, Tamil, Telugu and Urdu. There are seven main religions in India – Hinduism, Jainism, Buddhism, Islam, Sikhism, Christianity, and Zoroastrianism. Although the majority of the population are Hindus, around 10% of the population are Moslems. Christianity dates back to 52 A.D., when St Thomas is said to have landed on the western coast of India.

As in the case of the Irish flag, the main colours of the Indian flag are green, white and orange. The current Indian flag derived from the flag of the Indian National Congress, the political party that was at the forefront of India's independence movement – that earlier flag was green, white and red. In the centre white band of the Indian flag is a navy-blue wheel with 24 spokes. The wheel is known as chakra, and is associated with the Buddhist King, Asoka. The 24 spokes are said to represent the 24 hours of the day. It is also said that the green of the Indian flag represents faith, the white represents truth and peace, and the orange represents courage and sacrifice. The current Indian flag dates from 1933, and it was officially adopted as the national flag in 1947.

CONTENTS

1: IMPERIAL TIES

India and Ireland – two beautiful countries separated by over five thousand miles, separated by language and separated by religion, but joined together by an imperial past. During that imperial past, both countries had also been linked by bonds that were forged by Irish men and women who had travelled to India. Many of them were to find themselves enchanted, some for a short time and some for a life-time, by the far away country in the orient to which they had ventured.

The imperial histories of India and Ireland are well known. Since 1800, Ireland had been an integral part of the United Kingdom. India had been under British rule from a similar time period, and under its general influence since 1600. That influence arose as a result of the East India Company.

THE EAST INDIA COMPANY

The East India Company was founded in 1600 by a group of London merchants under Royal Charter. Its aim was to trade with India and parts of Asia. The company lasted around 350 years. By 1613, the East India Company had two trading stations, one in Surat in western India to deal with Indian affairs, and one in Bantam in the island of Java in the East Indies, to deal with the far east trade. The East India Company began to build its own ships, and by 1620 it had 76 ships and 12 trading stations in the east. At the time, it was one of the largest employers in Great Britain.

There is an unusual link between the East India Company and Ireland. Amongst the original members of the East India Company was a man called William Burrell, a shipwright by profession. One of his duties was to provide timber for the company, so that it could be used for shipbuilding. On his advice, in the early 1600s the East India Company bought and leased lands at Dundaniel on the Bandon River in the Irish Republic. The East India Company also established iron works there.

The Company planned to build all their new ships in that part of Ireland, but in 1615 the decision was reversed. The Company had about 300 English settlers there, and their total wage bill came to £40 per week. Three towns were especially built to house the settlers, these being called Thomas, Hope and Bantam (these were also the names of three ships belonging to the East India Company). The iron works in that area lasted till 1641. Dams and weirs were also built, but these caused resentment among the local people. Lord Boyle, mayor of Cork at the time, was also unhappy with the situation. In the 1620s, he acquired much of the land in the area, and he effectively became William Burrell's landlord. This factor, together with the dwindling supplies of timber, gradually led to the decline of the East India Company's presence in Ireland.

An Irishman from County Cork, by the name of Laurence Sullivan, worked for the East India Company, initially for a number of years in Bombay. He later returned to London and rose to the position of Company Chairman. He gained a reputation for being an efficient and fair-minded official of the company.

Unlike the English army in the 18th century, the East India Company never imposed a ban on Catholics entering its service. The Company had its own regiments, with recruiting offices in Ireland, and many of their soldiers were Irishmen – initially, they mainly comprised Protestants from Ireland but they later included a number of Catholics. The records of the Bengal army, run by the East India Company, indicate that from 1825 to 1850, out of the 7620 recruits 47.9% were Irish, whereas only 37.3% were English.

Many years later, the East India Company bought a large estate in County Down in Northern Ireland. One of the directors of the East India Company, who had no male children, wished for his shares to be somehow given to his niece. At that time, the rule of the East India Company was that women could not own shares in the company. So, instead, the Company sold his shares and bought several thousand acres of land in Northern Ireland with the money. This land was given to his niece, whose family lived in County Down. This estate, known as Mount Stewart, is now owned by the National Trust.

EYRE COOTE. *An Irishman who served as a soldier in India in the mid-1700s.*

IRISH COME TO INDIA

Many Irish men and women spent a large part of their life in India. Eyre Coote was an Irishman, born in Limerick in 1726. At the age of 28 years, he went to India, and he soon became captain of the 39th regiment, serving with distinction in Bengal. Around this time, a number of Irish soldiers were also in India, but on the side of the French! There had apparently been a tradition of Irishmen, especially Irish Catholics, being driven to join the French army due to repression in Ireland by the English and also due to the ban on Catholics serving in the English army. In 1756, when the English tried to drive the French out of India, it was an Irish officer with his Irish regiment who was employed by the French to defeat the English – the officer was Thomas Lally, originally from County Galway. He was however decisively beaten by his fellow Irishman Coote in a battle in 1761. Pondicherry, which was the main French stronghold in India, fell to the English and Lally was captured, along with his regiment. Coote himself came back to England, and was a member of Parliament for a number of years, though he returned to India in 1777.

Rajah Thomas

George Thomas was a remarkable young Irishman from Tipperary who went to India in 1781 at the tender age of 25 years. His story is told in detail in a book by Maurice Hennessy called the *Maharaja of Tipperary.* Thomas initially joined and then deserted the British Navy. He initially became the commander of an army of an Indian princess, Begum Somru, but he later changed his allegiance to the governor of a nearby territory. After that governor's death, he set himself up as a Rajah in his own territory in northern India, and he extended his territory with frequent raids. He was recognised as one of the great military leaders of eighteenth century India, particularly by his opponents, the officers of the British Army. When they captured him, they sportingly gave a dinner in his honour.

GEORGE THOMAS. *A young Irishman from Tipperary who went to India in 1781 and stayed as a soldier for many years.*

Thomas fell in love with many Indian princesses in his time. He had a love affair with the Begum Somru, who plotted his destruction after she was overthrown from her throne, even though he tried to reinstate her. In the territory that he ruled in northern India, Thomas had his own army and he pioneered welfare schemes for the widows and orphans of his soldiers. When fighting in battle, he led his men from the front rather than send them out ahead of him.

There were other Irishmen, similar to Thomas, who went it alone and served and gained distinction under the princely rulers of Indian states rather than in the regiments of the East India Company. One person of note was William Henry Tone, brother of the famous Irishman Wolf Tone. He initially joined the East India Company as a solider, but later joined the service of Indian rulers, reaching the rank of Colonel, before being killed during the storming of a fort.

The Telegraph Professor

In the early 1800s a remarkable Irishman came to India. His name was W. B. O'Shaughnessy who qualified as a doctor after studying in Edinburgh. He was sent to India where he became Professor of Chemistry in the Calcutta Medical College. As a doctor, he was the first to introduce intravenous fluids in the treatment of cholera. However, he also had many other talents, as was often the case for doctors of that period. He experimented with what was then called the electric telegraph. Lord Dalhousie – the then Governor-General of India – appointed Professor O'Shaughnessy as Director General of Telegraphs. In 1858, O'Shaughnessy initiated the laying of telegraph cables in Calcutta. This innovation was used to some effect – when a mutiny occurred in Meerut, near Delhi, the telegraph line was able to convey the news to Calcutta (the capital of India and of the British Raj at that time), which was 1000 miles away, and the mutiny could then be quelled. Queen Victoria was so impressed that she knighted him shortly afterwards.

Civil Service

In the 19th and 20th centuries, the Indian Civil Service was a prestigious service. Posts in that service were highly coveted, and are still much sought after in India today. Examinations for entry to the service were held in Great Britain as well as in India. The records of Queen's University, Belfast (or Queen's College as it was then known) note that in 1857, of the twelve places in the Indian Civil Service offered in that year throughout the whole of the United Kingdom three places went to students from Queen's College. The records also note that one of its graduates – David Barbour – entered the prestigious Indian Civil Service in 1862. He became secretary to the finance department of the Indian government in 1882, and financial member of the governor general's council in 1888. A number of Queens' University staff were examiners for Indian Civil Service entry examinations, including Professor George Craik (b.1798-d.1866) and Professor William Graham (b.1839-d.1911). The records of Queen's University also note that students of Indian origin attended the university – for example, documents for the academic year 1920–21 indicate several law students with names such as Susil Chaudhary and Suresh Sen.

Even in the 19th century, there were significant numbers of Irishmen in the Indian Civil Service and other fields such as the armed services. In fact, it is said that there were more individuals of Irish descent than of Scottish descent amongst the transient British population in India. The Irish were in fact at the forefront of the British presence, judging from the oft-quoted sarcasm about the British empire:

> The Irish fought for it, the Scottish and Welsh ran it, but the English kept the profits.

The proportion of Irish in the Indian Civil Service increased dramatically after 1855 (from 5% to 24%). 1855 was the date when competitive examinations rather than patronage were the primary selection mechanisms for deciding entry into the Indian Civil Service. In 1857, when Ireland's population was 20% of the United Kingdom, Irish universities supplied no less than 33% of the Indian Civil Service recruits for that year. Irish universities encouraged entry into the Indian Civil Service – in the late 1850s, Trinity College Dublin established chairs in Sanskrit and Arabic and began courses in zoology, all of which were subjects that were tested in the Indian Civil Service exams. Queen's University, at its college in Belfast, also had a comprehensive Indian language teaching programme. Its college in Cork offered courses in Indian history and geography, as well as in Hindu and Moslem law. The merits of work in the Indian Civil Service were acclaimed by Irish Newspapers – for example, the Connaught Telegraph of April 21, 1906 reported that the Indian Civil Service offered to young people in Ireland:

> A great, almost incredible, chance of passing from obscurity to glory, from grinding poverty to wealth…It was whispered that the salary began at the enormous figure of £800 per year.

Links between the governing establishment in India and Ireland remained strong in the second half of the nineteenth century. In the 1890s, seven of the eight Indian provinces (including Burma) were run by Irishmen. Sir Anthony MacDonnel, an Irishman who attained a high position in the Indian Civil Service in the 1890s, noted that this period was one "when Ireland had temporarily relieved England of the task of governing India". By the late 1800s and early 1900s, there was a gradual decline in the number of Irish men in the Indian Civil Service. This was due to a number of reasons, including changes to the recruitment procedures such that they now favoured those who came from English public schools. There was also the rise of nationalism in Ireland and the inevitable conflicts that resulted in the minds of Irishmen who would be supporting one imperial system abroad, while becoming more aware of efforts to overthrow a similar imperial system back home in Ireland.

MISSIONARY WORKERS IN INDIA

Irish religious workers first came to India in the early nineteenth century. These included Father John Fennelly who worked in Madras from 1842 onwards, and Father Daniel Murphy who worked in Hyderabad, also from the 1840s onwards. They helped to establish the Roman Catholic religion in the places where they worked. In addition to their missionary work, they established schools and hospitals that are still highly regarded in India today. Amongst the religious orders to have an influence in India were the Christian Brothers, the Patrician Brothers and the Loreto Nuns.

In 1911, an Irishman settled in Bombay, probably a missionary, wrote the following account in the *Catholic Bulletin:*

> There is revolutionary trouble in India, and there will be more of it...The revolutionary trouble is made by the educated classes. England sees that a great mistake was made in multiplying universities in India, but now the trouble cannot be remedied, and the country is over-run with young men who have honourably won their degrees. But there is no work for them. The Indian Civil Service provides snug billets for many English and Irish youths, and this aggravates the Indian, who is in every respect the equal of the imported official, so far as qualifications for the functions of the particular post are concerned.

The same writer, even though he was presumably in the business of converting Indians to Christianity, noted a piece of advice that was given much credence at the time –

> While the Indian stays in his own faith, he is content with a fistful of rice and a loin-cloth. But if he becomes a Christian, he'll want a beefsteak and a dress suit, and this darned country can't give it to him.

Some insights into the work of a Catholic missionary also come from another part of this account :

> Converts to Christianity are few and far between in India. It would mean social exile for a person to leave his form of belief and embrace Christianity. It certainly is a remarkable phenomenon that youths of both sexes will pass ten or fifteen years under the tuition of nuns and brothers and priests, and yet be uninfluenced in their religious views. What, then, is the good of labouring in their midst, some one will say? The Jesuit fathers, whose hospitality I shared and whose great kindness I was the recipient of in Bombay, explained the immense advantages resulting from Catholic education in India, apart from conversions: for all those who come under the influence of Catholic teaching know what the Church is and learn to respect Her. They afterwards become merged in the general population and occupy influential positions, and, if nothing else, give fair play to the Catholic Church, and dissipate the fabrications of bigotry and intolerance.

The Loreto Convent in India had its roots in Ireland, with the first Loreto institution being set up in Dublin in the 1800s. Thirteen brave nuns set off from Ireland for India in 1841, and after a four month sea-journey they arrived in Calcutta. They came with a dream of giving education to the masses in India who could not read or write, and of spreading the Christian message. The nuns were welcomed by the governor-general of Calcutta, Lord Auckland, who arranged living quarters for them. The nuns opened a school for the poor, and after some time seven girls' schools were opened in and around Calcutta. In 1846, a school was established in Darjeeling. The school in Darjeeling recently celebrated its 150th anniversary. Mother Francis Michael, who came to India as a young girl in 1936 and taught there for over 50 years, came all the way back from Ireland to take part in the celebration at Darjeeling. Today, there are around 19 Loreto convent schools throughout India, as well as similar schools throughout the world. Perhaps the most famous student of the Loreto order was Mother Teresa of Calcutta. She was Albanian in origin, though born in 1910 in Macedonia (formerly Yugoslavia). She went to Dublin in 1928 for a couple of months, at the age of 18 years, and spent that time with the Sisters of Loreto, mainly to learn English. She then went to Darjeeling, in northern India, where the Loreto Order had a base, and she underwent most of her training there. She spent most of her subsequent life in Calcutta, where she formed her own Missionaries of Charity, helping to alleviate poverty and spread the Christian faith.

A remarkable lady from the Irish Republic, Maureen Murphy, worked as a medical missionary in India from 1962 to 1982. She had in fact been born in Lahore in 1914, where her father was a civil engineer. Although Maureen Murphy received most of her education in Ireland, she spent much of her childhood and early life in India. She qualified in medicine from Trinity College, Dublin, in 1938 and worked both as an anaesthetist and as a child specialist. A few years after her husband's death in 1957, she returned to India under the auspices of the Church Missionary Society. Maureen Murphy worked for five years as Professor of Anaesthesia at the Christian Medical College, Ludhiana, in the state of Punjab in northern India. In 1967, she transferred to St Columba's Hospital in the town of Hazaribagh, a few hundred miles to the west of Calcutta in the state of Bihar. This hospital was supported by the Dublin University Mission. In 1982, Dr Murphy returned to Ireland, though she did occasionally return to India and Pakistan, doing medical locum work and revisiting the scenes of her early life. She died in Dublin in 1991. Shortly before she died, she completed a book about her life – *A Child of Two Continents* (1995, London, RSB Design).

Another remarkable individual from the Irish Republic pioneered the care of leprosy victims in India. The individual was Wellesley Bailey, who was born in Ireland in 1846 and spent most of his early years in Dublin. In 1869, he joined the American Presbyterian Mission in Ambala in the state of Punjab in northern India. It was around this time that he had his first contact with leprosy victims, an experience that had a major impact on him. With his wife Alice, he spent many years helping leprosy sufferers in India. He also set up fund-raising activities back in Ireland, and his friends in Dublin formed a society called 'The Mission to Lepers in India'. This organization grew from strength to strength, and in 1964 it changed its name to 'The Leprosy Mission'. This is now the major British charity working for leprosy victims throughout the world. Wellesley Bailey died in 1937.

Irish Presbyterian Church

Protestant Churches were also active in Indian missionary work. Since the early 1800s, the Church of Scotland and the London Missionary Society had kept a presence in the state of Gujarat, in western India. In August 1838, the Synod (special assembly) of the Presbyterian Church of Ireland had a special meeting in Belfast. After consulting with some of the Church of Scotland missionaries in Gujarat, they made a decision at this meeting to send two missionaries to Gujarat. Twenty ministers were asked to consider going, and from the seven who responded positively, two were selected. One was from Castledawson in Northern Ireland and the other was from Galway in the Irish Republic. The local congregation in Galway raised such a hue and cry that they succeeded in keeping their minister from going, so another one was chosen instead, this time from Portadown in Northern Ireland. The two ministers who went to India were James Glasgow, from Castledawson, and Alexander Kerr, from Portadown. In February 1841, they arrived with their wives in Bombay. Earlier missionaries in Gujarat had done some groundwork, such as translating the Bible into Gujarati, but a lot of work remained to be done. The two missionaries started working in the town of Rajkot. Within a few months, the kinds of sacrifices they would have to make soon became apparent – the Glasgow's infant daughter died, and shortly afterwards Alexander Kerr himself died. This was a severe blow to the mission, but others from Ireland came over to help out. By January 1843, four new missionaries had arrived, with mission stations opening in the towns of Rajkot, Porbandar (the birth place of Mahatma Gandhi), and Gogha. The first lady missionary from the Irish Presbyterian Church was a Miss Susan Brown, who came to Gujarat in 1874.

For these early Irish missionaries, times were difficult – infectious diseases were rampant, and medical facilities were limited. Twenty two Irish Presbyterian missionaries are buried in India, together with an unknown number of wives and children. The lives of the missionaries often involved the separation of children from parents, or husbands from wives. So it required a particular type of dedication to overcome such obstacles, together with making adjustments to climate, food, and the natural resentment amongst some Indians to foreign religious workers.

The first person to be converted to Christianity by an Irish Presbyterian missionary worker was reported to be a Moslem by the name of Abdur Rahman. He lived in Porbandar, and he was a distinguished and influential man in his own right. He had been a devout Moslem, regularly making a pilgrimage to Mecca, and he had to face a storm of persecution when he was baptised in 1843. He initially had to leave his wife and four children, though they later joined him in becoming Christians. In general, Indians who converted to Christianity had a tough time – many of them would be renounced by their families, would lose property and inheritance rights, and might even lose access to their spouses or children. In the light of these difficulties, the London Missionary Society, which had been working in Gujarat before the arrival of Irish Presbyterian missionaries, established a 'Christian village' in a place called Borshad. This would be a place where Indian Christians could live in peace and harmony. In 1859, the London Missionary Society handed over its work in Borshad to the Irish Presbyterian Church.

One problem that had to be overcome was that of caste – the converts to Christianity came from varied Hindu castes, and there was a natural tendency for people from different castes to live and eat separately. A difficult and brave decision was made for people from all castes, once they had become Christians, to mingle with each other. Quite often, Indian converts to Christianity still kept their Indian traditions – some kept their Hindu names, most continued to wear Indian dress, and some held onto traditions such as arranged marriages or segregation of the sexes in church.

Although Mahatma Gandhi was a devout Hindu, he admired the Christian religion and the work of the Irish Presbyterian Church. Gujarat was his home state, and he therefore spent a lot of time there. In 1920, he invited a missionary from that church, Mr J M Lyle, to teach English at his ashram (holy place), and the classes included a study of St Mark's Gospel. Mr Lyle was also influential in setting up the training of Christian workers, and in 1942 he helped to set up the Gujarat United

REV DR W G MULLIGAN, *on the left, who was a missionary of the Irish Presbyterian Church in India in the 1890s. He is shown in Gujarat, with his Indian assistant.*

School of Theology. Stevensons College in Ahmadabad, and Wilson College in Bombay, still have courses that retain the influence of missionaries trained by the Irish Presbyterian Church.

Ahmadabad, the largest city in Gujarat, had an Irish missionary presence from 1863 onwards. A mission school was built there in 1867 – the previous year, the government education department decided for the first time to give grants to mission schools, provided their programme included education that covered all religions. The opening of schools, often for children of lower castes, was a frequent avenue by which Christian influence was spread by missionaries. For example, the Dhed community, in the village of Anand in Gujarat, was provided with a school by Irish missionary workers and a Dhed Church Fund was in fact set up in Ireland, with donations being used to help build schools and churches. Schools were set up by the Irish Presbyterian Church in the cities of Surat, Ahmadabad and Rajkot, and these schools are still thriving today. Other skills were also taught – in 1932, a qualified agricultural missionary, Cecil Watson, was appointed and he helped farmers in Borshad improve their farming methods, e.g. by installing water pumps. Crafts were also taught – lace making was taught to the local Indian girls, using the latest patterns of Irish lace, and a flourishing cottage industry was set up.

Medical work by missionaries also helped to spread their influence. In 1890, two lady Irish Presbyterian missionaries – Miss S Roberts and Miss A Montgomery – started medical work in the village of Borshad. At first, they had difficulties in overcoming the suspicions of local women. One day, an Indian woman was brought to them unconscious, having suffered a snake bite. When she was restored to good health, the fame of the mission spread. Initially, the medical work consisted of dispensaries that gave away medicines. It was only later that clinics and hospitals were built.

The first missionary doctor from the Irish Presbyterian Church came to India in 1881 – he was Dr H D Obsorne, and he was stationed in the town of Gogha. Because of illness, he had to leave four years later, but he was followed in 1886 by the first woman missionary doctor, Dr Mary McGeorge. Sadly, she was drowned at sea in 1890, on her way back to India from leave in Ireland.

In 1899–1900, there was a great famine in Gujarat. This resulted in many orphans having to be cared for by Irish missionaries. In one area, 300 children died as a result of the famine, and the place where they died is commemorated by a Celtic cross. In 1900, there was also a cholera epidemic, and three Irish Presbyterian missionaries died in this outbreak. While saving the lives of the children was the first priority, many children later became converted to Christianity through their contact with the missionaries.

The first hospital to be opened by the Irish Presbyterian Church was in the village of Anand. It was opened in 1905 by Dr Neil Gavin. In 1919, a hospital was opened in the village of Borshad. This was run by Dr Sara McElderry. At one time, there was a great deal of lawlessness around Borshad. Local robbers were known as dacoits. On one occasion, Dr McElderry was called out by some men on an urgent maternity visit to a distant village. She rode her horse, alongside the men who had called her out. She asked them if they were not scared of the dacoits. 'Oh no', they replied, 'We are the dacoits!'

At one time, the Irish Presbyterian Church supported five hospitals in India. One of the doctors who worked in Gujarat in later years was Dr William Rutherford. He mainly worked in the town of Anand in the 1950s/early 1960s. He returned to Northern Ireland, and was to become famous for his work during the years of the troubles as consultant in charge of the casualty department of the Royal Victoria Hospital, Belfast.

The influence of the Irish Presbyterian Church continues to be felt, though indirectly and mainly through the activities of Indian Christians. It is estimated that in the State of Gujarat, 1% of the population are Christians, and that around 10% of these Christians have close links with the Irish Presbyterian Church. Many Gujaratis from India and East Africa now live in places such as Birmingham and Wembley, London. The Irish Presbyterian Church, in association with the Presbyterian Church of England, has maintained a presence in these communities, so that the needs of Gujarati Christians can be met.

The last serving Irish Presbyterian missionary in Gujarat was Dr Jean Shannon, who helped to establish a leprosy rehabilitation centre in the town of Prantij, near Ahmadabad. Dr Shannon came back to Ireland in 1990. Policies by the Indian government, which has discouraged missionaries entering India from other countries, and financial constraints, have limited the missionary work that was previously carried out. Christian churches in India are now self-sufficient and retain some links with churches in Ireland. Indeed, there is a feeling that Christian missionaries from India may be able to help in the reconciliation work in Northern Ireland, and in a sense do the reverse of what was done in India 150 years earlier.

At the time of writing, there were around 200 members of various Irish religious orders in India, though they are no longer called missionaries, and the work of active conversion stopped many years ago. Their main activities encompass work as teachers, doctors and nurses.

ULSTERMEN IN INDIA

A young Ulsterman, aged 25 years, went to India in 1781 as a colonial official. His name was Hugh Boyd, and he was born in Ballycastle, Co. Antrim, a small sea-side town on the north coast of Northern Ireland (the author's home town!). The Boyd family members were prominent landowners in Ballycastle, and were responsible for much of the development of that town. In addition to being a colonial official, Hugh Boyd himself was also a writer, and he wrote a few literary items in Indian magazines. During some of his time in India, Hugh Boyd was secretary to George Macartney, who also came from Northern Ireland and who was appointed governor of Madras in 1780. Macartney's time in Madras was considered by historians to mark a decisive phase in British imperial rule. Much of the financial corruption that had been present in India was put right by Macartney, and he helped to introduce a policy whereby the power of local Indian rulers was replaced by the power of British rulers.

In 1885, the Indian National Congress was formed in India – years later, this was to become the major movement that campaigned for Indian independence. The viceroy of India at the time was an Ulsterman, Lord Dufferin (born as Frederick Blackwood), an Ulster landlord and aristocrat with estates in County Down, Northern Ireland. He was also known as Baron of Clandeboye, and the Clandeboye estate is still in existence in Northern Ireland. Lord Dufferin saw similarities between the Indian National Congress and the Home Rule movement in Ireland – in August 1888, he commented that:

> Unless some definite line is taken in these matters, we shall soon have something like a Home Rule organization established in India, on Irish lines, under the patronage of Irish and Radical members of Parliament.

HUGH BOYD ESQ^{R}.

Supposed Author of Junius's Letters

HUGH BOYD. *An Irishman from North Antrim who was both a colonial official and a writer in India.*

Both Lord Dufferin and Lady Hariot Dufferin, who also came from County Down, were close friends of Rudyard Kipling's parents, and they also were well acquainted with Rudyard Kipling himself (Kipling's father was curator of the Lahore museum in Punjab). Both families would meet in Simla, which was the summer residence of the viceroy of India, and to where Kipling's parents were also accustomed to go during the hot summers. It is reported that Lord Dufferin's son twice proposed to Kipling's sister, but that she refused, commenting at a later date –

> I've always liked Irishmen, but I draw the line at marrying them.

LORD AND LADY DUFFERIN. *A County Down couple who held the highest colonial office in India, with Lord Dufferin as viceroy.*

Lady Hariot Dufferin did a great deal of medical charity work in India, and in particular initiated movements to provide proper medical and nursing care for women in India. This work was apparently at the instigation of Queen Victoria, for whom India was always a very special country. Lady Dufferin founded hospitals that were to be a lasting memorial to her – e.g. the Dufferin Hospital for Women in Nagpur was opened in 1888. She also raised money for charitable causes – the Dufferin Fund was still in place when she died in 1936, aged 93 years, her husband having died in 1900.

The Three Lawrence Brothers

Three brothers, John, Henry and George Lawrence, played an important part in political and military events in India. All three brothers had been educated at Foyle College, Londonderry. They were so devoted to the college and to the people they remembered in Londonderry that one Xmas, in 1851, they decided (together with another Foyle schoolfellow serving in Punjab, Mr Robert Montgomery) to send £50 to help an usher who had worked at the school and who was experiencing hard times.

Lord John Lawrence was later to become a viceroy of India. When he visited Lahore, the major city in the province of Punjab, he gave a pub-

LAWRENCE BROTHERS. *All three brothers had close links with Londonderry.*

LORD JOHN LAWRENCE. *Educated in Londonderry, he later became viceroy of India.*

lic address in which he told how the famous siege of Londonderry a couple of centuries earlier gave him inspiration during difficult and perilous times that he encountered in India. John Lawrence played a decisive role in the Indian mutiny of 1857, in which there was a rebellion in northern India of many native soldiers of the Bengal army ('sepoys'), helped by other Indian soldiers and by some of the local population. Cities such as Delhi and Lucknow fell to the rebels, with many Europeans being killed, but the mutiny was eventually quelled and the cities recaptured. John Lawrence helped to save the day for the British and to establish British military supremacy in India. His brother Henry Lawrence was made Assistant Revenue Surveyor in the North West Provinces of India, and was made Surveyor in 1835. Between 1843 and 1845, Henry Lawrence was resident in Nepal. During this period, he started the Lawrence Asylums for the children of European soldiers. His career in the Punjab, Rajasthan and Oudh was important in the establishment of law and order in those areas, but he was mainly renowned for his civil administration, reaching the position of agent to the governor general. Henry Lawrence died in 1857, having been fatally wounded during the siege of Lucknow – a small force of Europeans and loyal Indians was besieged by a huge number of rebels in the British headquarters in Lucknow, known as the Residency. It is said that his dying words were those associated with the siege of Londonderry around 200 years before – 'No surrender! Let every man die at his post'.

HENRY LAWRENCE. *Educated in Londonderry, he held a number of important civilian posts in India.*

HENRY LAWRENCE. *This picture shows him fatally wounded during the siege of Lucknow.*

His tomb in Lucknow reads – 'Here lies Henry Lawrence, who tried to do his duty'.

John Nicholson

JOHN NICHOLSON. *Born in Dublin, raised in Ulster, revered by his followers in India as a God.*

During the Indian mutiny of 1857, two other notable Irishmen met their deaths in the battlefield. One was John Nicholson, son of a Dublin doctor. He spent the first nine years of his life in Dublin. After his father's death, he moved with his family to Lisburn. He was educated at the Royal School, Dungannon and joined the East India Company's army in 1839. He led a company of British troops and Punjabi irregulars to confront mutinous soldiers in the Bengal army. He was killed during an assault near Delhi, which was eventually recaptured by the

British. He was regarded as a Victorian hero, and was considered to be a daring and ruthless soldier. Such was his reputation that he was given the status of a God by a local Hindu teacher as an incarnation of Hindu God Brahma. A sect of 'Nikalsainis' thus grew up – much to Nicholson's embarrassment, as he was a devout Christian! Even though he would whip and imprison his followers to deter them from worshipping him, the sect continued till his death in 1857. Some of the leaders of the sect even committed suicide on hearing of his death. It is reported that, in the 1950s, when John Nicholson's statue was being removed in New Delhi as part of the natural course of events after India gained independence, armed policemen were present. The police superintendent explained their presence by observing that –

> Jan Nikalsayn had been a very 'zubberdust' (fierce) man, and they could not be sure that his spirit would not return to mete out justice to those who disturbed his rest!

James Graham

The other Ulsterman was Dr James Graham, a doctor based at the town of Sialkot in north-west India. The Graham family originated from Lisburn, Northern Ireland, a town south of Belfast. Dr James Graham (born 1796, died 1857) was educated at the Royal School, Dungannon and qualified as a doctor in 1819. A year later he took up service as an assistant surgeon in the army of the East India Company

DR JAMES GRAHAM. *He worked as a doctor in north-west India. His family came from Lisburn, Northern Ireland.*

The story of the Graham family's connections with India around this time have been particularly well documented (*The Graham Indian Mutiny Papers,* Public Records Office of Northern Ireland, 1980). When the Indian mutiny took place in 1857, there were seven members of the Graham family in India – Dr James Graham, an army surgeon and his three sons, all of whom were in the service of the East India Company; his daughter and daughter-in-law; and a nephew. This nephew was also called James Graham – when he retired, he collected and organized the family's papers. The *Graham Indian Mutiny Papers* include letters written by members of the Graham family in India to their loved ones in Northern Ireland, describing events in India and in particular those associated with the Indian mutiny. The story of Dr Graham's death was reported in the Times newspaper of August 31, 1857. He was killed when the garrison at Sialkot mutinied. During the fighting, Dr Graham was driving his daughter to the safety of the fort in his gig (horse and carriage) when an enemy soldier on a horse rode up to him and shot him dead. His daughter seized the reins and drove screaming into the nearest compound with her father's body in her lap.

FOUR IRISH LADIES IN INDIA

Some Irish people made India their home, and were active in helping the under-privileged in India and in launching India's independence movement. Four were remarkable Irish ladies – Sister Nivedita, Annie Besant, Amy Carmichael and Gretta Cousins.

Sister Nivedita

Sister Nivedita was born as Margaret Noble in Dungannon, Northern Ireland on October 28, 1867. Her parents were of Scottish descent and had settled in Ireland. For a few years, she lived in Manchester as a child, but she had much of her schooling in Northern Ireland. When working as a young headmistress in London, she met Swami Vivekananda, a spiritual Indian leader, who happened to be lecturing in London, and she asked to join him in India. He wrote to her:

> Let me tell you frankly that I am now convinced that you have a great future in work for India. What is wanted is not a man, but a woman; a real lioness, to work for the Indians, women especially. India cannot yet produce great women, she must borrow them from other nations. Your education, sincerity, purity, immense love, determination and above all the Celtic blood, makes you just the woman wanted.

Yet, he also pointed out the hazards ahead –

> You cannot form any idea of the misery, the superstition, and the slavery that are there. You will be in the midst of a mass of half-naked men and women with quaint ideas of caste…shunning the white skin through fear or hatred and hated by them intensely…you will be looked upon by the white as a crank and your movements will be watched with suspicion.

Margaret Noble decided to go and live in India, arriving there in 1898. She became a Hindu, and she changed her name to Sister Nivedeta, meaning 'the consecrated one'. In 1899, she went back for a few years to England, but returned permanently to India in 1902. Although she was destined to live for only a further 13 years, dying in 1911 at the young age of 43 years, she had a major influence and inspiration on the Indians around her, both in her support for the Indian freedom struggle and also in her creative writings. She was involved in national movements in India, and in 1906 when floods and famine caused much distress in Bengal, she was actively involved in relief work. This resulted in her having malaria for a long period. Although the last year of her life was partly spent in England and America, she finally returned in 1911 to Darjeeling in northern India, where she had a major attack of dysentery. After her death, Rabindra Nath Tagore, the Indian Nobel laureate, described her as 'Lokmata' the 'mother [Mata] of Indian people [Lok]'. There is a memorial to Sister Nivedeta in the Darjeeling Cremation Ground, and it reads – 'Here reposes Sister Nivedita who gave her all to India'.

Annie Besant

Annie Besant, came to India in 1893. Both her parents were Irish, and she had previously been an active socialist in London. She was proud of her Irish blood, and she never failed to remind her English audiences that three quarters of her blood, and all her heart, was Irish! She had a brief and unhappy married life in London, marrying a Revd. Frank Besant in 1866. In 1875, the Theosophical Society was founded in London by a Russian born lady, Madam Blavatsky, who had come to England. Annie Besant was a disciple of Madam Blavatsky, and they both preached that Theosophy (the name for Blavatsky's brand of religious philosophy) was an eternal religion, and that "there is no religion higher than the truth". Theosophy was seen as part of a crusade against western imperialism. Around this time, Gandhi was in London as a Law student. He joined the Theosophical Society, and attended their meetings. He met leaders of the society such as Annie Besant, and he was heavily influenced by them. She was to spend 40 years in India. She established schools, wrote pamphlets and ran the 'World headquarters in Theosophy' at Adyar in Madras, southern India. An Irishman, James Cousins, was to become the Secretary of the Theosophical Society in Madras, and he took up the cause of Indian art around 1915. Cousins was editor of a journal, *New India.* He likened the excitement and intense interest aroused by Indian art to the days of the Irish Literary

ANNIE BESANT. *She was of Irish parentage and played a major part in the Indian freedom struggle.*

Revival in Dublin some years earlier. He thought that in both cases there was an awakening of a gifted nation to recognition of its artistic heritage.

Annie Besant was reportedly a close friend of George Bernard Shaw, and her particular brand of philosophy had an influence on Irish writers such as George Russell and William Yeats. Russell and Yeats were members of the Dublin Theosophical Lodge. Russell in particular was carried away by her 'Theosophy'. He believed in the theory of *karma* and the yogic power known as *kundalini,* a form of awakening that is regarded as the highest yogic experience. He described his own *kundalini* experience thus:

> It ran up like lightning along the spinal cord, and my body rocked with the power of it, and I seemed to myself to be standing in a fountain of flame, and there were fiery pulsations as of wings about my head, and a musical sound not unlike the clashing of cymbals with every pulsation.

Annie Besant conceived a movement on the lines of Redmond's Home Rule League in Ireland. She declared –

> I am an Indian tom-tom, waking up all sleepers so that they may wake, and work for the motherland.

Annie Besant wrote –

> It is not Great Britain against whom we are raising voices, but against the little men of the Anglo-Indian caste; they are the successors of those who had rejected the advice of Burke and Chatham and lost America.

Like Gandhi, she was firmly opposed to the use of violent means. In 1919, she wrote in the Times of India –

> The cutting of the telegraph wires, the derailment of troop trains, the burning of railway stations, the attacks on banks, the setting free of jail birds are not the actions of *satyagrahis* (passive resisters), nor even of casual rioters, but of revolutionaries.

Annie Besant also founded, in 1892, a college at Benares in northern India, called the Central Hindu College. In 1916, this college became the Benares Hindu University. At the time of its inauguration, she and Mahatma Gandhi both spoke from the same platform. She was actively involved in the Indian freedom movement. She was one of the originators of the Home Rule Movement in India, and she started this in 1916, soon after the Easter rebellion in Ireland. In 1917 she was elected President of the Indian National Congress, the major political movement that was clamouring for Indian freedom. She died in 1933.

Jawaharlal Nehru said of Annie Besant,

> India owes a very deep debt of gratitude for all she did to enable India to find her own soul.

One of the leaders of the Indian National Congress and a key figure in the freedom movement, Mrs Sarojini Naidu, even went so far as to remark,

> Had there been no Annie Besant, there would have been no Mahatma Gandhi.

Amy Carmichael

Amy Carmichael was born in 1867 in Millisle, County Down, on the east coast of Northern Ireland. Though her parents were prosperous, when she was a teenager she underwent a religious experience that led her into missionary work, firstly amongst the underprivileged 'factory girls' of Belfast and then amongst the poor of India. In 1895, she went to south India as a missionary for a Christian organization called the Keswick Convention, after having spent some time in Japan and Sri Lanka.

At the invitation of a Reverend Thomas Walker and his wife, who had been working in South India for the Church Missionary Society, she came to an area in South India and made her base in the village of Dohnavur. Dohnavur had previously been built as a village for persecuted Christians. She adopted Indian dress, and even the local Indians admired her taste in saris. She learned the Tamil language. She formed a small band of Indian Christian women to help her in her missionary work.

Amy Carmichael became famous for her work with the so-called temple children of south India. It was quite common for families to dedicate a child to a temple, perhaps because the child had been orphaned or simply in return for payment. Many of the girls who were donated to temples in effect went into a form of prostitution. Amy Carmichael was concerned to rescue such children before they might become temple children, and she formed the Dohnavur community to help achieve this goal. Finding out information about temple girls was not an easy task, and it required great determination on her part. She would have to defy not only elders in the temples, but also traditional secrecy in the local community.

One temple girl, aged seven years and called Preena, was given to a local temple after her father died. One day, feeling homesick and disliking the daily routine in the temple, she escaped and walked 20 miles back to her mother. The temple women followed her, and told her mother that the Gods would be angry if Preena was not returned. Preena's mother forced her to return to the temple, where the temple women branded her hands with marks as a punishment for defying them. Once again, Preena escaped. This time she was found by a Christian woman and taken to Amy Carmichael. The temple women soon appeared to claim Preena back. Amy Carmichael demanded proof

AMY CARMICHAEL. *Amy Carmichael with two of the young girls of her Dohnavur 'family' whom she had taken into her care.*

CHILDREN AT DOHNAVUR, EARLY 20th CENTURY. *Preena (left front), who was the first girl to be rescued by Amy Carmichael, is seen with two of her class mates.*

'TEMPLE GIRL', JANUARY 1997. *Yella, a six year-old girl, is being taken by her father to a temple in Southern India where she will be dedicated to the Goddess Renuka in an elaborate ceremony. The ceremony, which has been banned by the Government of India, takes place on a full moon and girls offered to the Goddess have to spend the rest of their lives in her service.*

that the child belonged to them. They could not give such proof, and so Preena joined Amy Carmichael and her friends at Dohnavur.

Amy Carmichael formed the Dohnavur family, which consisted of all those children who were taken into her care, and the volunteers who helped with their care. She herself was known as 'Amma' (Tamil for mother). She helped to provide medical care, education and training for those who became part of the Dohnavur family. By the 1940s, there were over 900 in the Dohnavur community. By then, the community included schools, a dairy farm, rice land, workshops, fruit and vegetable gardens and even a hospital to serve the sick. Often babies would arrive, and they would be given the names of flowers or jewels. The day that a new arrival came to Dohnavur would be its 'coming day', and in later years 'coming days' would be celebrated, rather than a child's birthday, since the date of a child's birth was often not known. Although initially catering for girls, her community later welcomed boys – they were often ones who had been trained to perform music or drama, and who had lives little better than the temple girls. In the early stages, with limited medical facilities and sickly children, there were occasions when infectious diseases resulted in the deaths of children there.

Amy Carmichael wrote many books describing her work at Dohnavur. In 1919, her services for the poor were officially recognised by India with the award of the Kaiser-i-Hind medal. The Governor of Madras wrote to her, indicating that this award was part of the Royal Birthday Honours List. She wanted to refuse the award, but her friends persuaded her to accept. However, she did not go to the actual presentation ceremony. One of Amy Carmichael's lasting memorials was that she succeeded in persuading Indians to pass laws forbidding the sale of children for immoral purposes. One of the first laws passed by the Madras State Legislature after Indian independence in 1947 was a law that made it an offence for anyone to dedicate children to temples as had previously been done. The lady member of the legislature who introduced the bill, Dr Mutthu Lakshmi, said that it was through Amy Carmichael's work that she had first seen that the temple women were a blot on the Hindu religion, and that it was the example of Amy's life that led her to work so hard to get the bill passed into law. In 1956, the Indian parliament made the practice illegal throughout India. Sadly, in some parts of South India similar activities continue to the present day. A report in *The Times* of January 23, 1997 noted that some parents in south India still take part in an annual custom of dedicating their daughters to be handmaidens to the goddess Yelamma. The children are taken to a temple in the town of Saudatti in the southern Indian state of Karnataka. They enrol as temple dancers, though in later years many appear to end up as prostitutes. The Indian Health Organization in Bombay estimates that every year a 1000 girls are dedicated to the Goddess Yelamma.

Amy Carmichael remained in the village of Dohnavur in South India till she died in 1951. Since 1931, she had in fact been crippled as a result of a minor accident, and she spent the last 20 years of her life largely confined to her room in the Dohnavur community. The story of Amy Carmichael is in fact now part of the syllabus for Primary Schools in Northern Ireland. The Dohnavur community is still flourishing in South India, and it has its British headquarters in London. The Dohnavur community continues the work in which it takes in and looks after abandoned or orphaned girls. It presently also looks after 50–60 physically or mentally handicapped women and girls in a small home 18 miles to the south of Dohnavur. Its hospital cares for 1000 inpatients in one year and has a yearly outpatient attendance of over 50,000. It also has a dental clinic and a leprosy clinic. In 1981, the Dohnavur Fellowship, in partnership with other Christians, formed the Santhosha Educational Charity to set up and administer a co-educational English-medium boarding school, primarily for the benefit of the children of missionaries of Indian nationality throughout India.

Margaret Cousins

A freedom movement of a different sort to that in which Annie Besant was engaged, but equally important, was one which fought for the emancipation of women in India. It was led by an inspirational Irish lady, Margaret Cousins, the last of the four Irish ladies.

She had much of her schooling in Londonderry, and went to India with her husband in the 1920s. Margaret Cousins (often known as Gretta Cousins), was born in the town of Boyle, County Roscommon in the Irish Republic, in 1878. In her autobiography, *We Two Together,* written along with her husband, she wrote –

> I always wanted to see over the edge, or round the corner of the road or into the other person's house or minds. I always wanted to change things into better shape. I was always ready to be a pioneer in making the change. I never shirked hard work.

When in Ireland, she was active in the Irish Suffragette movement. She spent time in prison for her civil disobedience, being sentenced to six months imprisonment for throwing stones at 10 Downing Street.

MARGARET AND JAMES COUSINS. *Originally from Roscommon in the Irish Republic, and educated in Londonderry, Margaret Cousins did much to improve the lot of the common woman in India.*

Gretta Cousins had a remarkable spirit. It is reported that her zeal for women's rights originated in an incident in her childhood. One of her descendants in Northern Ireland wrote:

> Gretta loved to ride horses. Following custom in the last years of the 19th century, she was as a young girl required to ride side-saddle. However, one day her saddle broke. She threw her leg over, like a man, and rode the horse to her heart's content. Little did she know that a friend of her father had seen this deviation from the accepted norm of the day, and he reported the event humorously to her father. However, her father did not take it so light heartedly. She was spanked soundly for behaving in such an unlady-like manner. She wrote about this incident – "That was my introduction to the inequality of opportunity which then belonged to being a girl. I was born a natural equalitarian and rebelled exceedingly from that early age against any differential treatment of the sexes." Gretta and her husband got to know Mrs Annie Besant, whose Theosophical Society held meetings in Britain and Ireland. After one of these meetings, Gretta Cousins had an overwhelming feeling that her husband Jim (who was a poet and writer) should write to Mrs Annie Besant and offer himself as a journalist for Mrs Besant's work. Mrs Besant immediately invited them to come to India and stay with her. Indeed, she even sent them the money for the passage. When she and her husband first arrived in India in 1915, they settled in Madras in southern India. Gretta worked as a teacher in a high

school attached to a college that was founded by Annie Besant. Her husband worked as a literary sub-editor of the magazine New India. He later became actively involved in promoting art in India.

In 1917, she helped to found the Indian Women's Association, and in 1923 she became the first lady to become a magistrate in India. In 1919, she was the founding head-mistress of the National Girls' School in Mangalore in Southern India. In 1932, she was also imprisoned for a year in Bombay as a result of protesting against emergency powers that were then in force. She founded the All India Women's Conference in 1926. The All India Women's Conference was supported by many of the leaders of the Indian freedom movement, including Mahatma Gandhi. Margaret Cousins and her husband carried out many charitable activities during her life in India. She suffered a stroke in 1943 after a two-mile walk to a mother-and-child welfare centre. She recovered, but later fractured a hip in a fall, while trying to chase away a cow that had wandered too close to her. She died in India in 1954, and her husband died a couple of years later.

Then And Now

One of Margaret Cousins' descendants is a General Practitioner, Dr Keith Munro, who currently practises in Londonderry. Dr Munro addressed an annual meeting of the All India Women's Conference in Lucknow, India at the beginning of 1994. This organisation now has around 200,000 members and 500 branches in India. It has helped introduce reforms in a range of areas, including child marriage, women's right to divorce and remarriage, maternity rights, etc. It teaches village lady folk a range of skills, including reading, writing, growing vegetables, etc. It helps in the provision of women's hostels and children's day care centres, helps leprosy-affected mothers, and teaches rural women how to install tiny solar-energised cooking stoves. The use of smokeless fuel combats damage to eyesight that can be caused by old-style cooking smoke in confined places. The organisation also helps educate those who live in slums of large cities, such as Bombay, about diseases such as AIDS. The organisation has branches all over India, and plans to set up a branch in Londonderry, Northern Ireland. Its President, Mrs Shobana Ranade, visited Londonderry in September 1994 and also went to Dublin where she met the Irish President, Mrs Mary Robinson. Mrs Ranade also unveiled a plaque on the wall of the house in Roscommon where Margaret Cousins was born. She also gave at talk to the local Indian community at the Indian Community Centre in Belfast.

While women folk have had a traditional, 'background' role in both Indian and Irish societies, these four women represented a striking departure from that trend. In more recent years, there have also been remarkable instances in both countries of the advancement of women. India had its first woman Prime Minister in 1966, Mrs Indira Gandhi, many years before Britain had its first woman Prime Minister. Ireland elected its first woman President in 1990, Mary Robinson.

STRUGGLE FOR FREEDOM: INDIA FOLLOWS IRELAND

> India has quite a lot to do with the wage earners of Britain. The Lancashire cotton operatives have found that out all right. One hundred thousand of them are on the dole already; and if we lose India, if we had the same treatment from a Home Rule India that we have had to our sorrow from a Home Rule Ireland, it would be more like two million bread-winners in this country who would be tramping the streets and queuing up at the Labour Exchange. *[Sir Winston Churchill, in a radio broadcast on India that took place on January 29, 1935].*

India gained its independence in 1947, with the formation of two separate countries, India and Pakistan. The links between the two independence movements were patchy but real. Early links between India and Ireland can be traced to the beginnings of the freedom movements for each country, beginnings that had their origins in the 19th century. An interesting book, written by a British Brigadier-General, has compared the Irish and Indian freedom movements as they developed in the first part of the 20th century – Crozier, F.P. (1931). *A Word To Gandhi. The Lesson of Ireland.* Williams & Norgate, London. At the beginning of Chapter One of his book, Crozier comments:

> There is some similarity between the struggles of Ireland and India for self-expression. Both countries were in turn occupied by England for gain. Both became 'planted' [settlers who were introduced into the country]. Both became permanently entwined in the mesh of English economics and finance. Both countries provided an outlet for the sons of English gentry in the realms of soldiering, sport and administration. Both countries gained from the advent of English culture, and eventually set up educational, legal, medical and economic schools of their own. Both countries were subjected to violent upheavals from time to time and both suffered accordingly. Both countries were, and still are, divided by religion, of which England has never been slow to take advantage. Geographically, both countries are all important in the strategic sense to the welfare of England. But a friendly Ireland or India is a greater asset to England in times of trouble than ever either of those countries can be in a disgruntled condition.

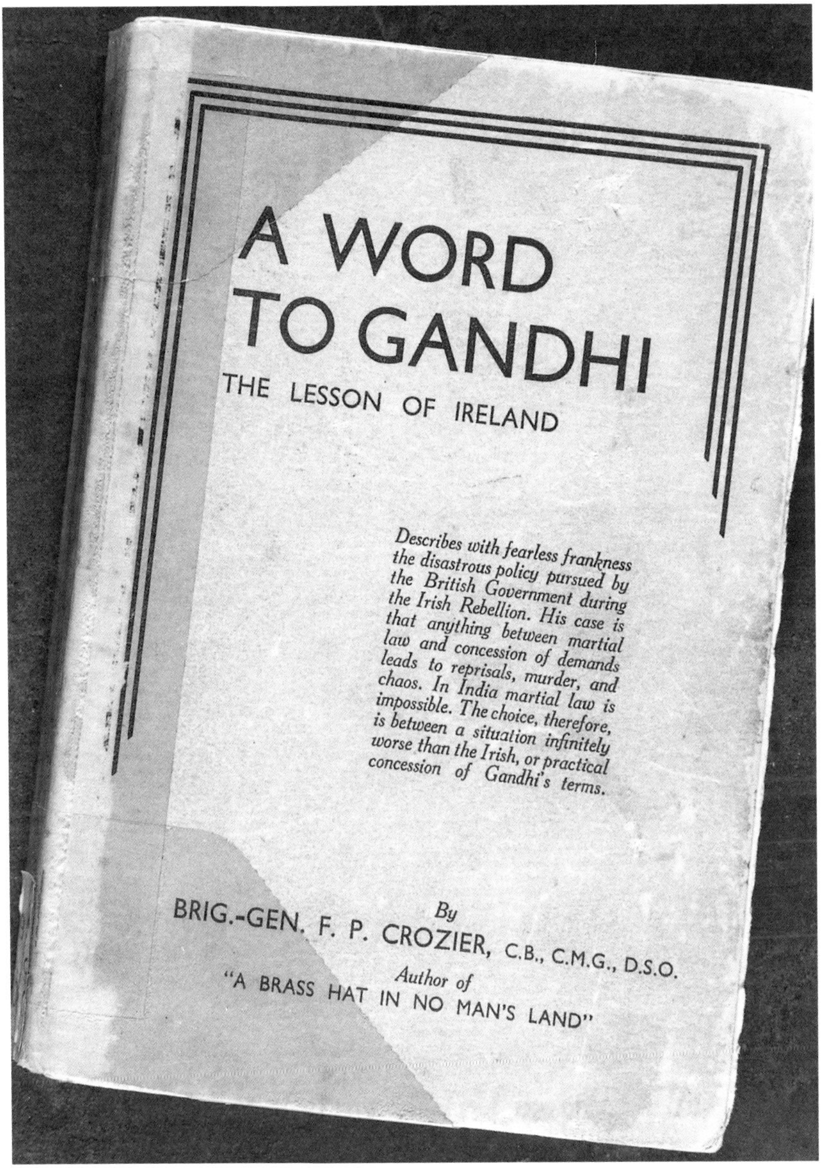

CROZIER'S BOOK ABOUT IRELAND AND INDIA. *Crozier's family originated from Ireland.*

Indian Societies In London

In July 1872, the London Indian Society was formed. Its aim was 'to bring into closer union the Indians residing in England, and to furnish an opportunity for the interchange of thought and feeling on all matters connected with India'. It was to this society that Frank Hugh O'Donnell, the Irish MP, made approaches. He had plans for forming an Irish-Indian organisation for bringing the grievances of India before the British parliament. At that time, there were a number of Irish MPs sitting in the House of Commons, their role being to represent Ireland and the needs of the Irish people. Many Indian nationalists were in turn interested in the Irish Home Rule Movement and the Irish Parliamentary Party, and by the mid 1870s Indian Nationalists and Irish MPs began to develop an alliance. In 1875, O'Donnell and four other Irish MPs, together with two Indians living in London, J C Meenakshya and G Tagore, formed the Constitutional Society of India. O'Donnell himself was a close friend of Tagore, a Bengali citizen who came to England and who was the grandfather of the Nobel prize winning Indian poet, Rabindra Nath Tagore.

In 1883, O'Donnell formed a formed another lobby group that included Indians and which was intended to press Parliament for reform in India. Neither of these initiatives got very far, perhaps due to O'Donnell's rather maverick reputation, although they did help to encourage educated Indians living in London to start thinking about pressing the British government for reform in India. People such as Frank O'Donnell saw the potential benefits of cooperation between Indians and Irishmen – Irish MPs could speak on behalf of Indians, while they could also use Indian issues as delaying tactics in parliament. The idea was even floated of four Indians being adopted to represent Irish constituencies in parliament, and to speak for Irish Home Rule on all Irish questions. In return, Irish MPs would support Indian legislation. However, this proposal came to nothing. It should also be added that some Indians thought it unwise to be associated with Irishmen whose words and deeds were not held in high regard by the British, since the Indians felt that this might work against their interests and aims in persuading the British of their views.

In 1905, the Indian Home Rule Society was formed by a small group of radical Indian students in London. It was based at India House, 65 Cromwell Avenue, Highgate, North London. The leader of the group was a young man called Vinayak Damodar Savarkar. He was known as Veer Savarkar (veer meaning 'brave'). The group was rather extreme, and was prepared to support any means to gain independence for India. Some of the students even took part in revolver-shooting at a rifle range in Tottenham Court Road, London. At their public meetings, they tried to work alongside Irish Nationalist groups, but their activities were closely scrutinised by the police.

The Indian student group's agitation reached a climax on July 1, 1909 when one of the group, Madan Lal Dhingra, assassinated Sir William Curzon Wyllie, a prominent Anglo-Indian, at the Imperial Institute in London. Madan Lal Dhingra was subsequently hanged in Pentonville Prison a month later. Savarkar himself was arrested in London in 1910 and held in Brixton jail. While he was in prison, some Irish and Indian revolutionaries jointly plotted a rescue operation with the help of a certain Mrs Dryhurst and the Sinn Fein leader Maud Gonne. An ambush was laid for the police van which was used to carry Veer Savarkar from the prison to court and back. But the plan failed, as the van that was attacked by them turned out to be an empty one, Savarkar having been taken to his destination by a different route! Some time later, Savarkar was deported to India.

In June of 1920, a remarkable event also took place in Punjab, one that was to bring home to the British rulers the links between the struggle in Ireland and the struggle in India. Men of the Connaught Rangers, who were stationed at the towns of Jullundur and Solon in the Punjab, refused to obey orders and raised the green, white and gold flag of the Irish Republic over their barracks. The leaders of this mini mutiny argued that their regiment was repressing the people of Indian, just as the British army was doing in Ireland. The mutiny was soon put down, with one of its leaders being killed and others sentenced to prison. However, the mutiny did two things – it reminded the British of the links between the freedom movements in Ireland and those in India, and it also reminded them that at least some of their soldiers in India could not always be trusted with unremitting loyalty.

Jinnah

Both Indian and Irish freedom movements resulted in a partition that was agreed by the British rulers only after significant pressure from one, largely religion-based, section of the community that had conflicting political aspirations from the other section. In the case of India, the Moslems – led by their leader Jinnah – urged the creation of the separate state of Pakistan, although many Moslems eventually chose to remain behind in India after partition. In Ireland, the corresponding scenario comprised many Protestants, led by Sir James Craig, who wished to form a separate state that was to become Northern Ireland. In the early part of the 20th century, there were reported to be links between the two respective 'freedom movements', Sinn Fein and the Indian National Congress. The name 'Sinn Fein' means 'ourselves alone', and there was a movement in India with the exact same title – *Swadeshi,* which is Gujarati for 'ourselves alone'.

Jinnah himself was very aware of the similarities between the situation in Ireland and in India, and he appeared to exploit these similarities for the maximum gain. The Protestants in Ireland had been able to gain special status, through the Government of Ireland Act in 1920 which created Ulster as an integral part of the United Kingdom. He was proposing that the Moslems in India have a similar deal, with a separate country after the British had left India. His awareness of the similarities with the Irish situation is shown by the following quote from one of his speeches:

> The Nationalist leader, Redman, met Carson, Ulster leader, and told him, "Look here, can't we come to some settlement? Why do you want to separate from Ireland? Mind you, there is not one-millionth part of the differences between the people of Ulster and Ireland". What was Carson's reply? "I do not want to be ruled by you."
>
> My reply to Mr Gandhi is, "I do not want to be ruled by you".

Thus, Jinnah had a clear aversion to be ruled by someone he saw as being fundamentally different in religion, mores, ways of thinking, etc. and he saw the Irish precedent as a vitally important one to look towards and one to guide his thinking.

DYER, O'DWYER AND THE PUNJAB MASSACRE

One of the most notorious involvements of Irishmen in imperial rule in India was that of General Reginald Dyer and Sir Michael O'Dwyer. Sir Michael O'Dwyer was one of 14 children born in Ireland, near Tipperary. Like many other Irishmen, he sought to mark out his career in India, joining the prestigious Indian Civil Service. He was Lieutenant Governor of Punjab from 1913 to 1919. Despite his Catholic background, Sir Michael O'Dwyer had little sympathy for Indians who were pressing for reform and independence. Dyer was born in the Punjab in 1864, being the son of an Irish brewer, and he was educated at Midleton College, County Cork (Dyer was no relation of O'Dwyer).

Although Gandhi was preaching nonviolence around this time, there was considerable agitation in Punjab. Violence broke out in the city of Amritsar in the Punjab, involving the killing of some Europeans and the beating up of a female English doctor, Marcia Sherwood. This led to ruthless counter measures by the British commander, Brigadier-General

GENERAL DYER. *Dyer served in the British army in India. Though born in India, his parents were Irish and he was educated in County Cork.*

INDIAN ORDERED TO CRAWL IN AMRITSAR STREET. *This order was made by General Dyer in response to an attack on an English doctor.*

Reginald Dyer. An order was issued by Dyer that any Indian using the lane where Dr Sherwood had been attacked must crawl along it. (When Gandhi visited Oxford in 1931, he recounted this to his host – the wife of the master of Balliol college. She was so horrified that she offered for her and her husband to crawl on their belly 50 times in expiation. Gandhi replied that there was no need for such an unusual demonstration of sorrow for what had happened!)

On April 13 1919, Dyer was involved in confrontation with an unarmed crowd of Indians at Jallianwala Bagh in Amritsar, in the Punjab. Dyer ordered his troops to open fire, apparently thinking that he was penned in and at risk of being overwhelmed by the crowd of around 10,000, who were protesting against the arrest of two Congress leaders. The official death toll is that 379 people were killed, and 1,200 were injured, but unofficially the toll is considered to be closer to 600 killed. Many of those killed and injured included women and children. Some of the casualties died while flinging themselves down a deep well in an attempt to escape the bullets. Although O'Dwyer was in Lahore at the time, and was not responsible for the action of his Brigadier-General, he made known his approval of Dyer's action (The massacre is described in a book by Robert Furneaux entitled *Massacre at Amritsar.* The West

Indian film-maker, Horace Ové, made a short film for British television about the whole event, the film being called *The Equalizer*).

The government set up a committee to examine the massacre, and the Hunter Committee censured Dyer who was invited to resign from the army in 1920. Sir Winston Churchill, who was the Secretary of State for War at the time, announced in the House of Commons that Dyer had committed an error of judgement. Dyer was retired on half-pay. When Dyer's fate was discussed in the House of Commons, it was the Irish Unionist leader, Sir Edward Carson, who rose to Dyer's defence, having been briefed by O'Dwyer. It is also notable that the issue caused considerable controversy in Britain, and that one of the newspapers at the time, the *Morning Post,* launched an appeal on behalf of Dyer that raised £26,000 for him. Both O'Dwyer and Sir Edward Carson, were amongst the first contributors to this appeal.

After O'Dwyer left the Punjab in 1919, the Princes and others in that state raised around £20,000 for a memorial to his work there. He asked that it be used to establish two soldiers' clubs in Lahore, one for British soldiers and one for Indian soldiers.

Revenge

A young man called Udham Singh had been a 16 year-old water carrier at the scene of the massacre, giving water to some of the survivors, and he swore to avenge the deaths of his fellow Indian citizens. General Dyer himself had died of natural causes in 1927. On March 13 1940, Singh went to a meeting that was being held in Caxton Hall, London. This meeting had been organized by the East India Association, and O'Dwyer gave a lecture at the meeting. At the end of his lecture, Singh called out O'Dwyer's name. O'Dwyer turned round, smiled at him, and then turned back. Singh produced a revolver and shot him

MICHAEL O'DWYER.
O'Dwyer was born near Tipperary, in the Irish Republic, and served as governor of Punjab.

dead. Singh was overwhelmed by members of the audience, many of them women. Singh was tried and hanged at Pentonville Prison in 1939. When sentenced to death, he reportedly proclaimed,

> I say down with British imperialism...I do not care about the sentence of death. I do not care about dying or anything. I do not worry about it at all. I am dying for a purpose....Machine guns on the streets of India mow down thousands of poor women and children...I have nothing against the English people at all. I have more English friends living in England than I have in India. I am against the Imperialist government.

When he turned to leave the dock, he reportedly spat across the solicitor's table. His actual speech from the dock was in fact suppressed by the authorities, perhaps because at the time (1940) Britain was at war and the war effort was being aided by a large number of Indian soldiers.

Only recently have some of the papers from the case been made available to the general public. They indicate that at the time of his trial Singh changed his name to Mohammad Singh Azad, and he insisted that it should be kept as this, even though the court changed his name back to Udham Singh. Perhaps by changing his name Singh was trying to identify himself and his deed with all the people of India, and not only the Sikhs. When Udham Singh's body was eventually returned to India many years later, it was given a state reception at New Delhi airport, attended by the President of India and other national leaders, and Singh was given a hero's funeral.

NEHRU IN IRELAND

Jawaharlal Nehru, the first Prime Minister of India and one of its leading freedom fighters, was a student in Trinity College, Cambridge at the beginning of the 20th century. Nehru visited Ireland twice in this period. The best documented of his visits was in 1907. In the summer of that year, he went for the first time to Dublin, staying there for a few weeks. It is said that he avoided Belfast, since there were riots there at the time. He was impressed by a book *The New Ireland.* It was written by an English journalist, Sydney Brooks, and published in 1907. It outlined the ideology and strategy of Sinn Fein. Nehru was also reported to be impressed by Sinn Fein, and by their more forceful protest movement. He wrote to his father, Motilal Nehru, that Indians should be similarly forceful in their freedom movement. In his letter to Motilal of November 7, 1907, Nehru likened Jinnah to the Indian 'Sir Edward Carson'. After the Irish Uprising of 1916, Nehru is reported to have commented –

> But was that not true courage, which mocked at almost certain failure, and proclaimed to the world that no physical might could crush the invincible spirit of a nation.

Some years later, in 1932, when Jawaharlal Nehru was to find himself in prison in Dehra Dun, in northern India, the superintendent of the jail turned out to be a Captain Falvey, a former pupil of Eamon De Valera, the Irish freedom fighter and the first President of Ireland. Captain Falvey did everything to alleviate conditions for Nehru while was kept in jail.

Indian and Irish constitutions and parliamentary democracies have many similarities, and it is said that those who drew up the Indian constitution in 1947 based it on that of Ireland, which had gained its independence a number of years earlier. In fact, a committee of Indians was set up in the 1920s to consider a constitution for India. It was called the Nehru committee, since it was headed by Motilal Nehru, father of Jawaharlal Nehru. The Nehru committee noted in one of its deliberations that India was most like Ireland among the dominions of the British Empire, and they used the constitution of the Irish Free State as one of their guides. On the last night of British rule in India, August 14–15 1947, the Irish Prime Minister Eamon De Valera and his Foreign Secretary Frank Eaken were guests of Lord Mountbatten, the last Viceroy of India.

After Indian independence, Nehru became Prime Minister of India and he made several trips to Ireland. One was a brief stop-over that he recounted in one of his letters to his daughter, Indira Gandhi, who was later to become Prime Minister of India. Nehru wrote in his letter, dated May 3 1949:

> I spent several hours in Dublin and had a warm-hearted welcome there. The Irish are a loveable people and Dublin is a charming city.

Nehru was not the only distinguished Indian to visit Ireland. VV Giri, who was President of India from 1969 to 1974, studied law at University College, Dublin between 1915 and 1925. He got involved with Republican sympathisers, and was apparently sent back to India because of his contacts with them. Chaman Lal Chaman, one of the early Indian freedom fighters, was expelled from India by the British authorities in the early 1920s. He came to England, then went to Ireland for a few months. He acquired an Irish passport, and from there made his way to South America.

SUBHAS BOSE AND THE INDIAN NATIONAL ARMY

The Irish Republican Army had its counterpart in India, the Indian National Army, though the Indian movement was much smaller, less popular and less influential than its Irish counterpart. The Indian National Army was led for some time by an Indian called Subhas Chandra Bose. Bose went to Germany at the beginning of World War II. He in fact met Hitler in 1942 in an effort to enlist Nazi support for his movement, but failed in this endeavour. He then turned to the Japanese for help. He went by German and Japanese submarines to the Far East. Here he formed an anti-British military force from British Indian army soldiers taken prisoner by the Japanese. Bose led this army against British forces in Burma. He died in an air crash in Taiwan in 1945 while trying, after Japan's surrender to the allies, to seek refuge in the Soviet Union.

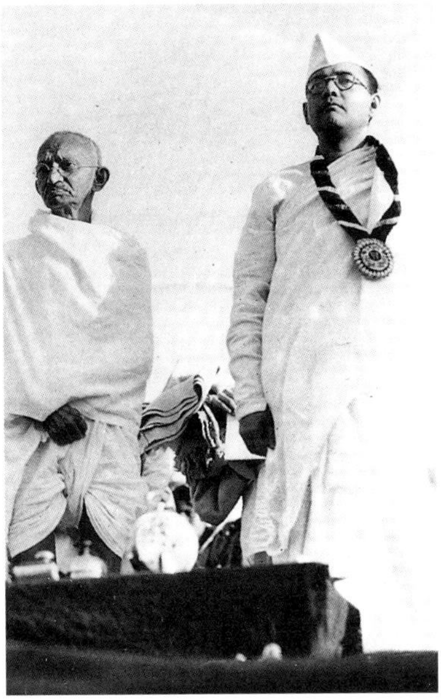

SUBHAS BOSE, 1938. *Subhas Bose, the Indian freedom fighter who had links with his counterparts in Ireland, is seen standing to the right of Gandhi. Around his neck is the badge which signifies his position at that time as President of the Indian National Congress, the movement that played a major part in India's freedom.*

In his speeches, Bose drew many parallels between India and Ireland. For example, shortly before starting a prison sentence in the late 1920s/early 1930s because of his freedom activities, Bose stated:

> The resolution setting forth complete independence as our ideal has been passed but it will have to be probed as to how far the same will prove useful. As regards its ability, the history of Ireland provides a very pertinent example. The Irish Nationalists not only passed a resolution setting forth independence as their goal but also declared complete independence. Some of them who were instrumental in making that declaration have stated in their memoirs that only a handful of men supported that declaration yet it was essential at that time because the nation could not be roused unless such an ideal was placed before it. After that the whole

> national outlook of Ireland underwent a complete change...The British government had tried to deceive the Irish people by convening an Irish Convention but the intelligent and farsighted Sinn Feiners did not walk into the trap. They boycotted the Irish Convention and continued to fight for freedom until the time when the British government decided to negotiate for peace with the Sinn Fein party alone. Unless the Congress [party of India] was in a position to speak for India by itself – the Congress could never negotiate successfully with the British government.

In the early 1930s, there was considerable repression by the British authorities in Bengal, and in numerous speeches Bose compared this repression to that in Ireland under the infamous Black-and-Tans – a body made up largely of ex-servicemen who were brought in by the British to suppress the IRA.

In 1936, Bose was visiting Paris when he decided to go to Ireland. He did not want to go through Britain, risking trouble with the immigration authorities in England. He therefore went directly from Le Havre to Cork. His first act on arrival in Cork was to pay homage at the grave of Terence MacSwiney, who had died as a martyr in a British prison, and who was greatly admired by Bose. Hunger strikes by prisoners were commonplace in India, and to a lesser extent in Ireland. Gandhi was renowned for his hunger strikes. Terence MacSwiney was the Lord Mayor of Cork in the early part of the 20th century. He used the hunger strike as a weapon against British rule, and has a place in Irish history because of this. He was a member of the Irish Volunteers, a freedom movement that was formed in Ireland in 1913. He was elected Mayor of Cork in 1920, and in his inaugural speech he remarked, in memorable words similar to those used by Gandhi –

> It is not those who can inflict the most, but they who can suffer the most who will conquer.

SARAT BOSE AND EAMON DE VALERA IN CALCUTTA, 1947.
Sarat Bose and his brother, Subhas, were actively involved in the Indian freedom struggle, and felt a lot in common with De Valera and his efforts to gain Ireland's freedom.

He was constantly on the run from the British, and his wife was to write after his death –

> He really could not be with me at all. He could not be where they might find him at night. I hardly ever saw my husband, to tell the truth.

He was arrested in 1920 and sentenced to two years in prison, most of this to be spent in Brixton prison in London. He went on hunger strike, and after 73 days of his hunger strike he died on October 25, 1920, aged 41 years. Terence MacSwiney's body was returned to Ireland, and he was buried in Cork amidst scenes of great sadness and great resentment against the British.

De Valera met Bose on three separate occasions during Bose's ten day stay in Ireland. Around this time, there was in fact an organization called the Indian-Irish Independence League, and Bose met some of its officers during his visit. After his visit, Bose wrote to Mrs M Woods, Secretary of the League –

> I often think of the days I spent in Dublin. It is like a dream and those went so quickly.

When in Dublin, Bose also met a Col. JH Smith, who had been – as part of the British establishment – his former jailer in Mandalay Jail in Burma.

Bose also met De Valera on the midnight of January 16, 1938 – Ireland had by then become a republic, and they discussed and compared the political destinies of India and Ireland. There is no record of their talks, but it is interesting that the *News Chronicle* called Bose 'India's de Valera'. Sarat Bose, the brother of Subhas Bose, was also an active freedom fighter. In one of this speeches, he pleaded for India to be free from British rule, and he quoted the words spoken by the Irishman Roger Casement during his trial for treason (for which Casement was subsequently hanged) –

> I am proud to be a rebel and shall cling to my rebellion with the last drop of my blood.

In 1938, Sarat Bose also visited Dublin with his wife and children. They met the President of Ireland, Sean O'Kelly, and the Prime Minister, De Valera.

Although the Japanese tried to lure Bose's army into supporting them against the allies when World War II extended to south-east Asia (they dropped thousands of leaflets on to front-line Indian soldiers telling them that the Japanese would help them get independence from

Britain), the Indian National Army never had the same influence or prominence as the totally peaceful movement that was led by Gandhi.

Members of the Indian National Army were put on trial in Delhi after World War II. The trial did give some respect to the army and its leaders, and it brought home to the British that the foundation of their rule – the Indian Army – could not be completely depended on for support. Some historians regard Bose as having shown the potential to achieve more than Gandhi. During its trial in 1945, the Indian National Army was enthusiastically supported by both Muslims and Hindus alike. There was a view amongst some Indians at the time that it could have forged an alliance between the two communities that Gandhi failed to achieve, and could thus have avoided the partition of India.

GANDHI TALKS ABOUT IRELAND AND TERRORISM

Mahatma Gandhi was much admired in Ireland during the period of India's freedom struggle, but less so amongst some quarters in Britain. In a remark that was to become infamous, Churchill described Gandhi as that 'half-naked fakir' – the word 'fakir' is generally used to describe a wandering, penniless, holy man.

Gandhi himself was very much aware of the similarities and differences between the plight of those in Ireland and those in India. In a speech to students in Bombay, on November 14 1920, Gandhi reminded the students that his non-cooperation had no similarity with the non-cooperation movements of Ireland, even though the motive was the same. Some in Ireland preached violence, while he was against it. He warned them that the use of the sword, or force or abuse against an opponent, was morally equally culpable and that they all amounted to violence.

He made a number of astute observations on Ireland throughout his life, and these have been documented in the published volumes of his writings and speeches (*published by the Publications Division of the Ministry of Information and Broadcasting, Government of India*). Here are a selection –

> The Sinn Feiners resort to violence in every shape and form. Theirs is a 'frightfulness' not unlike General Dyer's. We may pardon it if we choose, because we sympathise with their cause. But it does not on that account

MAHATMA GANDHI. *This picture shows Gandhi outside 10 Downing Street in 1931. Einstein made a memorable comment about Gandhi in 1949, after meeting the Indian Prime Minister, Jawaharlal Nehru, who visited Einstein at Princeton University the year after Gandhi was assassinated – 'Generations to come, it may be, will scarcely believe that such a one as this ever in flesh and blood walked upon this earth'.*

differ from General Dyer's act...We must therefore seek to guard English life as our own. We must constitute ourselves as self-appointed volunteers guarding English life from violent hands. And our success depends upon our ability to control all the violent and fanatical forces in our midst.
Gandhi, 1/9/1920 [Volume XVIII, 219–220]

Ireland gained absolutely nothing through the policy of harassment and obstruction; and remember, it had an able leader like Parnell to fight for it. In despair, it has now taken to the method of violence. This also, I believe, is a mistake. I have cited the instance of Ireland only to show that obstruction leads nowhere.
Gandhi, 18/7/1920 [Volume XVII, page 56]

Lord Reading has flung Ireland in our faces. Let us contemplate for a moment that romantic nation. I would like the reader to believe with me that it is not the blood that the Irishmen have taken which has given them what appears to be their liberty. But it is the gallons of blood they have willingly given themselves. It is not the fear of losing more lives that has compelled a reluctant offer from England but it is the shame of any further imposition of agony upon a people that loves its liberty above everything else. It is the magnitude of the Irish sacrifice which has been the deciding factor...And England has yielded when she is able no longer to bear the sight of blood pouring out of thousands of Irish arteries.
Gandhi, 15/12/1921 [Volume XXII, page 17]

INDIAN CULTURE MEETS IRISH CULTURE

Over the broad range of literary and artistic pursuits, one can occasionally glimpse similarities between Indian and Irish cultural traditions. This can be seen in some of the dance styles, musical instruments and melodic tunes. Literary figures in both countries admired each other's work, as in the following examples.

SRI AUROBINDO. *An Indian, talented in English literature, who wrote about the links between India and Ireland.*

Aurobindo

Sri Aurobindo was an Indian who started off as a poet and a professor of English. He was later to become actively involved in Indian politics. Like Annie

Besant, he became President of the Indian National Congress. He was fascinated by Celtic culture and by the nationalist movement in Ireland. At the beginning of the twentieth century, he wrote an editorial in a magazine that he edited. The editorial was entitled, 'An Irish Example', and it was in response to the rejection by Irish politicians in London of an offer by the then British government of limited Home rule. The government at the time was formed from the Liberal Party. He wrote -

> By accepting the Liberal offer, the great ideal of an Irish nation for which Emmet died, for which O'Connell and Parnell planned and schemed and which the Sinn Fein movement is making more and more practicable, would either have been entirely frustrated or postponed for another century. Instead of a separate nationality with its own culture, language, government, the Irish would have ended by becoming a big English county governed by a magnified and glorified Parish Council...The refusal of the Irish Parliamentary Party under Mr Redmond's leadership...is a step on which we may congratulate the Irish people.

He was in fact inspired to write a poem entitled, '*Lines on Ireland: 1896*':

How changed, how fallen from her ancient spirit!
She that was Ireland, Ireland now no more,
In beggar's weeds beyond at England's door
Neglected sues or at the best returned
With hollow promise, happy if not spurned
Perforce, she that had yesterday disdained
Less than her mighty purpose to have gained.

Tagore

In the case of Rabindra Nath Tagore, his great liaison was with the Irish poet William Yeats. Yeats was considered to have been attracted to Indian literature and philosophy throughout his life. He found inspiration for much of his poetry and plays in Indian mythology, dance and religion. He wrote an 'Introduction' to Tagore's famous work, *Gitanjali,* that was to win Tagore the Nobel Prize for Literature in 1913. It was through an English writer, William Rothenstein, that Tagore came to know Yeats. Rothenstein was the first to read Tagore's manuscript of poems. He contacted Yeats, introduced Tagore to Yeats and other writers, and arranged for the publication of *Gitanjali.* He also looked after Tagore's needs when Tagore visited London. It is no wonder, therefore, that Tagore dedicated *Gitanjali* to Rothenstein.

> Yeats first met Tagore in London on June 27, 1912, over dinner and at Rothenstein's behest. On July 10, 1912, a dinner was held in Tagore's honour at the Trocadero restaurant in London. This was organized by Rothenstein, with Yeats proposing the toast and reading three poems

RABINDRA NATH TAGORE WILLIAM YEATS

Yeats and Tagore were close friends and had a mutual admiration for each other.

> from *Gitanjali.* Within a week, Yeats was at work selecting and arranging the poems and making pencilled corrections for Tagore to consider. In his Introduction to *Gitanjali,* Yeats wrote of the work, "I have carried the manuscript of these translations about with me for days, reading it on railway trains, or on the top of omnibuses and in restaurants, and I have often had to close it lest some stranger would see how much it moved me. These lyrics display in their thought a world I have dreamed of all my life long". Yeats invited Tagore to Dublin in 1939, but due to the outbreak of World War II around that time, Tagore could not make the trip. Yeats himself was awarded the Nobel Prize for Literature in 1923.

Yeats was one of those who strongly recommended Tagore for the Nobel prize. He corresponded with Tagore, assisted him in translating and publishing his works, and Yeats produced one of his plays in Dublin's Abbey Theatre. Tagore's play – 'The Post Office' – was first performed at the Abbey theatre in Dublin in 1913. Tagore founded a school at Shantiniketan, India that was modelled on Pearse's St Edna's school in Ireland (Pearse was an Irish freedom fighter who set up this school, named after the Irish Saint, St Edna. Pearse was also headmaster of the school. St Edna's school was intended to include a good deal of Irish language and culture, since many schools in Ireland were biased towards British-style education).

Most of Tagore's works can be found in the Tagore Collection in Alexandra Palace Library, Haringey, north London.

Yeats himself held views that overlapped with those of other Indian leaders. Thus, he once asserted that the spiritual history of the world has been the history of the conquered races. The idea that defeat conferred a spiritual strength superior to the conqueror's materialism also finds echoes in Gandhi's teachings, where nonviolence and passive resistance are seen as important political and moral weapons against those who may be physically or materially stronger.

In addition to these links in the area of literature, it is interesting to note that Dublin's Chester Beatty Library houses one of the world's finest collections of Moghul miniature paintings.

2: FIRST INDIAN SETTLERS IN IRELAND

WANDERING FROM INDIA TO IRELAND

Early links between Ireland and India can be traced back over a number of centuries. Around the tenth century AD, Gypsies – or Romani, to use the more correct term – ventured out of India into countries further west. The word Romani itself is presumed to derive from a term to describe low-caste musicians from the aboriginal Dravidian tribes of northern India *(Plate 1, p. 57)*. It is thought that the Romani left India because of conflict with the Hindus, who were the major religious force there. This conflict may have been due in part to their customs – Romani were meat eaters, whereas most Hindus were strict vegetarians. Their language, called Romany, has at least some of its roots in Hindi. This is evident by common words that exist between the two languages – e.g. 'ek' is Hindi for 'one', and the equivalent Romany word is 'eck'; the word 'bal' is Hindi for 'hair', and the equivalent Romany word is also 'bal'. The Romani arrived in middle-eastern countries between the 10th and 14th centuries, and reached Europe around the 14–15th century. When they arrived in Europe, people thought that, because of their dark skin and dark hair, they must have come from Egypt. Thus, the term 'gypsy' derives from 'Egypt'. A large number of Romani settled in countries such as Romania, but a number did come as far as Ireland, and they began to settle in Ireland around the 15th century – one report is that the first band of Romani came in 1490. Romani still exist in India today, mainly in the north-western state of Rajasthan.

Early Mentions

There are only a few isolated accounts of Indians who were present in Ireland in the 1700s/1800s. The most famous of these Indians – Dean

Mahomet – is described below. Amongst the other accounts are the following (reference to Indians is in *italics*)–

1750 – "At a concert in the Crow Street Theatre, Miss Rachael Babtist to be accompanied in Recitativo by an *Indian Gent*, lately arrived, who condescends to show himself in Publick on this Occasion, and the two Performers hope to convince the Publick that the Flower of Musick is not confined to Colour." (*Dublin Journal*, 1750, March 17–20).

1767 – "Eloped from Eyre Evans Crow, Esq., at Aughrim near Ballinasloe, on Wednesday the 4th instant, a mulatto *East India Boy*, answers to the name of Tom, he went off in a blue Frock Coat, a Silver Laced Hat, is about fifteen years of age, about five feet two inches high, wore his hair which was not very long." (*Dublin Journal*, 1767, February 7–10).

1767 – "Run-away from Captain Tate of Sprucefield near Lisburn, on Thursday last, a *black Boy*, aged about 14 or 15 years. He is a *Native of Bengal*, has long black hair, is in-knee'd, badly limbed, and answers to the name of Will." (*Belfast Newsletter*, 1767, September 25).

1770 – "The case of Armstrong v. Coffee in Dublin, in which the plaintiff (Armstrong) accused the latter of stealing away his servant or slave, an *East Indian Black*." (*Dublin Mercury*, 1770, July 10–12).

1772 – "An *East Indian Black*, shown holding a pony belonging to Gerald Fitzgerald Esq., in a painting by Thomas Roberts."

1840s/1850s – "*Indian cook* from William IV's kitchen, came to Bruff in Limerick as servant to Lord Carberry's brother, became chef at the Carberry Arms in Bruff; died there." (M. Carberry, *The Farm by Lough Gur*, Cork/Dublin, 1937, pages 267–268).

DEAN MAHOMET: SHAMPOOING SURGEON TO KING GEORGE VI

One of the earliest documented contacts made by an Indian with Ireland was that of a man called Dean Mahomet [Much of this account is taken from the excellent article by M Fisher (1996). Cork's Dean

Mahomet. *Journal of the Cork Historical and Archaeological Society*, Volume 101, pages 81–96]. Dean Mahomet, was born in 1759 in Patna, a large city several hundred miles to the west of Calcutta. He was only 11 years old when his father died, leaving his mother to look after him and his elder brother.

At that time, Calcutta was the capital of India and headquarters of the East India Company. Dean Mahomet's family came from a military

SAKE DEAN MAHOMET. *He was one of the first Indians who is known to have settled in Ireland for an appreciable period of time.*

background. He himself was always keen to enter the service of the East India army, and he often eagerly watched the procession of soldiers as they went into the barracks in Patna.

In 1769, as a young boy of 10 years in India, Dean Mahomet joined a British soldier as a 'follower', a form of assistant. The soldier in question was a Godfery Baker of the East India Regiment. His mother was not at all keen on this move, and she pleaded with Baker to let her son come back. However, Dean was so enthusiastic that Baker successfully re-sisted her pleadings. Baker's father was well-established in Cork in the Irish Republic. Baker himself became captain in 1781, and Dean Mahomet rose to the rank of lieutenant. Mahomet took part in numerous military engagements with Baker. Baker appears to have had a fairly distinguished career, marred only by a court martial conviction and being the subject of allegations from local villagers that he had tried to extort money from them. Both Baker and Dean Mahomet subsequently resigned from the army and moved to Cork in 1784.

Within a year of returning to Cork, Baker married into an influential family, the Massey family. Sadly, Baker died the following year, and his wife remarried a year later. It seems, however, that the Massey family looked after Mahomet.

In Cork, Mahomet went to college to improve his English. At college, he met a pretty fellow student, Jane Daley, with whom he ran away and got married! He deposited an amount of money ('a wedding bond') with the local church. It seems, therefore, that he had been quite successful up to that time. Dean Mahomet and his wife returned to Cork after their elopement, and they lived in a prosperous part of Cork, probably in Godfery Baker's house. It is uncertain what occupation(s) he had while in Cork. It appears that, from his important contacts within Cork society, he must have been able to gain some income and perform some respectable duties, perhaps as a manager of a large house.

In 1794, he published his first book, called the *Travels of Dean Mahomet*. This was a major undertaking for him. In those days, books were often published by individuals rather than by publishing firms. In addition, it was common for a prospective author to appeal to potential buyers of the book to sponsor the book's printing by paying a subscription in advance towards the book. This appeal for money would be in the form of a series of public advertisements. Mahomet's book itself would cost five shillings and five pence to 'subscribers', and one shilling more to others. In all, around 320 people 'subscribed' to the book before it was printed, each parting with half a crown (two shillings and six pence, 12.5 pence in today's money, but a considerable sum at that time). Many of these subscribers were influential people in Cork society, and a good number had contacts with India, perhaps having served as officers in the army of the East India Company. Having secured monies in advance, Dean Mahomet was then in a good position to go to a printer to get the book printed and bound. He would probably have printed 400–500 copies of the book. The book was probably also intended to be a guide for the many Irishmen who would find themselves working for the East India Company in India. While it might have made him some money, it was just as much intended to establish his place in Cork society. The names of the subscribers were printed at the beginning of the book. Mahomet dedicated his book to William A Bailie, Colonel in the service of the East India Company. He ends his dedication with the words, "Sir, with the most profound veneration, your much obliged and devoted humble servant, Dean Mahomet."

The book is written in the form of letters to a friend, with 58 letters in all. It is in two volumes, though these volumes are set within one cover that is only seven by five inches. The book itself deals with many aspects of life in India, in addition to Mahomet's own experiences in the army. The book also describes the cities of New Delhi and Bombay, customs relating to marriage and death amongst the 'Mahometans' (the clan that Mahomet belonged to), and it even has one letter describing elephants. It covers Dean Mahomet's travels up to the point that his ship reached England in September 1784. The English in the book is immaculate, considering that when he arrived in Ireland Dean Mahomet would probably not have been fluent in English. In the book, Mahomet takes pains to have a glossary of terms for those unfamiliar with India – e.g. he gives meanings of the words 'begum' (princess), 'brahmin' (priest) and 'bazar' (market). The book is now out of print, but one copy is available in the library of the British Museum, London.

Godfery Baker's brother, Major William Massey Baker, had also served as a soldier in India. He returned to Cork in 1796, sold the original Baker family house in Cork and bought one in another Cork estate. It is possible that Mahomet and his wife set up their household on that estate. There is a report that in 1799 Mahomet met an 'Indian traveller' during his time in that estate. There is a more detailed account of a meeting he had with another Indian called Abu Taleb who landed in Ireland, as his ship was prevented from landing in England due to stormy seas. Taleb happened to meet Major Baker while dining in Cork. Baker invited him to his house, and there Taleb met Mahomet. In his subsequent account of his visit to Cork, Taleb noted that Mahomet had several beautiful children from his marriage.

Move To England

After spending 17 years in Ireland, Mahomet moved to England in 1801. There is no clear indication why he did this – it is possible he did not get on well with Major Baker's wife. In England, he initially opened a café called 'The Hindustanee Coffee House' – perhaps the first Indian takeaway in Britain! This proved unsuccessful, and he moved to Brighton around 1814. He set himself up selling exotic oriental treatments, such as tooth powder. These treatments, and medicinal springs, had been popular in the Cork area, and so Mahomet established Mahomet's Baths, steaming baths that were used for the cure of all sorts of ailments. Brighton was a logical place to start such a business – it was a fashionable health resort, since sea-bathing for rheumatic ailments was popular, and it was close to London. Mahomet would refer to himself as a 'Shampooing Surgeon'. In those days, the word 'shampooing' meant

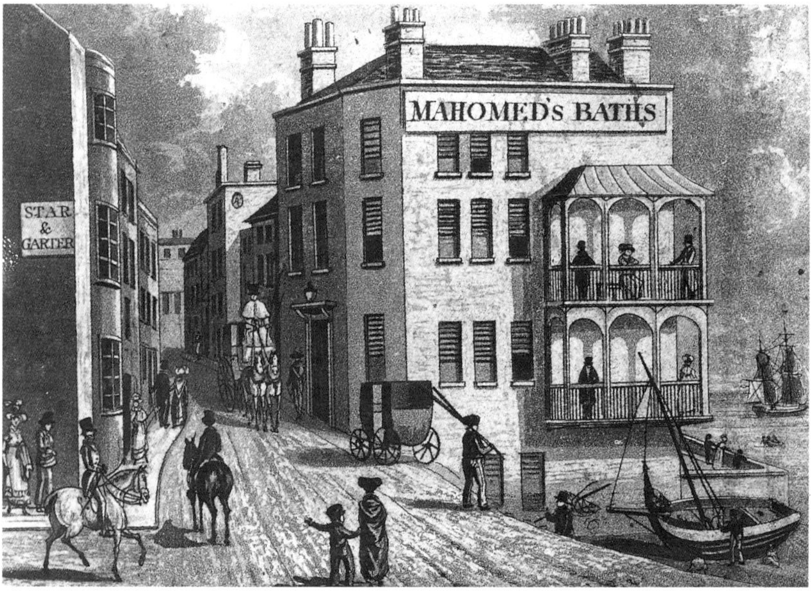

MAHOMET'S BATHS. *When he moved to England from Ireland, Mahomet may well have changed the spelling of his name to Mahomed. This picture shows his baths in Brighton.*

much more than simply washing hair – for example, it might involve things such as steaming, aromatic baths (as in modern day saunas) or vigorous massage.

Mahomet initially offered his 'treatments' free of charge, so as to encourage the public to try them out, and so as to give his practice some publicity. His fame soon spread, and in 1830 he opened a second establishment in London. His baths were advertised as being open daily, except Sundays. An 'Indian Medicated Vapour and Shampooing Bath' would cost six shillings (30 pence in today's money, though probably equivalent to several pounds in those days). In the advertisement for the baths, it was noted that there was a separate department for ladies, that invalids who required a bath could be attended in their own home, and that the charges that were listed did not include the cost of having an assistant present. The rich and famous flocked to him, and his clients included the Prime Minister Sir Robert Peel and King George VI, who appointed him as his personal 'Shampooing Surgeon'. In 1822, Mahomet published a second book entitled, *Shampooing or Benefits Resulting from the Use of Indian Medicated Vapour Bath.* The book contains cases successfully treated by him, including cures for ailments such as asthma and rheumatism.

In later years, Mahomet reportedly tried to hide the fact that he spent time in Ireland, perhaps because of the stigma attached to Irish immigrants. His marriage appears to have been happy, and it lasted 65 years until his wife's death in 1851. Dean Mahomet himself died a couple of months later. He is buried alongside his wife in St Nicholas's churchyard in Brighton.

A grandson of Mahomet, a Frederick Akbar Mahomet, was a doctor who was born in Brighton in 1849. He went to Cambridge University, and worked at Guy's Hospital, London. Sadly, he died of typhoid fever at the age of 35 years.

A CRICKETING PRINCE COMES TO IRELAND

A later contact by an Indian citizen with Ireland was that by the famous cricketer Ranji, who was both an Indian prince and also a cricketer of international renown. His full title was Colonel, His Highness Shri Sir Ranjitsinhji Vibhaji, Maharajah Jam Saheb of Nawanagar, GBE, KCSI (born: September 10, 1872; died: April 2, 1933). He was born in Sarodar, a small town in the western Indian province of Kathiwar. He studied at

RANJI AS CRICKETER. *He played for Sussex and for England.*

Trinity College, Cambridge. He played cricket for the county of Sussex, making a century on his first appearance. He first played for England in 1896, also making a century in his first test match. During Ranji's early cricketing years, the great cricketer (Dr) W G Grace was still alive. Robert Thomas, one of the leading umpires of the period, remarked: "The prince is a greater cricketer than the doctor". So prolific was Ranji at getting runs in cricket matches that the satirical magazine, Punch, nicknamed him 'Run-get-sinhji'.

(Plate 1) ROMANIES ('Gypsies') IN THEIR ORIGINAL HOMELAND OF INDIA. *Gypsies still roam freely in India, cradle of the Romany people. They are mostly found in the north, particularly in the desert state of Rajasthan in north-west India. Still nomadic, they are often seen travelling on wooden-wheeled cars, with highly ornate metallic decoration, advertising their skills as smiths and metal workers.*

(Plate 2) BALLYNAHINCH CASTLE HOTEL. *The exterior of this building is much the same as when it was the residence of Ranji in the early 1900s.*

(Plate 3) RANJI IN HIS FULL INDIAN DRESS. *This portrait still hangs on the walls of Ballynahinch hotel, the Irish Republic.*

(Plate 4) AREA OF LAHORE KNOWN AS BHATTI GATE.
A number of the families who came to Northern Ireland originated from this part of Lahore, and many in fact came from the same street.

(Plate 5) 1940s/1950s DWELLING IN RAILWAY QUARTER OF NEW DELHI. *Employees of the Indian Railways, and their families, would live in flats that had been specially built for them by Indian Railways. Rent would be fairly cheap, and the place of work would usually be close-by. This is one such flat, Number 2, located in Kishan Gunj, one of the poorer parts of New Delhi. It was occupied by a family who later moved to live in Northern Ireland.*

(Plate 6) A SHIP USED BY INDIAN SETTLERS WHO CAME TO IRELAND. *The Caledonia, depicted as she is setting out from Bombay.*

(Plate 7) A SHIP USED BY INDIAN SETTLERS WHO CAME TO IRELAND. *The Jal Jawahar.*

In 1907, Ranji was installed Jam Saheb of Nawanagar, and from that time till his death in 1933 he played an important part in Indian affairs. During World War I (1914–1918), he served on the Western Front. In 1915, he lost his right eye in a shooting accident – while out shooting in Yorkshire, he was hit by a shot from a member of the shooting party. Ranji received a letter of sympathy from the king at the time, King George V. In fact, Ranji continued to play some cricket for a few years after the loss of his right eye. He had a glass eye made, and in one of his palaces in India there are reportedly five spare glass eyes on display.

In 1921, Ranji presented two pairs of lions to London Zoo. Although they were African in origin, they were born in his home district of Nawanagar. All four lions were sent to Bombay, and then shipped to London on the ship SS Chanda. It berthed at Tilbury docks. Three lorries had to be contracted to take the lions from Tilbury to the zoo at Regent's Park, London. They were reported to have arrived in good condition, and to have fed well throughout the long journey.

In the summer of 1924, the Ballynahinch estate of thirty thousand acres in Connemara, in the west of Ireland, came on the market. Ranji had come to know of Ballynahinch on account of its famous fisheries. He was a wealthy man, owning property in England and also owning palaces in India. He initially rented the estate, and later bought it from its owners, the Berridge family. It was in Ballynahinch Castle (*Plates 2 and 3, p. 58–59*) that Ranji stayed, and he was greatly attracted to the salmon and sea-trout fishing in the vicinity.

He would come there every summer, around June. Before coming to Ballynahinch he would buy five motor cars, two limousines and three smaller cars. He would buy these in the nearby town of Galway. When leaving for India in October, he would give the cars to the locals as gifts – perhaps one to the parish priest, one to the local vicar, etc. He would do this every year!

Ranji would spend hours trying to outwit fish at spots where no one else would think of catching them. When Ranji first went to Ballynahinch, the troubles surrounding the partition of Ireland were still in recent memory. On his arrival in Dublin, he found a civic reception awaiting him, arranged by the then Prime Minister of Ireland, William Cosgrave. This was followed by an official dinner by the Irish government, which was reciprocated at a later date by Ranji giving a similar dinner at the Shelbourne Hotel, Dublin. When he went to Ballynahinch, his large entourage of Indian servants would accompany him, as well as relatives and a few close friends. His supple wrists, previously of such value in the cricket field, found a new use in his agility with the fishing rod when he was fishing for salmon.

The people of Connemara were grateful to him, not only for the employment he gave to over a hundred men, but also for the encouragement he gave to local activities such as the breeding of Connemara ponies, support for light industries and his interest in local Church affairs. The local population and his many Indian servants seemed to co-exist happily, and two of his nieces went to school at nearby Kylemore Abbey. Ranji took back with him to India a set of dinner plates, each portraying a different view of the castle, lake, river and hills of Connemara. He was responsible for most of the landscaping of the gardens and woods, and also the erection of the fishing piers and huts along the river. The avenues to the castle were covered with marble chips, which were raked every day.

On his birthday, September 10, he would always give a free day with full pay for the castle staff and estate workers, and he would organise a party during which he would personally serve a seven-course lunch to his staff. The party was held in the billiard room (now the bar of the hotel), and Ranji had a truck outside the door to take home the well intoxicated staff! Ranji had his own train carriage from Galway to Clifden, and this stopped off at Ballynahinch station (the Galway-Clifden line closed down in 1936). As Ranji neared Ballynahinch station, the locals would place fire crackers on the line as a sign of welcome.

Alan Ross, in his book about Ranji published in 1983, eloquently describes the nature of the love that Ranji had for his abode in Ireland –

> It is strange to think of an Indian prince holding sway over this remotest of areas, miles and miles of peat bog stretching uninterrupted between the stone flanks of the Connemara hills. Yet, in a real sense, this has become Ranji country, not only because of his love for it but because it complements that other paradise, the Kileshwar hills in India. In climate, there could scarcely be two more contrasting areas, but in the contours and colours of the landscape, the stony dispositions of foothills and outcrop, they are mirror-images of each other. To walk among the Connemara woods and hills, and along the banks of the teeming rivers, is to realise how soothing the memory of it all must have been to Ranji sweating it out in the burning droughts of Kathiawar (page 236).

Ranji looked to his Ballynahinch estate for peace and repose from the turbulent politics of India in the 1920s and from the sometimes oppressive climate of that country. After Ranji died, the castle passed into the hands of his nephew Duleepsinhji, who sold it to the McCormack family from Dublin. Duleepsinhji also auctioned off much of its contents. In 1946, the Irish Tourist Board took it over. For the first time it ceased to be a private family home and became a hotel. In the 1950s, it was bought by an American businessman, who in turn sold shares in the hotel to many friends and business associates. It remains a hotel, largely under American ownership, and it has been host to the former U.S. President, Gerald Ford and his wife, and to the former British Prime Minister, James Callaghan. Piers and huts built by Ranji are still in evidence in the vicinity of the hotel. In 1983, one of the most famous 'gillies' (fishing guides) ever to work in Ballynahinch, Frank Cummins, died. The day before he died, he was still remembering fondly the pair of ruby cuff-links that Ranji had given him over 50 years before.

Although it seems that Ranji occasionally toyed with the idea of retiring permanently in Ireland, the actual contacts he made were more those of a regular visitor. Similarly, the Maharaja of Baroda had a stud farm in the west of Ireland, where he bred horses, but this again was a contact that did not consist of primary settlement into Ireland. We have to look farther afield, in fact several thousand miles to the west rather than to the east, to unravel the origins of Indian settlement in Ireland.

AN INDIAN STOWAWAY FROM CUBA

The year was 1920. The place was Cuba. There were a number of bonded Indian labourers working in a sugar cane plantation in Cuba. Indian labourers had for decades been 'exported' from India by the British, usually to work in colonies where there was a shortage of labour. The conditions and work in this particular plantation in Cuba were reported to be harsh. One of the labourers, by the name of Mohammed Ali, decided to escape on the next ship bound for England. He managed to get away by hiding in the ship's hold, arriving in England as a stowaway. He realised that in England he would be a wanted man. To avoid his capture by the police, he was advised by people whom he met to go to Ireland. He was told that this was a pleasant country, only a night's journey by boat from England. Remember that Ireland was about to gain its freedom, and that it was presumed to be a safe haven for someone in Ali's position.

Probably Ali had never heard of Ireland. Nevertheless, he decided to go there and he landed there safely. He made his way to Dungannon, Northern Ireland and settled in a nearby town called Castlecaulfield. He lived on people's charity for a while. He was advised by a priest to earn his living by selling ties, scarves, socks, handkerchiefs, etc. at the local fairs. There were cattle fairs in different towns on different days of the week, and he would sell his goods at these fairs. He started earning his living and managed to get somewhere to stay in the town. He wrote to his friends in Cuba and also to his relatives in India, singing praises of Ireland, 'a pleasant and friendly place where it was easy to make a living'. A number of his friends and relatives then followed him, and settled in different towns in Northern Ireland. By the mid-1920s, there were friends and relatives of Ali living in Belfast, Ballymena and Londonderry. In the 1940s, two old men by the name of Ali lived together in relative seclusion in the town of Castledawson, Northern Ireland and it is possible that they were related to this original Ali. The relative of Ali that lived in Ballymena came from a small village (Kot Dadal Khan) in the Jullundur district of the state of Punjab, in north-west India. Sad to say, however, the long arm of the law eventually caught up with the original Ali, and he was deported from Britain.

Charlie Verma And Others

There was another Indian living in Cuba who also ventured to Northern Ireland, possibly summoned by Ali. It seems that it was he who started the major chain of settlement that was to result in a succession of further immigrants to Northern Ireland. His name was Jamna Das Abroal. He soon brought his two brothers over to Northern Ireland. These two brothers, Takar Das Abrol and Mansur Ram Abrol, came to Londonderry in Northern Ireland in the 1920s. Takar Das Abrol came first, followed by Mansur Ram. It is rumoured that Takar Das Abrol had also spent some time in Cuba, and that he may have known Ali, but there is some uncertainty on this point. A nephew of Takar Das Abrol and Mansur Ram Abrol was a young man called Pyare Lal Bucher. He came from a village in India called Musapur, in the Jullundur District of northern India. He had worked for a time in Kenya, in East Africa. His job was painting and repairing railway wagons. When he came to Northern Ireland, Pyare Lal Bucher decided to change his name to Charlie Verma, to make it easier for the local Irish population to remember his name. In 1929, Pyare Lal Bucher came to Londonderry to join Jamna Das Abroal and his other uncles there.

In Northern Ireland, Charlie Verma started off a business by selling scarves and other minor clothing items at local fairs. This type of work was not easy. He initially started off on a bicycle, and some years later he bought a van. He himself never drove the van, since he never learned to drive. Instead, he employed a driver to do this. He was based in Letterkenny, living in lodgings there. Charlie Verma was already married when he came to Ireland, but it was not possible for his wife to join him. In 1948, he went back to India along with another Indian settler in Ireland, Bal Makund Mehan. They both tried to start a factory in Bombay that made hosiery material and scarves. After four years, Charlie Verma returned to Ireland. He went back to India permanently in the early 1960s, to his home village of Musapur in the Punjab. He died in 1978.

Charlie Verma had persuaded five of his friends in Kenya to join him in Northern Ireland. One of these friends was called Barnarsi Das Chada. Banarsi Das Chada came to Northern Ireland in 1932. A few years earlier, in 1928, Banarsi Das had gone directly from India to Kenya, and he had worked in a railway workshop in Nairobi. He originated from a village called Hadiabad in the Jullundur District of Punjab, and this particular part of north-west India was to become a rich source of further migrants to Northern Ireland. Another of Charlie Verma's friends was Salag Ram Vij. It is reported that the decision by Salag Ram Vij to come to Ireland was prompted by the fact that Charlie Verma wrote a letter to his father in Talwan. His father, not knowing how to read, took the letter to the Vij family members, who lived nearby and who could read. When they read the contents of the letter, which stated how good life was in Northern Ireland, they thought – why don't we send one of our family there to make a fortune as well? And so it happened that Salag Ram came to Ireland! Although it is not known for certain, it was probably Salag Ram Vij who helped to sponsor someone else from Talwan, a Bal Makund Mehan, who in turn was influential in bringing over a number of Indians from northern India. Salag Ram Vij himself lived in Londonderry for a number of years, but he eventually moved to Liverpool where he died in the 1950s.

LIFE IN INDIA

Life in India for Dwarka Nath Kapur was very different from that in Britain. His father was a clerk in the railways, and Dwarka Nath also had a job there. The job that Dwarka Nath had in the late 1940s/early 1950s was fairly routine. He would get more fun out of flying a kite or playing cards than from his job.

He grew up in Lahore (*Plate 4, p. 60*) with his three brothers and four sisters. Growing up in India in the 1920s and 1930s was more eventful than in Britain, often tragically so. Once, when bubonic plague was rife in Lahore, Dwarka Nath saw a rat in his house. He dared his sister to touch the rat. She touched the rat. A few days later, she caught the plague and subsequently died.

Snakes were also plentiful in parts of Lahore. When one of Dwarka Nath's relatives left a house vacant for a long period of time, he returned to find it infested with snakes, and a snake-catcher had to be called to empty the house of snakes!

When Dwarka Nath moved to Delhi after the partition of India into India and Pakistan, he got another job in the railways and lived in the 'railway quarters' in New Delhi. This was an estate of two story buildings that comprised small flats (although the word 'flat' is rather an over-generous term to use). It was built solely for railway employees, and was one of the 'perks' of working for the railways.

These were flats that had windows without window panes, and doorways without doors (*Plate 5, p. 61*). There was also a lack of running hot water. Electricity was available, but there were frequent power cuts. Nonetheless, they were homely flats. The streets were narrow, so you could talk to your neighbour across the road by shouting at them from the front 'window'. Dwarka Nath not only had his wife and four children to look after, he also had to take care of his aging father and mother. His father would stand in the street on a hot summer's day, and would give out cool water to passers-by.

Being a man with gambling instincts, quite often Dwarka Nath would have his hands read by a palmist. Some palmists would say 'You'll be rich one day'. He would tell this to his wife, who would usually reply – 'What rubbish. You've only got a simple, menial job. How will *you* be rich one day?'

Those who came from the Indian subcontinent to Ireland in the 1930s and 1940s had usually been accustomed to living a fairly basic existence in India. Beds were not ordinary beds that you find in the west. They were called 'charpai', these being wooden frames joined together by a tough interwoven string. While some family members would sleep inside, it was more customary – especially for the adults – to sleep on the roof of the dwelling. There was no need for a pillow or a blanket. At the most, a cool winter's night might necessitate a sheet. Whenever the monsoons came, however, it was wiser to sleep inside for fear of getting soaked!

Milk came straight from the buffalo or cow that was in the milking station on the estate. There was no pasteurised, bottled milk! Brushing one's teeth was by means of a stick, called a 'datun', which was actually the twig from a tree called the 'neem tree' – this twig gave out juices that helped to clean the teeth. Radios had only just arrived, and few families in the estate had them. Televisions were non-existent on the estate. Children went to school, but it was often an outdoor school, with classes in an clearing. Luxuries were few and far between. Most children never knew what it was like to eat chocolate – that was a real luxury preserved for the rich classes. Cars were also reserved for the very rich – usually Maharajas or foreign diplomats. Most Indians got around by walking or on bike.

Most of the Indian settlers who came to Northern Ireland in the 1930s and 1940s had little in the way of formal qualifications. Those who had such qualifications, or who had held important jobs in India, would have found it difficult to get these recognised in Ireland, where practices and work routines would inevitably be very different from those in India. The backgrounds of those who came from India to set up business in Northern Ireland were varied. Some were in business, some held clerical posts, some were in government positions, and some came from farming families. In most cases, they were only able to afford a relatively simple standard of living, with little prospect of wealth in their own country. By contrast, those who came to study or to work as doctors often came from well-to-do professional or business families. In most cases, Indians had come to Ireland to earn more money than they could hope to earn in India. They could thus have a higher standard of living for their families, and also indirectly for the families that they left behind in India, since they would inevitably send back money and goods to their loved-ones in India. Many had also come to Britain in order to give their children a good education and thereby give their children better opportunities for gaining a higher standard of living than they would have expected had they been brought up in India. In order to come to Britain, an Indian would have to be 'sponsored' by an Indian who had already settled there. If this was done, then a visa would usually follow without any major difficulties.

SCENES OF VIOLENCE AND UPHEAVAL AS A RESULT OF THE PARTITION OF INDIA AND PAKISTAN IN 1947. *A number of the Indian families who settled in Northern Ireland were Hindus or Sikhs who lived in Lahore, and who had to move to India during the time of partition. Around 300,000 of the population of Lahore were Hindus or Sikhs, and it is estimated that 75% of them fled to India.*

Destruction of part of Lahore as a result of riots there.

Crowds of Hindu and Sikh refugees in Lahore railway station, waiting for trains to take them to India.

Hindus and Sikhs on a crowded lorry heading for India.

A column of Hindus and Sikhs leaving Pakistan.

SURVIVING THE NIGHTMARE OF PARTITION

> In 1947, we lived in a Hindu enclave within a Moslem area in Lahore. Lahore, which was the major city in Punjab, would become part of the new country, Pakistan, that was to be formed. We thought we would be safe, since many of our closest friends and neighbours were Moslems. However, we began to learn that they were killing Hindus and setting fire to their houses. From the roof-top of our house, we could see fires burning around the city. At the last minute, we decided to leave for India. We packed up all that we could take with us. We had to leave behind our property and many belongings. My wife, my parents and my three sons managed to get onto the last train that was leaving from Lahore to Delhi. Some of the earlier trains from Lahore to India had been attacked, with many of the Hindu occupants stabbed to death by marauding Moslems, and so the journey was a very risky one. But we managed to reach Delhi safely. *[An Indian settler who arrived in Northern Ireland in the early 1950s]*

In the case of those who came directly from India in the 1940s or early 1950s, this was for many of them the second major upheaval within a few years. In the summer of 1947, as a result of the partition of India into two countries, India and Pakistan, there was a major transfer of population. The actual partition itself took place in August, 1947 – it had initially been planned by the British to take place over a period of 18 months. However, it was decided by Lord Mountbatten, the last viceroy of India, to try and push this through over a period of five months. He had been authorised by the Labour government, headed by Prime Minister Clement Atlee, to implement the British withdrawal from India. Millions of people, mainly Hindus, headed east from what was to be the new state of Pakistan to India. Another equally large number of Moslems travelled west from India to Pakistan. Truck-loads of Moslem refugees would be taken to a temporary camp, and from there they would be transported from India to Pakistan. The same would happen for Hindus who were trapped in Pakistan. It is estimated that up to a million people were killed during the period of partition, one of the most horrific man-made disasters of the 20th century outside of the two world wars. The apparent hasty and poorly planned retreat by the British from its Indian empire has been blamed by some historians, such as the British historian Andrew Roberts, for the huge loss of life that took place in India and Pakistan.

Many of the Hindus who fled to India came from the city of Lahore. This was the capital of the state of Punjab in pre-partition India, and this state was to be divided into two parts. Lahore was to be located just inside the Pakistan side of the border. It was a largely Moslem city. It was therefore a city from which thousands of Hindus would wish to flee.

CHAMAN LAL TREON. *Before coming to Northern Ireland, he had a lucky escape during the disturbances around the time of the partition of India and Pakistan.*

Two of the Indians who came to Northern Ireland had vivid stories to tell of their escape from Lahore to India.

"I Fled By Bike"

Chaman Lal Treon, a 25 year-old sanitary inspector at the time of partition, had the following experience –

My wife and two sons left Lahore a few months before me. A few days before partition, in August 1947, they went by train from Lahore to Saharanpur, a town across the border in India – my sister was there. I myself stayed on in Lahore till November. The house in Lahore that I inhabited was my mother-in-law's house. Some of my Hindu friends tried to disguise themselves as Moslems and got killed by Hindus. I too was disguised as a Moslem, and I kept my beard (most Moslems wore beards).

I fled by bike from Lahore to Amritsar, a distance of 35 miles. Amritsar would be in the newly partitioned India, whereas Lahore would become part of the new Moslem state of Pakistan. When I reached Amritsar, I was held up by several Sikhs. The Sikhs immediately took me for a Moslem, since I had been disguised as a Moslem. They threatened to kill me in spite of my pleading that I was really a Hindu. They asked me for proof that I was a Hindu and not a Moslem. I then recited the Hindu mantras (holy prayers) to them. That convinced them that I really was a Hindu, so they let me go. They then took me to a barber to get my beard shaved off!

My father and sister had come from Lahore in a truck that carried refugees. They were in Amritsar in my cousin's house. They all stayed there for a few days, and then they went on to Delhi. At that time, when I arrived in Amritsar, I did not know whether my wife and my two sons were dead or alive. They had left Lahore by train, and around that time many trains had been held up and the occupants had been killed. Fortunately, my wife and children had in fact reached across the border to Saharanpur safely. The train that they came on was crammed to overflowing, and they had to sit in between the carriages of the train. After my wife had arrived in Saharanpur, she constantly checked the trains that arrived from Lahore to see if I was on any of the trains. I myself only found from announcements on radio that my wife and children were alive – at that time, regular announcements were made on the radio indicating the names of those refugees who had successfully made it across the border into India.

GETTING OUT OF INDIA

Getting a passport and visa was no easy task. It often meant giving bribes to officials. In addition, you had to show that you had enough money in the bank to maintain yourself and your family in Britain. In the case of a visa, you had to have sponsorship from someone in Britain. I refused to consider giving a bribe to get my passport. When I applied for one, I was told that I did not have enough money in my bank account to take my family on a holiday, never mind to go and settle in Britain. I tried to see if my doctor could write a letter to indicate that I needed to go to Britain for treatment in relation to the loss of sight in my left eye. But he indicated that my left eye was a hopeless case – there was a detachment of the retina at the back of the eye, and nothing could now be done about it. Therefore, he could not write any such letter. I happened to mention all this to a friend who was a catering contractor to the railway station where I worked. He told me that he had contacts, and that if I gave him the documents, he would get me a passport in a few days. A few days later I got my passport! I had to cash in my pension in order to raise money for the journey to Britain. We did not have much in the way of jewellery left that we could sell – we had sold some of it a few years earlier when my nephew travelled to Northern Ireland. At that time, my wife pawned precious jewellery that she had been given as a wedding gift to help pay the cost of his fare. *[Experience of a first generation Indian who came to Northern Ireland in the early 1950s]*

JOURNEY FROM INDIA TO IRELAND

The boat on which we travelled was French, and the main thing that we could get to eat was long French bread rolls and black tea! Fortunately, we had taken with us a supply of food that might last us for the few weeks of the journey. Our parents were concerned that we should eat well on the journey to Ireland, and they made us a large tin that contained 'pakora' (a form of fried vegetable), 'mitee' (a type of large savoury biscuit), 'pinee' (a type of Indian sweet), etc. Our parents prepared these particular sorts of foods since these items were very nourishing and filling.

When the three of us arrived in Ireland in 1934 after our journey from India, we initially stayed overnight in a hotel in Portadown, Northern Ireland. It was the Queen's Hotel. After our stay, the landlady – knowing that we had come by boat from India – presented us with a 'bill for three sailors'. This may have been because we looked so scruffy! Presumably, the bill we got was a special rate, different than the normal rate. *[Accounts by two early settlers from India to Northern Ireland]*

Until the 1950s, the journey from India to Ireland was invariably by boat. Many ships plied the line between India and Britain in the 1930s, 1940s and 1950s – the P & O Line was one of the major shipping lines, with Bombay being one of the stops on the regular run taking emigrants between Britain and Australia. French, Polish and Italian ships were also used by Indians to get to Britain from India. The P & O ships were reported to take the shortest time, around two weeks for the trip between Bombay and a British port such as Southampton, with the other ships taking rather longer. Around this time (the early 1950s), the one-way fare was £45 (worth several hundred pounds in today's money). The ship would usually stop at ports in the middle east, such as in the Sudan or the Suez canal.

After Indian independence in 1947, ships with Indian names became more common, and these included the *Jal Jawahar* *(Plate 7, p. 62)* (*Jal* means water, and *Jawahar* derives from the name of Jawaharlal Nehru, the first Prime Minister of India and one of the leaders of the freedom movement). This boat belonged to the Scindia Shipping Company. Other boats included several ships of the Anchor Line, such as the *Circasia*, the *Caledonia* (*Plate 6, p. 62*) and the *Celicia*.

Usually, the boat journey was from Bombay to one of the British ports, for example Southampton or Liverpool. In a few cases, individuals went from Bombay to Colombo, the capital of Sri Lanka (or Ceylon as it was then known). Then they took a boat on a French shipping line to Marseilles (one such boat was called the *Aramas*), travelled overland to Calais, and went by boat to Dover. Some Indians who travelled this way took the opportunity to stop over in Paris for a few days.

In the case of the Italian shipping line, one such journey was made by an Indian family in 1960. They went on the ship *Roma* that sailed from Australia to Genoa, calling at Bombay. Their stops on the way included Port Said in Egypt, Malta, Naples and then Genoa. At Port Said, for the sum of £5 they were allowed to get off, have a tour of the pyramids, etc. and then join the ship at a port further up the Suez Canal.

Getting Prepared For Arrival

The boat passed through the Suez canal, through the Mediterranean Sea and via the Bay of Biscay. Journeys were occasionally rough, especially the part of the journey through the Bay of Biscay, with a number of settlers from India reporting that they were sea-sick on that part of the journey. Often the passengers were given lime to help with their sea-sickness. In those boats that had an Indian crew, it was usually possible to obtain Indian dishes. Many Indian settlers would have been vegetarians, and some would bring food along with them to do their own cooking while on board the ship. One Indian was asked by one of his friends in Ireland to bring mangoes with him from India. He took 200 mangoes along with him onto the ship, but by the time the journey was half-way through the mangoes had been eaten up by him and by his fellow passengers!

For those who did not know English well, time on the journey from India to Britain would occasionally be spent learning English. There was also the matter of learning things about the British way of life, such as the currency. In India, it was 'rupees and 'annas', whereas in Britain it was 'pounds, shillings and pence'. After around two-three weeks on ship, they would feel wobbly with their first few steps on dry land, since this was usually the first journey by boat for most of the Indians!

When the ship was approaching England, some of the Sikhs on board would use this opportunity to shave off their beard and cut their long hair. The beard and long hair, with the turban over the hair, would have been kept on the outward journey so as to please relatives in India. However, once they were back in Britain the Sikhs found that this aspect of their religious tradition would sometimes be a handicap. One of the Sikh businessmen from Northern Ireland, on his journey back from India to Ireland, still kept his beard and turban. A close friend, who had already settled in Ireland a few years earlier and who had called him over to live in Northern Ireland, had decided not to write to him in India to ask him to shave his hair, since this would probably have discouraged him from coming to Ireland. Instead, he wrote a letter to him c/o his ship (the *Jal Jawahar*). The letter in fact reached him when the ship stopped in Port Said, Egypt. In his letter, the close friend in Northern Ireland strongly advised the Sikh gentleman to get rid of his turban and his beard, since this would work against him when he was selling goods to the local Irish people, who might be scared by such an unusual appearance. However, the young Sikh decided to ignore this advice, perhaps still feeling the pressure from his parents and other close relatives whom he had just left behind in India.

The trip to Northern Ireland was usually from Liverpool to Belfast, though in a few instances a boat was taken from Holyhead to Dun Laoghaire (which in those days was called Kingston), with a train connection to Northern Ireland. One Indian settler had, as his first experience, a train ride from Belfast to Londonderry where the train was full of Orangemen, presumably going to the Apprentice Boys' celebrations in Londonderry. The Orangemen were playing their drums, and he vividly recalls the bloodied hands of the drummers as a result of the repetitive beating of the drums.

Those arriving in Ireland without anyone to meet them at the station were in a vulnerable position if anyone wanted to take advantage of their innocence. One Indian arrived at Londonderry railway station and wanted to get to 4 Simpson's Brae, which he knew was the main base for Indians in Londonderry. Little did he know that it was just a few hundred yards away from the station. He took a taxi, that duly took him to his destination, and charged him half a crown for the journey – equivalent to £5 today.

THE VARIETY OF NEW SETTLERS

> I ventured to Dublin because I remembered reading the works of Shaw and Yeats at school in India, and I was fascinated to go to their country of birth. *[Indian student going to Dublin to try and get into medical school]*

It was not easy starting work in a new country, one that was different in language, culture, climate and in many other ways. Most of those who came had little in the way of formal qualifications. Those who had such qualifications, or who had held important jobs in India, would have found it difficult to get these qualifications recognised in Northern Ireland, where practices and work routines would inevitably be very different. In many cases, Indians had come to Northern Ireland to earn more than they could in India. They could thus have a higher standard of living for their families. They could also help to raise the standard of living of the families whom they left behind, since they would usually send back money and goods to India. Many had also come in order to give their children a good education and to give their children better opportunities for gaining a higher standard of living than they would have expected, had they been brought up in India. Some of the Indians who settled in Northern Ireland initially came to England, and were told of better opportunities in Northern Ireland by friends or relatives.

READY FOR BUSINESS. *An Indian settler, F C Sumra, standing in the doorway of the van that he used for selling clothes to the local Irish community in Londonderry, Northern Ireland.*

Many of the Indians who left India to come to Ireland had some contacts with earlier Indians who went there several years earlier. In the case of Indians from the Jullundur district of northern India, many Indians who settled in Northern Ireland came from the same villages in this district – usually the villages of Talwan or Phillaur. This provided the link that made others follow. For example, one of the Indians who came in the 1930s, Fakir Chand Sumra, was friendly with a solicitor in his village (Phillaur). The brother of this solicitor was called Bal Makand Mehan, and Bal Makand was already in Ireland working in the clothing business. He therefore sponsored Fakir Chand Sumra to come over to Britain. When Fakir Chand Sumra did come and settle in Londonderry, he came to be known to the locals as 'Paddy Sumra'.

The early settlers, especially those who did not have any personal contacts and who came on their own initiative, were of the adventurous type. The imperial links with Great Britain were ever present, and so Great Britain was the obvious place to go if someone living in India was thinking about a trip abroad in search of a better life. Often, these Indians went to England first of all, and then made their way to Ireland. The decision to go to Ireland could have been as a result of curiosity or, more often, as a result of meeting others who had been to Ireland and who spoke well of it as a place to earn a living and as a place where the inhabitants were friendly.

Many Indians, especially those who came in the 1930s and 1940s, were unmarried. Even if an Indian was married, he invariably left his wife and children behind in India, simply because he could not afford the cost of taking them along or of supporting them in Ireland. In the early days of working in Northern Ireland, this meant long hours of work in order to earn sufficient money with which to bring a family over from India.

A few Indian men did develop friendships with local Irish ladies, though the more orthodox Indian men would generally frown on this. In one instance, one Indian businessman, after seeing his uncle have affairs with local Irish girls, insisted that any of his brothers in India who ventured from India to Ireland first got married in India and then came to Ireland, bringing his wife with him!

Those who came to Ireland can be divided into four broad categories –

(1) Self-employed businessmen: these formed the majority of those that settled in the 1920s to 1950s. During that period they were particu-

larly prominent in Northern Ireland, and almost all were in the textile clothing business;

(2) Students, most of whom had intended to come and study for a short while and then return to their country of origin, which was to India or to one of the British colonies with large Indian populations;

(3) Professional workers, such as doctors, engineers, chemists, etc. Many of these individuals came to Ireland for a period of post-graduate study or training, though a few came with the direct aim of settling down Northern Ireland;

(4) A miscellaneous group that included restaurant workers, sailors whose ships berthed in Ireland, embassy staff, Hindu priests, etc.

A large number of Indians have spent some time in Ireland in a temporary capacity. It is impossible to list each and every category of transient settler. Students and doctors gaining post-graduate experience perhaps form the largest group within this category. Many of these went back to India or went on to North America, and excelled in their respective fields. They remained proud of the experience and knowledge that they had gained in Ireland. One such person was a Dr Chopra, who came to the Royal Victoria Hospital to gain experience in Neurology. He subsequently went back to India, and he is now one of the leading neurologists in the country, having been for many years Professor of Neurology at the Postgraduate Medical Institute in Chandigarh, northern India.

Because of the shipyard and docks in Belfast, Indian sailors have occasionally passed through Northern Ireland. In the early 1960s, a group of around a dozen Indian sailors 'jumped ship'. Some eventually married local Irish girls and settled in Northern Ireland.

Some cricketers from India have, for a limited time period, joined local league teams in Northern Ireland, gained relevant experience, and then returned to India.

'INDIA TO IRELAND VIA PINEWOOD STUDIOS'

Most of the first Indian settlers from India to Ireland were young men who had previously lived in village communities in India, who did not have great wealth to bring along with them, but who had qualities of hope and determination that saw them through tough times. This is the story of one such man, Ram Gupta (born 1910, died 1994).

RAM GUPTA.
One of the first Indians to set up a clothing business in Northern Ireland.

My name is Ram Gupta. I grew up in a village called Talwan, near Jullundur, in north-west India. My father owned a general store, where I was an assistant. In 1936, when I was 26 years old, I travelled to England with a friend who had relatives in Birmingham. My first stop was in London, where I obtained temporary employment as an extra in the film 'Elephant Boy', starring the famous actor Sabu, which was being made at Pinewood Studios, Middlesex at this time. I had a minor disagreement with the director, the famous Sir Alexander Korda, who would not let me wear a hat with my dhoti (white Indian loin cloth). I then resigned after only a few days work on the film!

Next, I made a brief excursion to the west of England, visiting Taunton in Somerset, before reaching Birmingham, where I parted company with my friend. I then travelled alone to Preston. In Preston, I embarked on my first business venture. This was selling clothes in pubs, and I carried my merchandise in a suitcase. I lived in rented lodgings which I shared with a Moslem friend. Two English couples, a Mr and Mrs Fletcher, and a 'Bill and Nancy' befriended me. I maintained contact with them for many years.

In the meantime, I had also kept in touch with a Fakir Chand Sumra, whom I knew in India, and who had also travelled from Jullundur to England, though at a separate time. As a young man, Fakir Chand was an adventurous sort and he initially planned to go to East Africa. He made his way to Bombay, but when his mother got to hear of it, she dispatched her younger son to fetch Fakir Chand back.

When Fakir Chand came to England, he initially went to Liverpool. He knew someone from Jullundur who had been successful in the retail clothing business in Northern Ireland, a Mr Bal Makund Mehan – who had settled and was working in Londonderry. In fact, in 1931 I had spent a year with him in Ireland helping him out with his clothing business. Bal Makund had encouraged Fakir Chand to come to Ireland. Bal Makund's brother was a solicitor in Talwan. This solicitor and Fakir Chand had been good friends in India. Fakir Chand and I did not want to disadvantage Bal Makund Mehan and other Indians in Londonderry by setting up a competing business and encroaching on their 'territory' in Londonderry, and we therefore took lodgings in Omagh, which was some distance away. Fakir Chand and I travelled to Omagh in 1937, to try and sell clothes there.

Our way of working was to carry a small suitcase, filled with clothing items such as shirts, socks, ties, underwear, etc. (i.e. non-bulky items). If the suitcase was not carried by hand, it would be mounted on the rear of a bicycle. We would travel within Omagh and its surroundings, covering 10–15 miles a day, knocking on doors and trying to establish regular customers. Our typical working hours would be from 9 o'clock in the morning to 7–8 o'clock in the evening, Monday to Saturday. Fakir Chand and I pioneered the system of selling clothes on interest-free credit, where the customer would make a regular weekly payment of, say, 4 or 5 shillings (20–25 pence in today's currency), which would allow him/her to purchase goods up to the value of £5. We did not have much difficulty in securing a number of regular customers, especially in country areas, because the majority of working people had no form of transport.

I recall that in those days, around 1937, the typical wages for an average working person in Northern Ireland were £1 per week. I had a sales turnover of £25–30 per week, with a profit level of around £3–4 per week. From this amount, I was able to pay for my accommodation and meals, and also other living expenses. Every month, I could still send the sum of £8 to my family in India – that would have been regarded as a large sum of money in those days.

Fakir Chand and I worked six days a week, for nearly 10 hours a day, travelling on our bicycles in all weather. My Sundays were spent both in the usual household domestic chores, in making up accounts and in writing out orders for goods that were needed for the following week. The goods were purchased by means of orders made by post from wholesalers in London – new orders were posted out on Sunday, and the parcels of goods would arrive in Northern Ireland by Tuesday/Wednesday. At that time, there were no clothing wholesalers in Belfast to whom we could turn.

After a year, I moved from Omagh to the town of Armagh, and Fakir Chand went to Londonderry. I took up lodgings in Dobbin Street, Armagh. During the days, I would be on my bike with my suitcase of clothes. In the evenings and on days when I was free, I would just walk around Armagh and occasionally stand in the market square. One day a shopkeeper, who had probably noticed me standing in the square on certain days, brought me into a nearby clothing shop that he owned. His name was Marcus Martin. We got talking, and he was quite impressed by my coming all the way from India and working so hard to survive in this country. When Marcus found out how I used to send money to Glasgow to get my stock of clothes, he decided to take me with him to Belfast. Marcus introduced me to his wholesale suppliers in Belfast. He acted as a guarantee for me, and the wholesale suppliers therefore allowed me to open an account with them. I was probably the first Indian businessman to open an account with Belfast wholesale merchants – I myself then acted as guarantee for other Indians, who were then able to open accounts in Belfast. Together with other Indians, I am greatly indebted to the kindness of Marcus Martin for helping our businesses get established.

SAT PAL KAPUR. *Known locally as Paul Kapur, he was one of the first Indians to settle in the northern part of Northern Ireland, settling in the town of Coleraine. A large number of Indian families came to Northern Ireland as a direct result of his efforts.*

'FROM PEN-NIBS TO PULLOVERS'

Sat Pal Kapur, or Paul Kapur as he was known in Ireland, grew up in Lahore, India (now in Pakistan). His mother had died when Paul was a young child, and his father had remarried. As was the custom in India, Paul was subsequently raised not by his father and step mother, but by a close relative. In this case, it was his father's brother, Dwarka Nath Kapur, who brought up Paul. Dwarka Nath treated him as his own child. He helped to educate him, and in later years he also bore all the responsibility for arranging his marriage and the actual wedding.

Paul initially wanted to be a soldier in the Indian army, but his family strongly disapproved and arranged for him to be 'bought out'. Paul then decided to import pen nibs from England, with the idea of putting these nibs onto pens in India and then selling the pens abroad. Pen nibs in India were either not available or of very poor quality. He therefore set up a company with his close friend Sat Pal Kher and with a cousin. Paul went to London to try to purchase pen nibs. Sat Pal Kher's father helped with putting up cash for the venture. Paul Kapur made two trips to London. His venture proved to be a failure, partly due to the fact that the market price for pens fell around this time. After his second trip to London in May 1947, Paul set off back to India, a rather disheartened young man. By chance, on the ship that was going back to Bombay, he met a young man from India, Fakir Chand Sumra (whose story is told above – page 81–82). Fakir Chand was going back to India to get married (his first wife had died suddenly). The two men got talking to each other. Paul told him about his unhappy experience in trying to deal in pen nibs and pens. Fakir Chand told Paul about the much better opportunities that were in Northern Ireland where he himself had been in business for around ten years. He told him how friendly the people were, and how there were many opportunities to set up a clothing business that was based on door-to-door selling techniques. He suggested that Paul come to Northern Ireland. So Paul went to Northern Ireland later in the year, August 1947. He in fact went on the same boat as Fakir Chand Sumra and Fakir Chand's wife, and they celebrated Indian Independence Day on the boat (August 15, 1947).

Occasionally, the trip between India and Britain resulted in new friendships that were to lead to a major new settlement of Indians to Ireland. The chance meeting between Paul Kapur and Fakir Chand Sumra was one such occurrence.

It is interesting to note that both individuals involved in this chance encounter had personal histories that were marred by tragedy, in each case the sudden death of a loved one (Paul Kapur's mother, Fakir Chand Sumra's first wife). In those days, death at an early age was quite commonplace in India, mainly due to the widespread occurrence of infections and also the inadequate treatment facilities for these and other conditions, illnesses that would now not prove fatal. Out of tragedy can come good fortune, and this proved to be the case in the tale of these two settlers.

'FROM A FARM-WORKER TO A FACTORY OWNER'

Nizam Dean worked as a farmer in a small village called Jagraon, near Faisalabad in north-west India (now Pakistan). He also happened to be good at stitching clothes. However, he had little education, and he knew little English. His family was quite poor. He knew someone who was settled and doing well in Ireland, and so he decided to make his fortune there.

When he came to Ireland in 1932, at the age of 35 years, he was already married, but it was not feasible to bring his wife along with him. When he arrived in Northern Ireland, he settled down in Belfast, renting a bedsit in an area in north Belfast. Ironically, this area is close to the part of Belfast that now houses a Hindu Temple (though Nizam himself was a Moslem). Like most of the other Indians who came around this time, he started a door-to-door business, carrying around his suitcase full of clothes. He would walk and also occasionally use the bus. He later acquired a bicycle. Nizam went out in all

NIZAM DEAN. *He came from India to Northern Ireland in the 1930s. After the formation of Pakistan in 1947, he chose to be a Pakistani citizen. He was one of the first people from the Indian subcontinent to set up a factory in Northern Ireland. This picture, taken on November 19, 1966, shows him on the right, with a white cap. He is seen close to Ayub Khan, the President of Pakistan, who is the centre figure with a moustache.*

weathers, riding his bike for 5–10 miles a day. On one occasion, the snow was so heavy when he was out on his bike meeting some of his customers that he had to stay in a farm house overnight. After 2–3 years, he bought a van.

His bed-sit in Belfast had no running hot water, and no bath. If he wanted a wash, he would have to heat some water on a stove and fill a bucket with hot water. After a few years, he moved to his own house in a street in a neighbouring area of Belfast. At that time in the 1930s, he was the only person on the street to own a motor vehicle.

Nizam was in Belfast throughout World War II, and during the bombing of Belfast he would seek shelter in the nearby hills. At the end of the war, in 1945, Nizam opened his factory. This was the first factory to be owned by someone from the Indian subcontinent. He made mens' shirts and ladies' dresses, and these items were exported to England and to Scotland. Initially, he employed 4–5 people. At its peak in the early 1960s, his factory employed 70–80 workers.

Nizam was well known and well respected, both in Northern Ireland and also in England. When the President of Pakistan visited Edinburgh in 1965, Nizam was invited to meet him. He was introduced to the President as one of the Pakistanis who had done exceptionally well in Britain.

GRAVESTONE OF NIZAM DEAN. *He was one of the most successful Pakistani citizens to settle in Northern Ireland. He is buried in a cemetery on the outskirts of Belfast.*

While Nizam Dean was by all accounts a brilliant businessman, and could converse in English, it is reported that he never learned how to read or write English fluently. Yet, he would often be seen smartly dressed, with a copy of the *Times* newspaper under his arm! It is also reported that some of his suppliers were very impressed by how promptly and efficiently he paid his debts – he apparently had the habit of going to his supplier in person, taking along his cheque book and the bill in question, and asking the supplier to write out the amount of cheque that he required. Little did the supplier know that Nizam could not write cheques due to his limited knowledge of English!

Nizam Dean died of cancer on October 13 1967, aged 67 years, and his body is buried in a cemetery on the outskirts of Belfast. On the gravestone reads the following inscription –

REMEMBER MAN AS YOU PASS BY
AS YOU ARE NOW, SO ONCE WAS I
AS I AM NOW, SO YOU MUST BE
PREPARE, O MAN, TO FOLLOW ME

Nizam's brother – Jamal Dean – came to Northern Ireland in 1947, and he also opened a factory, one that made knitwear. This factory in fact started by chance – Jamal was owed some money by a local Irish man, who could not or would not pay up. This man did however have some knitting machines, and Jamal took these in lieu of money for the debt he was owed. He used these knitting machines to help start his factory.

'FROM A MATHS TEACHER IN INDIA TO A MATHS TEACHER IN IRELAND'

I arrived in Sligo, on the west coast of Ireland, on a snowy January evening, in 1953. I had cycled in the snow from Bundoran with my suitcases, containing all my worldly possessions. I was without my wife, who throughout my life has been my soul companion and my source of moral encouragement. I had left her behind in Punjab, to be sent for when I was settled.

When I arrived wet and shivering at the cafe run by Maggie and Anne McGowan I must have been a sorry sight. This was my first experience of snow. It was certainly their first experience of a non-white arriving in their midst. If this caused them alarm, they didn't show it and I was welcomed into The Cosy Cafe where a blazing fire and a good Irish tea soon revived me. This was the beginning of my lifelong friendship with

JOHNNIE CHADA. *He came from the Punjab to settle in Sligo, on the west coast of the Irish Republic. Johnnie Chada was a keen football fan, and this photograph shows him on the right with Jackie Charlton, when Charlton was manager of the Ireland football team.*

Ireland.

Although I graduated from the University of Punjab with a teaching degree in maths, I had to start on a different path of life here. So I started a business from scratch selling clothes, at first travelling by bike. For years I did a forty mile radius of Sligo into Manorhamilton, Bundoran and out as far as Skreen. This was done on the bike, with my wares in suitcases. In all those years of travelling I met nothing but goodwill and kindness. I honestly believe that the notion of racial prejudice does not exist in the Irish psyche.

Anyway, back to my early days. I had decided on my business venture. It remained for me to establish a place in which to live, so that I could send for my beloved wife. Here again, I was fortunate in the generosity of the Irish character. I was having a mineral in "Molly Noone's" (Connelly's Bar) when I came across Mattie Scanlon. Without hesitation, when he heard my predicament, he offered me the key of a house in Holborn Street. I sent for my wife and daughter and there we lived happily for many years. What can I say about the neighbours in Holborn Street except that they were the salt of the earth? All of them. The Mitchell family in particular were outstanding. At that time, my wife was a lonely stranger with very little grasp of the language. But everyone got together to make her feel part of the neighbourhood as much as themselves.

Of course we had our sad times, and it was hard work selling from a bicycle. But the happy times were made all the happier by contrast. Funny incidents? Anyone who deals with the public for a living should be able to write a book of funny incidents. There's one in particular I recall. After I got my first car, I was travelling in the dark after a day's selling, when a slight accident put paid to one of my lights. I was duly stopped by the local sergeant.

"You have no light," he said sternly.
I hopped out of the car and shrugged uncomprehendingly.
"Me no light?" I said slowly.
We repeated this interchange a few times until the sergeant gave up.
"Come on," he sighed to his colleague, "This gentleman has no English."

The following day I was selling my wares to a kind lady. We were bargaining in her kitchen when ... you guessed it! ... in walked her husband, the very sergeant who had stopped me. "Beglob," he said dryly "Your English improved greatly since last night." Luckily he had a sense of humour and we had a good laugh.

In 1960 we moved to Circular Road. This was another example of the generosity and trust of the Irish. Although I was a non-national this made no difference to the builders, Noonan and Co, Dublin, when I set about getting a house. They took me at face value and accepted my deposit. The next hurdle was looking for a mortgage from the Irish Permanent Building Society. At that time, one dealt directly with Dublin. The then managing director wanted bank security and two references for security on the loan. I sought a personal interview, which he kindly granted. I looked him straight in the face and told him that I knew nobody and had no assets in the bank. "My honesty and your kindness will be the only security for my request for a loan," I told him. He returned my look with equal candour. "The loan is granted," he said. I will never forget this stupendous act of kindness. So I settled with my wife and children in Circular Road and the neighbours there proved as kind and caring as those in my earlier home in Holborn Street.

Well, even though I was happy selling clothes, I never gave up my yen to get back to my first love of teaching maths. While I enjoyed my business of selling clothes and had built up a large clientele of truly lovely people, I never lost the hope that one day I could return to my first chosen profession. In 1968, my break came with the offer of two morning classes in the local college, Summerhill College. Then, in 1969, I was accepted for full-time employment provided I could fulfil the Department of Education requirement that I pass a test in Oral Irish. I was determined that nothing would stop me and so I crammed for six months and passed the Oral examination. I was then registered with the Department and could teach with full equality. I was overjoyed.

In the meantime, I and my family – now numbering my wife and two sons and two daughters – were integrated fully into the Sligo community. There was never a sense of isolation for us. In fact I was elected Sligo Man of the Year in 1987. I have been very involved in local activities notably working with the mentally handicapped, the physically handicapped and of course with my great love – the local soccer team, Sligo Rovers. I was chairman for five terms and am currently treasurer, having held that position for many years.

I went to college in Jullundur, northern India, in 1942 and during this time I also took part in the movement for independence or 'freedom struggle' as it was called. During this time, I got to know some of the famous players in that struggle – Mahatma Gandhi, Jawaharlal Nehru, Rajendra Prasad, Sardar Patel, etc. I got to know Nehru in particular, and our families became friends. When I visited India in 1977 with my wife, I wrote to Indira Gandhi that I knew her father and that I was coming to India on a visit. She replied to me, and my wife and I met up with her in Delhi. When I met her, I presented her with a book of poetry by Yeats, who was a close friend of the Indian writer and Nobel Prize winner Tagore. I also met Nehru's sister, Madam Pandit, when she visited Dublin in the early 1960s – at that time, she was Indian High Commissioner to Great Britain and honorary Ambassador to Ireland before the embassy in Dublin was formally established.

Would I change anything in my life? No. I started out poor, but was determined to succeed. I can say that two factors contributed to that success, the faithful love and moral support of my wonderful wife and the goodwill of the Irish people. My philosophy is simple and echoes the teachings of Christ, which can be brought down to two principles: "Love God, love your neighbour". When you put money in the bank it earns interest, but when you do a good turn for someone you are opening an account in the heavenly bank where the interest is paid by God in the form of health and domestic concord, and of course eternal happiness when it's time to pass on. *[Based mainly on an interview given by Johnnie Chadda ('Dina Nath Chadda') with Dympna McNamara and also in part on an interview given with the author]*

'A SAILOR JUMPS SHIP TO A NEW LIFE'

Lal Khan was born in the village of Badali between 1901 and 1906 (there being some uncertainty as to the exact year). This village was in the District of Mirpur, which was then part of north-west India, but which now forms part of Pakistan. Lal Khan's mother and father died when he was young, and he himself had to bring up the younger five children in the family. He therefore had little schooling, and he could not read or write. He was a sailor on a merchant ship. He jumped ship with

LAL KHAN. *Lal Khan came from India to a country area in the southern part of Northern Ireland. He set himself up largely single-handed, working very hard in all sorts of conditions. He is shown with his wife, three small children in front, and his wife's younger brother on her left.*

a few other Indians when the ship docked in Glasgow in 1938. The reason for jumping ship was simple – to seek a new life in Britain, with a better standard of living

Lal Khan laid low for a while, and in 1939 he went to Northern Ireland along with two other Pakistani men, also called Khan but not related to him. It is possible that he already knew of a Pakistani, called Shah Mohammed, who had been living in Cookstown, Northern Ireland and that this was the reason for his coming to Northern Ireland. He initially stayed in Cookstown for a few months, then Dungannon, and then a place a few miles away called Castlecaulfield. He lived there with his two Pakistani friends, one of whom not only plied a clothing business during the day but was a barber in the evenings and also a tailor in his spare time!

Around this time, Indians in Northern Ireland had good reason to have links with Glasgow – not only because of the many Irishmen, from north and south, who went to live there, but for their own particular reasons. They would buy items for their clothing business from wholesale stores in Glasgow, they would get Indian groceries or Indian dresses for their wives from Glasgow. They might also have cause to go to Glasgow since it would (until the 1960s) be the closest city on the mainland with its own crematorium, where Hindus could take their deceased.

Lal Khan started his clothing business in Castlecaulfield. For the first two years, he walked, suitcase in hand, establishing new customers in all weathers. His 'territory' included the Sperrin mountains, and many a time he had to brave heavy snow and driving rain. After a couple of years, he purchased a bike to use in his business, and he had this for 1–2 years. He was then taught how to drive a car by one of the local Irishmen, and he bought a second-hand Austin 10 car for £125.

Lal Khan would get his clothing stock from wholesale firms in Glasgow or Belfast. Even though he could not read or write, he had a remarkable memory. He was able to keep in his head information about his many customers, details of the various orders that they had placed with him, how much each had paid, etc. When he came home each day after visiting his customers, he would relate to his wife information regarding orders, payments, etc. She would write it down in a book. On some days, this would have meant Lal Khan keeping in his head information relating to 30–40 customers, though some customers would write down specific clothes measurements on a piece of paper and he would pass this written message on to his wife. Around once a month, his wife would go out with him to customers to see if the accounts that she kept in her book tallied with the accounts that many of the customers themselves kept for the goods they had bought.

One of his customers was a very stout lady with an arm measurement of 27 inches (around 66cm). Every 12th of July (a holiday in Northern Ireland, when Protestant marches take place), she would regularly order a frock from Lal Khan. He would have one specially made by a fellow Pakistani, Gulab Mohammed, who had a clothing factory in Belfast.

Lal Khan was very popular with the local citizens. He himself was quite impartial and even oblivious to the religion of his customers. Once, around the 12th of July, he went out of his way to make sure that an order for a dress arrived in time for another lady customer so that she could wear it that day. He made a special journey to Belfast to get the order, and he went to her house on the morning of the 12th of July. However, he did not realise that she was a Catholic and would definitely not be celebrating on the 12th of July!

Lal Khan would go out of his way to please his customers. One of them was a semi-recluse lady who had in fact lived most of her life in the USA and was called 'the Yankee'. She lived in a hut in an isolated field. During a very severe winter, around 1948, he took pity on her and left her a pair of his own boots, his shoe size being the same as hers. On another occasion, he took the only clock he had in his house and gave it to her. At the time, his wife joked to a friend that the next thing he would give to the old lady would be their own bed!

Lal Khan met his wife, a local Irish girl, in 1941 and he married her in 1942. She retained her Catholic traditions, while he retained his own Moslem religious values and habits, and they both respected each other's customs. He was a strict Moslem, and therefore did not eat any pork. Nor did he smoke or drink. He himself killed and prepared the lamb and chicken that his family ate, since this would ensure that the meat was 'halal'. He was a proficient cook, having learned cooking during his time as a sailor.

Lal Khan kept in touch with his own family in India, sending them money, and returning on occasions for a visit, usually for three months. His wife would carry on the business while he was away, and she would send him money when he was in Pakistan. His two sisters were both widowed, their husbands having drowned at sea while working as sailors, and Lal Khan took particular charge of providing money for them so that they could bring up their children.

When Lal Khan received a letter from his family in Pakistan he would have to take it to Belfast to have it read by one his Pakistani friends who could read Urdu. He would also ask one of his friends to write a letter in Urdu to his family. Because of his limited fluency in English, he would rely on his wife for many things. In the case of letters, forms, bills, etc. in English, his wife dealt with these. Lal Khan would vote at elections, but since he could not read, he simply spoke his choice of candidate to the presiding election officer who was present in the election booth. This was called having 'an open vote', and was apparently fairly common in rural parts of Northern Ireland where a number of voters could not read or write.

Lal Khan built up a successful retail clothing business, and he was able to raise 12 children (one of whom sadly died in a road traffic accident a few years before he himself died in 1976). For the last seven years of his life, he only had vision in one eye, and he also suffered from heart trouble, but he carried on his business right to the very end. His wish was that, when he died, he would be buried in Pakistan, but sadly this was not to be. At the time of his burial in the local cemetery, his grave had to be re-dug so that his body faced in a different direction – that is, facing the city of Mecca, which is the holy city for Moslems. The Irish grave diggers, when they had been preparing the grave, would of course not have been aware of this formality. It was Lal Khan's Moslem friends, who came down from Belfast for the funeral, that pointed this out and asked for the grave to be re-dug. *[Based on an interview given by Lal Khan's wife, Mrs Mary Khan, to the author]*

(Plate 8) WORSHIP AT HOME. *For many Hindus, having a ready place of worship is important. If they have space at home, it is therefore common for a part of a room, or even – as here – a small room, to be set aside as a place of worship. This particular room is on the ground floor, next to the front door-way.*

(Plate 9) HINDU TEMPLE IN BELFAST. *Before becoming a Hindu temple, this was once a Presbyterian church. Building regulations do not permit the external structure of the building to be changed.*

(Plate 10) A HINDU CEREMONY. *A 'Havan' is the collective term given to a Hindu ceremony of thanksgiving/prayer, and – as in this case – the havan involves the lighting of a fire and the offering of prayers to God.*

(Plate 11) PRAYER ROOM OF BELFAST HINDU TEMPLE. *The front of the prayer room contains an array of Hindu Gods and Goddesses.*

(Plate 12) HANUMAN, THE MONKEY GOD, IN THE BELFAST HINDU TEMPLE. *In the mythical story that forms part of the Hindu religion, Hanuman fought a 10-headed monster in order to help the hero Ram get back his wife Sita, who had been carried away by the demon king Ravana.*

(Plate 13) VISHNU, AND HIS CONSORT LAKSHMI, IN THE BELFAST HINDU TEMPLE. *Amongst Hindus, Lakshmi is the goddess of wealth and is worshipped at the time of Diwali – this is the Hindu equivalent of Xmas, and occurs around the beginning of November.*

(Plate 14) DURGA, GODDESS OF POWER, IN THE BELFAST HINDU TEMPLE. *Durga is worshipped during the ten-day festival called Durga Puja/Dussehra that precedes Diwali – puja is Hindi for worship.*

(Plate 15) LORD SAI BABA, IN THE BELFAST HINDU TEMPLE.

(Plate 16) LORD KRISHNA, AND HIS CONSORT RADHA, IN THE BELFAST HINDU TEMPLE.

(Plate 17) HARE KRISHNA CENTRE, BELFAST. *The Hare Krishna faith is a branch of Hinduism. This temple in Belfast was established in 1979.*

(Plate 18) SHRINE ROOM OF HARE KRISHNA CENTRE, BELFAST.

(Plate 19) BRIDAL PARTY, HARE KRISHNA WEDDING, BELFAST.

(Plate 20) HARE KRISHNA CENTRE, DAME STREET, DUBLIN.
The Hare Krishna Centre in the Irish Republic was first set-up in the mid 1970s, and it occupied these premises in Dublin city centre in 1982.

(Plate 21) MAIN SHRINE, HARE KRISHNA CENTRE, DUBLIN.

(Plate 22) SIKH TEMPLE ('GURDWARA'), LONDONDERRY.
This building was once a primary school, and is in fact near to the house in Londonderry where some of the first Indian settlers lived.

(Plate 23) SIKH TEMPLE ('GURDWARA'), DUBLIN. *This building was once the Oscar Theatre in Dublin, and it was acquired by the local Sikh community in 1986.*

(Plate 24) SHRINE OF THE SIKH TEMPLE ('GURDWARA'), DUBLIN.

(Plate 25) DUBLIN MOSQUE CENTRE. *Like the Hindu temple in Belfast, this was once a Presbyterian church.*

(Plate 26) PLANS FOR NEW ISLAMIC CENTRE, DUBLIN.

(Plate 27) BELFAST ISLAMIC CENTRE. *This Islamic centre is a large town house that has been adapted to the needs of the Moslem community.*

(Plate 28) FIRST FLIGHTS TO INDIA. *This poster shows a 1930s advertisement for Imperial Airways (the first airline to offer flights to India from Britain). India was an important destination, since it was still part of the British Empire, and it therefore featured prominently in ads such as this one. Imperial Airways later became part of the British Overseas Airways Corporation, which later merged with British Airways.*

3: COPING WITH A NEW LIFE

FINDING A PLACE TO LIVE

> I arrived in Dublin as a young medical student with the princely sum of 11 shillings and six pence (around 55 pence in today's currency). I initially stayed in the Salvation Army Hostel, which charged two shillings and six pence for bed and breakfast (twelve and a half pence in today's money). After I left the Salvation Army Hostel, I went with a friend of mine to take up board in a lodging place not far off. *[Sumanth Jeawon – a young Indian student coming to Dublin to study medicine]*

> When we arrived in Londonderry in March 1934, we were met at the station by the person who was to be our landlady – a Miss Mary Grant. She met us with transport. This transport was a pony and trap! There were four of us from India who were staying with the landlady. After a while, she even learned to speak some Hindi! The facilities at these lodgings were quite comfortable, and we had the luxury of inside toilets. Each of us had a suitcase that we filled with clothes which we would sell during the day. Since we were in lodgings, we could not have a separate store room for keeping such clothes. A few weeks after we arrived, I saw snow for the first time. [*One of the first generation Indians arriving in Northern Ireland from his village in India*]

When Indians came to Ireland for the first time, many of them found themselves looking for lodgings and staying in rented accommodation, but some stayed with landlords and landladies who provided bed and breakfast. In many cases, the landlords and landladies became loyal friends whom the Indians in turn would help out in later years. Compared to today's prices, rents in the 1930s appeared to be relatively cheap. For example, two Indian businessmen shared lodgings in Omagh, Northern Ireland at a rent of £1 per week. In 1951, one Indian settler was renting a room, with three meals a day, for the sum of £2.75 per week.

4 SIMPSON'S BRAE, LONDONDERRY. *This was the house to which many of the first Indian settlers to Northern Ireland in the 1940s would first head after their arrival. A typical car from that period (Ford 10) is shown parked outside the house.*

In the case of Indian settlers who arrived in later years, they were more likely to have contacts with Indians who were already settled. This often meant that they could move straight into a house where other Indians were living. In those early years, newcomers would often stay with a core 'family', usually a group of Indian businessmen. This household would inevitably become host to many different Indians over the years. There had to be a lot of tolerance and sharing between different individuals. When they were in India, the settlers had been accustomed to living with a number of families in the same household, so this was not a great novelty for them.

In the early years (1930s and 1940s), men would invariably be living together in a house without any ladies present. Their long working hours, difficult domestic conditions (e.g. no running hot water), and little income to start with, meant that it was simply not feasible to have wives or children present. It also meant that the men folk shared many domestic chores, including cooking, cleaning the house, washing clothes, etc. This was a new experience for those men who had been accustomed to living in a joint family system in India. (The joint family system in India consisted of brothers/cousins and their wives living under the same roof, often with grandparents present as well. Domestic work would have been done by the ladies of the household or by servants.)

THE THREE VIJ BROTHERS.
All three brothers came from a village in northern India to settle in Northern Ireland. This photograph was taken around 1950. The brothers are, from left to right – Tilak Rai Vij, Lakhpat Rai Vij and Tara Chand Vij.

Up till 1936, it would seem that the largest congregation of Indian settlers in Ireland lived in Londonderry. Mr Suchet Singh Nagra obtained the first rented house from Londonderry Corporation at 4, Corporation Street, in July 1936. He was joined by three Sikh settlers – Ujagar Singh, Daleep Singh and Bawa Singh, who moved in with him.

Mohabat Rai Vij was the second person to secure rented accommodation in Londonderry, this being in August 1936 at 4, Simpson's Brae. He later bought this house. Although Mohabat Rai Vij himself returned to India in the 1940s and stayed with his family in Bombay, the house in Londonderry remained with the Vij family for 55 years. In the early 1950s, three Vij children were born during their parent's residence in this house. This was a new event for a house that traditionally only housed single men, and after the third child was born there was understandable pressure for the parents and children to move out to their own house elsewhere. The house at 4, Simpson's Brae was a great meeting place for the Indian community in Londonderry and also for those Indians who came to Londonderry from other parts of Northern Ireland. The ground floor front room would be used to store clothes and as a sort of shop. It was quite common for customers to come on Sundays to buy goods from the store.

In India, where labour and land was relatively cheap, it would always be the dream of an Indian family to build their own home to their own specifications. This was more difficult for the settlers who came to Britain, but nonetheless many did try to build their own house. The first house to be built by an Indian settler was in Buncrana, County Donegal by Mr Bagwan Das Dhand. This house was built in 1950. The second house was built in 1954 in Londonderry by Mr Manohar Lal Chada and his brother. They built two bungalows side by side. One bungalow was given the name Shanti Niketan, after the name of a school in Calcutta that was set up by Rabindra Nath Tagore, the Nobel prize-winning Indian author.

One Indian businessman managed to save up enough money to buy his own house in 1954, only three years after he had settled in Ireland. He bought this three bedroom house for the sum of £1600.

LIVING TOUGH

> We did not have any bathroom when we moved into our first house in Portstewart, Northern Ireland, in the late 1940s. My husband Paul Kher and his friend Paul Kapur made a make-shift bathroom out of wood. This was constructed outside at the back of the house. We would boil hot water over a coal fire or a stove, pour it into a tub mixed with cold water, and then take the tub out to the make-shift bathroom. *[Mrs Savitri Kher, a young Indian housewife]*

Living conditions for many of the early settlers between the 1920s and 1950s were primitive by today's standards. Many historians refer to the 1930s as the 'hungry 30s', because of the widespread unemployment and poverty that was present in Britain and many other countries. Up to the 1950s, Indians would have to be content with living in conditions where there was seldom hot running water nor central heating. Many of the rooms would have to be heated by coal fires. In some houses, the coal fire was also used for cooking food. The coal fire would have to be lit first thing in the morning. Toilets were often outside the house. In a few houses, the water supply itself was only available from an outside pump. Soap boxes would often be used as chairs, and boxes or trunks (metal suitcases) would be used as sofas.

GOING ON A PICNIC. *Three Indians in Northern Ireland setting out for a picnic. The person on the left is Sat Pal Kher, the person on the right is Hans Raj Passi – both of these were recent settlers to Northern Ireland. The person in the middle was visiting from India at the time.*

A single house would hold not only the semi-permanent residents, but also those new arrivals who were passing through before they found more permanent accommodation. Bedrooms therefore had to sleep several people at once. Where bathrooms were present, they had to be similarly shared. There would often be a rota system for things such as cooking meals, each person taking it in turn to do so. All of this would have required considerable sacrifice on the part of those living in the house. Some Indians even resorted to taking baths in local hotels, or in council baths. One of the Indian settlers reported that when living in Belfast in the 1960s he would take a bath for 10 pence in the Grove Public Baths, Belfast. He also pointed out that the house in which he had been living only had an outside toilet, and that during cold nights he and others living there would be obliged to use an empty milk bottle as a urinal!

> It was autumn 1952, and I had been in Northern Ireland only a few months. I was based in Coleraine in the northern part of Northern Ireland. However, the 'territories' in this area had already been taken up by other Indian businessmen. So I had to travel by van to towns on the north-east coast of Northern Ireland, such as Cushendall, Cushendun and Ballycastle, to find customers and to set up my business. I would leave for Cushendall on Monday, and come back to Coleraine on Friday. During the week, I would stay in a bed-and-breakfast guest house in Cushendall. This would be my base for finding customers in other towns along the coast. I had to cope with a number of handicaps and difficulties. I had only one eye, having lost the sight of the other eye a few years before in India. It was around this time that I needed to get my teeth taken out and have false teeth. The inconvenience and pain of regular visits to the dentist had to take second place to the busy schedule I had trying to find customers. Around this time, I also lost the hearing in my left ear. I was a strict vegetarian, not even eating eggs. I therefore had to make do with cooking my own meals in the guest house where I was staying or eating what I could get in the local cafes. Much of the area that I covered meant travelling over hilly terrain, and in winter the roads would often be impassable due to snow drifts. I had never driven a car before in India, and with my limited sight and hearing, I had to be extra careful. *[Dwarka Nath Kapur, who came to Northern Ireland in the early 1950s]*

It is ironic that many of the Indians who came to Ireland were in fact refugees from communal conflicts relating to the partition of India and Pakistan, and that they came to a country that was itself partitioned. However, this also meant that few of the Indian settlers were therefore newcomers to dealing with tragic events. Coming as many of them did from village communities or rather poor backgrounds, quite a number had already been exposed to personal tragedies in India. These ranged from the traumas relating to partition, to family tragedies such as deaths of loved-ones due to infectious disease. A certain toughness and resilience, therefore, was to some extent part and parcel of those early Indian settlers. This stood them in good stead for any hardships that came their way during their initial years in Ireland.

One instance of such a hardship bravely endured was that borne by Lakhpat Rai Vij who came to Londonderry in 1939. A few years later, he developed tuberculosis infection in his foot. He was reluctant to have his foot amputated, and the infection subsequently spread to the rest of his left leg. He was told that he would die unless he had his leg amputated. After he had this operation, and was given an artificial leg, he was determined to get back to work. Not only did he walk many miles to recruit customers for his business, he also went round by bike, carrying a heavy parcel on the back. Although based in Londonderry, he often made his way across the border to Donegal on his bike. He was also a keen swimmer – in spite of his artificial leg he would go swimming every morning, something he did for twelve years.

TRYING TO MAKE A GOOD CURRY!

> We had difficulty in obtaining Indian food. We often had to make do with locally produced vegetables. However, as time went on we were able one way or another to get some Indian food. We got this from a variety of sources – by post from India and from places on the mainland, This would usually be London and Glasgow, where there were already sizeable Indian communities. Sometimes if anyone went to India or Scotland, or to India, they would usually bring back lots of ingredients for Indian dishes. They could bring large quantities of dry food (lentils, nuts, etc.) in parcels, but it was not feasible to bring fresh vegetables. Initially, posted food parcels consisted mainly of lentils ('dal'), chillies and rice. At that time, there was no wholemeal flour for making Indian bread ('roti'). Instead, we used white flour. It was only much later that we were able to buy wholemeal flour by post. When I initially went back to India, I would usually eat those things that I really missed and that I could not get in Northern Ireland, such as fresh mangoes or certain spicy dishes. *[One of the young Indian housewives in the 1950s]*

Even up to the late 1940s, there was only one main Indian grocery source in London, a store called Raja Brothers. Fresh Indian vegetables would be out of the question. It was therefore a question of compromising with locally grown vegetables. Most of the Indians were Hindus – some would have been pure vegetarians, and those who ate meat would invariably not eat any beef at all, as the cow is a sacred animal in the Hindu religion. Being a vegetarian was not a simple matter, since many tinned foodstuffs such as soups contained a small amount of

COOKING DINNER. *An Indian lady, wearing western dress, cooking an Indian meal in her new home in Northern Ireland in the 1950s.*

animal fats or similar products derived from animals. Some Indians would always check the ingredients of tins of soup that were bought. If a tin of soup was found to contain animal fats, they would angrily throw the tin in the bin or in the fire!

One of the first shops in Northern Ireland to sell Indian grocery items was run by Nand Lal Mehan in Londonderry in the late 1950s. He ran a Post Office downstairs, and upstairs he had a small store of grocery items, some of which included Indian foods. In the 1960s and 1970s, a few grocery shops opened in Belfast that specialised in selling Indian groceries, in addition to western food. These were usually run by Indians.

During World War II, such difficulties were accentuated with the rationing that was imposed – butter, sugar, eggs, tea, sweets, cigarettes, etc. were strictly rationed. As might be expected during such times, there was also a 'black market' for many of the items that were rationed due to the war. Occasionally, it was possible to get round this, either by going across the border to the Irish Republic (or the 'Free State' as Indians were accustomed to call it) or by coming to some arrangement with a customer who was also a farmer. For example, eggs or potatoes would often be given as part payment for an item of clothing that was sold to him by the Indian settler.

Food Problems

One Indian gentleman, after first arriving in Ireland in the early 1950s, found himself looking at a slice of bread for the first time – in many parts of India, especially in the villages, sliced bread was not to be seen. Indian bread ('chapatti') was made at home, out of wholemeal flour, and was round. When he sat at the table in Ireland, this Indian did not recognize the slice of bread as bread and started cutting it into small squares, in the same way that Indian sweets were usually cut up. He was soon scolded by his fellow lodgers, who had to teach him what western bread looked like and how bread was eaten!

For those Indians who were Moslems, and for Pakistanis, not only was pork forbidden, but the meat had to be prepared in a certain way – 'halal' meat was traditionally prepared by cutting the animal's neck so that all the blood drained out, and at the same time reciting a Moslem prayer (Ziba). Halal meat was not available in shops till the 1960s/1970s, and prior to then other arrangements had to be made. Sometimes meat was brought over from England or Scotland, or obtained from any shops in Ireland that catered for Jewish tastes, since Jews also consume only Halal meat. Importing meat was strictly speaking illegal, because of the restrictions imposed by the Northern Ireland Department of Agriculture regarding the import of animal and food stuffs to Northern Ireland. If Indians were caught bringing in meat, it would be confiscated and a fine would be imposed. Even to the present day, some Moslems in Northern Ireland take animals to the butchers, and stand over the animal while the animal's neck is being cut. Usually, one or two members of the Moslem community have a license, issued by the local council, that enables them to sacrifice animals by Moslem traditions.

It was also customary for a Moslem to have an agreement with a local farmer to supervise the killing of, for example, a chicken at the farmer's premises. The animal would then be taken home and skinned by members of the family. On one occasion (in 1989), an Indian had to plan for around 40–50 Moslems who would be attending his son's wedding. He found himself having to prepare 120 chickens before the wedding. He wanted this chicken meat to be halal meat, and he therefore went with one of his Moslem friends to a local chicken farm – they spent most of the evening killing chickens and plucking feathers from them!

BRINGING UP CHILDREN

> My main reason for coming to Northern Ireland from India was so that I could give my children a fine education. In India, British education was thought to be the best in the world. With a fine education, my children would have a much better start in life than they would ever have had in India. *[Dwarka Nath Kapur, who settled in Northern Ireland in the early 1950s]*

NEWLY ARRIVED, 1953. *A family recently arrived from India pose for a family photo which they can send back to relatives in India (from left to right, Dwarka Nath Kapur, Phulan Rani Kapur and their three children.*

Bringing up children in Ireland presented its own unique challenges to Indian settlers. Should they be taught to speak an Indian language when they were at home? Should they follow the same food habits as their parents? Should they be encouraged to follow the Hindu or the Christian religions? For the Indian ladies, whose major role it was to bring up the children, this responsibility in fact helped to relieve them of the boredom and distract their mind from the stresses/strains that accompanied living in a new country. With the absence of the joint family system (whereby lots of families would live together in the same house), there was not the warmth nor number of family interactions that children would have enjoyed in India.

When children from the more religious Indian families went to school, they were under strict instructions not to eat beef at school meals. This would inevitably cause some difficulties for the children, as even to the trained eye it would have sometimes been difficult to know if a meat product contained beef, as opposed to lamb or pork. At school, children would also be exposed to Christian beliefs. This meant that even though teachers might not oblige them to go to church/chapel, the children would inevitably end up learning about Christianity and reciting some Christian prayers.

Since the dialogue between parents was usually in an Indian language, usually Punjabi or less commonly Hindi, the children of Indian settlers would pick up some fluency in the understanding of an Indian language. Children would seldom be fluent in speaking an Indian language, apart from those who were born in India or whose parents made a specific effort to make them speak in an Indian language. Indian parents would find that local Irish children were not as obedient as children in India, and this tended to rub off on their own children. However, most accepted such changes as a necessary consequence of coming to live in a new country.

AN INDIAN LADY'S LIFE

I generally stayed at home, looked after the children, did the cooking and did the housework. It was quite lonely at first. I looked forward to Sundays, since I would get together with several Indian families. It was a chance for lady-folk to meet and share experiences in this new country. When telephones became more widely available (in the 1950s), that made a great difference. I could then talk to other Indian ladies, and that took away much of the loneliness during the day.

Clothing was more a problem for us than for the men folk. Our traditional Indian dress was the sari. This is quite a light dress, and is more suitable for warm climates. For several months after we first arrived in Northern Ireland, a few of us did wear western dress, usually frocks, and occasionally slacks. This was mainly so that we did not stand out when we walked outside. When we initially went out wearing a sari, we would usually be greeted with long and puzzled stares from the local population. Children would come and tug at our saris, to feel what they were really like. Eventually, after a number of Indian ladies had arrived in Northern Ireland, most of us were quite confident about wearing saris.

Trying to obtain saris was difficult. There were, of course, no local shops that sold them. Saris would be obtained from India, and later from England. In the meantime, a few of us, when we were really stuck, used fine curtain material and made this into saris!

IRISH GIRLS IN INDIAN DRESS. *Local Irish girls were fascinated by the Indian saris worn by Indian ladies. This photograph shows a group of girl guides being shown how to wear saris by the three Indian ladies on the right.*

> I had been in the Girl Guides in India, and I made friends with the local Girl Guides group in Londonderry. I was invited to show how a sari was worn at a local meeting of the group. I was complimented on wearing such a nice 'evening dress', even though the dress itself was one that was worn throughout the day and not just in the evenings.
>
> It was some time before I went out of the house on my own. My brother-in-law, with whom my husband and I lived when we first came, was very strict. He was regarded as head of the household, since he had been here before the rest of us in Northern Ireland. He did not like Indian ladies going out by themselves. It was a tradition in India that ladies rarely went out on their own. It was only after a number of months, when I needed to go to the doctor or to the chemist, that I actually went out on my own. *[Several Indian ladies who arrived in Northern Ireland in the late 1940s/early 1950s]*

Indian women first came to Northern Ireland in any significant numbers in the late 1940s. One of the very first women who came was Mrs Vidya Wanti Chada, wife of Banarsi Das Chada. She arrived in Northern Ireland in 1937, and she was here during the war years. When she first came to Northern Ireland, she initially wore a sari. After a few months, she realised how much she stood out amongst the locals, and so she took to wearing a western dress in public. Sadly, she was also one of the first widows, her husband dying in 1947 while she was in India arranging the marriage of one of her daughters.

One photographer in Londonderry, who ran a business in the town, had taken a photograph of a young Indian family, which included a young housewife wearing a sari. The photographer found the picture to be so novel and beautiful that he had an enlargement made and he displayed it prominently in his shop window for passers by to see.

Home

The Indian ladies were the ones who had to cope at first hand with any difficulties regarding food, bringing up children, washing clothes, etc. A few of them would have been accustomed to having servants in India. In India, this could often be easily afforded, since servants were plentiful and cheap. Thus, when they arrived in Ireland, doing all the domestic chores by themselves would have taken some adjustment on the part of the ladies. Eventually, when their husbands were bringing in a regular and important income, they could afford to have a maid-servant of their own in Northern Ireland. This person would do things such as cleaning the house and washing/ironing clothes. In the 1950s this would be for a wage of around £2 a week. In those days, washing machines were hardly to be seen, and there was no such thing as disposable nappies. The person would also help to look after children, but she would not do the cooking, since cooking Indian food required skill and experience, e.g. in using spices. Needless to say, there was some adjustment involved in dealing with such home-helps, since the relationship with servants in India was usually a fairly authoritarian and rather demeaning one. This was partly due to the caste system, since servants in India would usually come from the lowest castes. (The caste system in India had developed over many hundreds of years, and is partly based on religious doctrines. People are born into specific classes or castes, often revealed by the person's surname, with the highest castes including the Brahmins and the lowest caste being the Untouchables.) By contrast, in the west there was pressure for 'servants' to be treated as equal citizens. In the case of those Indian families living around Londonderry, such a maid/servant would often come from Donegal, since labour was cheaper and more plentiful there. This person might even live with the Indian family, if that family was a large one and if the house was large enough to accommodate her. Occasionally, the local police in Northern Ireland would check some of the houses of Indian families, since some of the maids/servants might not have a work permit to work in Northern Ireland.

Ladies would tend to have more of a communication problem than men, especially on occasions such as being in hospital – e.g. when giving birth.

They would have less opportunity to learn a new language because of their limited need to interact with the local community (remember that television was a rare commodity in the 1930s and 1940s). As a result, they also suffered loneliness more than men. A few of the Indian ladies might have learned to speak English fluently when in India, but this would have largely depended on the circumstances of the particular family. As a rule, in the 1920s and 1930s, it was customary for most boys to stay in school till the age of 15 years, and for most girls to stay in school till the age of 13 years. These were the age-limits laid down by the local authorities – notice the different policy for boys and for girls. It was assumed that girls would not need much education, since they would usually end up as housewives, whereas it was assumed that boys would need more schooling to give them a better basis for a career. A few Indian ladies who came to Ireland were quite fluent in English –

> I came from a middle class family in India. My father was a school inspector. I trained as a teacher at a training college in Lahore. At the time of partition, we escaped from what was to become Pakistan and had to leave all our possessions and property behind us. We settled in Ludhiana in Punjab. I taught in the Government Girls' High School in Jullundur, and I later taught in an English school called St Thomas' School in Simla, a town in northern India at the foothills of the Himalayas. This school was exclusively for English children. Thus, I had a good grasp of the English language when I came to Northern Ireland in 1947. *[Mrs FC Sumra, who was one of the first Indian ladies to come to Northern Ireland]*

Since most of the menfolk who were in the clothing business had their clothes stores at home, some of the ladies would sometimes help in marking items of stock and counting money that had been collected during the day. If they were fluent in English, they would also help in serving customers. On a number of occasions, the menfolk would often end up coming home late at night, since their business on a particular day might take them to some remote country areas, and some customers might not be in their home till late in the evening. On those occasions, the lady folk would invariably have an anxious wait at home for their husbands to arrive back. If the weather was bad, as it sometimes was, there would be the added worry lest something had happened – in those days, cars were less reliable, the areas where the businessmen travelled were often remote from any significant habitation, and telephones were much fewer than at the present time.

COMING TO IRELAND TO TRAIN AS A DOCTOR

> My name is Sumanth Jeawon. I was born in South Africa. My grandfather

came to South Africa from northern India in 1860 as an 'indentured' labourer. My grandfather died when my own father was only six years old. My father had no formal schooling and he had to educate himself. He started off his working life as a simple carpenter. He gradually worked his way up to be a building contractor of repute in South Africa, and he was eventually included in the Indian 'Who's Who' of South Africa. He had a great knowledge of the eastern religions and philosophies, and this had a considerable influence on me.

My burning ambition in life was to become a doctor. In South Africa, I had done some work as a teacher and as an assistant librarian. Getting into medical school or even getting any university education was extremely difficult for non-whites in South Africa, so I set off for London at the age of 21 years. I arrived in September, 1951 at the port of Southampton with £23 in my pocket, and I made my way to London.

OVERSEAS MEDICAL STUDENTS IN DUBLIN. *Sumanth Jeawon is on the front row, second from the left, and Tilak Rai Vij is immediately behind him.*

When I arrived in London, I found that priority for getting into medical school was being given to ex-servicemen from World War II. So after three days, I ventured to Dublin to see if I could gain entry to medical school there. I arrived with the princely sum of 11 shillings and six pence (around 56 pence in today's currency). I stayed in the Salvation Army Hostel, which charged two shillings and six pence (10.5 pence in today's currency) for bed and breakfast. Ironically, it was located just across from the Royal College of Surgeons in Dublin. The logical place to try to get into medical school was the Royal College of Surgeons, since they allotted one third of their places to students from developing countries. I tried on a number of occasions to gain an interview with the Registrar of the Royal College of Surgeons, a Norman Rae. I finally managed to see him. I told him of my background, my limited financial means and my ambitions. I also chatted to him about how Indians came to live in South Africa, and he was quite interested in this. He had spent some time in Sri Lanka, and he was perhaps more sympathetic than others to students from developing countries, and in particular to Indians. However, he told me that I had been foolish to leave South Africa and to arrive, somewhat unannounced, on his doorstep. He advised me to go back to England, and from England perhaps to go to America to study medicine.

In order to get entrance into the Royal College of Surgeons' medical school, students had to sit their entrance exam. In those days, this consisted of English, another language, maths and one other subject. I asked Mr Rae if I could at least do the entrance exam. "No," he said, "If I let you do the entrance exam, and if you pass, then I'd have to take you in!" "At least let me do the entrance exam, just for practice," I pleaded, "You need not take me in if I am successful." He relented! That moment, when he allowed me to sit the entrance exam, was without doubt the happiest moment of my life.

I then got a form, and entered for the exams, which were to take place in 17 days' time in December. There was not a long time to prepare for the exams, which in my case were English, Maths, Latin and Biology. I moved out of the Salvation Army Hostel where I was staying for a week, and I moved in with an Irish family (in later years, I in fact ended up treating my landlady in hospital). I had little money left. I therefore promised to pay my landlady with money from South Africa if she allowed me to stay. I studied from eight o'clock in the morning to four o'clock the next morning – a total of 20 hours a day. I usually studied in the city library till it closed at ten at night, since this was a warm building, and Dublin was now in the beginning of winter. After studying in the library, I would come back to the lodgings where I was staying. I did not have much to eat in those days. Post-war rationing was still in force, with coupons for tea, butter, etc. I largely ended up drinking soups. In the house where I was staying, lights went off at ten o'clock, after which I studied by candle-light. I had been used to studying by candle-light as a child in South Africa, since our family had been quite poor for a while. So working by candle-light in this house in Dublin was not such a new or difficult experience for me. Nevertheless, this was winter, and in the middle of the night it was pretty cold in the room where I was living.

One hundred and thirty three students sat the exam. When the results were announced, I was top of the class, and I gained a first class honours in Biology! I went back to see the Registrar of the Royal College of Surgeons, Norman Rae. I said, "Sir, thank you very much indeed. I am taking your advice. I will be going back to England and I will then work my way back home to South Africa or to America. But, just in case you want to know how I fared in the entrance exam, it might please you to know that I got, in the 17 days that you offered me to prepare for the exam, a first class honours in Biology, and I was also first in the whole class." "Did you, really?" he exclaimed. "Look, he said, you're troubling me. Get out."

"Thank you very much indeed," I said. Then he added, "But, I want you to start medicine next October!" You can imagine how I felt. I then had nine months in which to look for a job, so as to earn enough money to pay my fees, lodgings, etc. for the first year of my studies.

I looked for work in Ireland, and went about getting advice on how to find work. I met the son of an MP in the Irish Parliament. The MP was called Mr Briscoe. He later became Lord Mayor of Dublin. I went to the MP to seek advice about getting a job. "My son," he said, "There are 92,000 unemployed people in the Irish Republic. Your best bet would be to take the boat to London with the rest of the sons and daughters of Ireland." At that time, there were around 5,000 people a week leaving Ireland to seek work in Britain. Needless to say, I was reluctant to take up this advice. The first job I got was near Dublin, and this involved cutting turf for fuel. This was very hard, laborious work for a mere pittance, and after a couple of weeks I gave this up and went to London.

I went straight to the Indian Embassy and had an interview with Mrs Vijay Lakshmi Pandit, who was then the Indian ambassador (she was also the sister of the Indian Prime Minister, Jawaharlal Nehru). She introduced me to the medical advisor at the embassy. He got me a job working in the mortuary at St Bart's hospital in central London. At that time, I was living in Earls Court. The famous Indian politician and freedom fighter, Krishna Menon, had set up Indian students' bureaus in London, and there was one in Earls Court. I stayed there and also got a job working as a waiter in the evenings. Since I was mixing with Indian students much of the time, I was able to use that experience to improve my Hindi. For a while, I was doing both the mortuary job as well as the 'waitering' job. I subsequently took a telephonist's course. This was a four month course, which paid me £4–6 per week, and at the end of this I worked for a few months as a telephonist. Through jobs such as these, I was able to save enough money for my first year at medical school. Life was quite tough for me in London, and post-war England still had rigours that had to be endured. I remember our landlord once telling us during supper – Do you realise you're eating Irish horse? We had been eating horse-meat imported from Ireland, and we did not even know it!

I entered medical school in 1952. I got some money from my family in South Africa, this being around £40 every couple of months. I initially stayed with an Indian family in Dublin that had originally come from South Africa. The head of the family was a Dr Mistri. He was a physician in Scotland whose family had moved to Dublin so that their children could get an education. They rented part of their house, and I stayed in there for 18 months. After this, I moved into a bedsit, and I stayed there for 18 years. My landlord was an Irishman called Jerimiah Donaghue. After I sat my exams in June, I would go to England to work for three months during the summer vacation. I simply had to pass my exams at the first go in June, so that I was then free to work during the summer to earn money to keep me for the next year. Having to resit any exams would have been a disaster. Together with a number of other students from Dublin, I mostly worked in a canning factory near Norwich, England. I would earn £17 for a 92 hour week. I did this summer work every year till my final year in medical school. In that year (1958), I found myself short of money. It was not possible for money to be sent from South Africa, due to the introduction of apartheid. For a few months, I therefore had to work at night. My landlord at the time was a bus driver, and I was able to get work washing down buses from 11pm at night to 7am in the morning. Then I would head straight to a clinic where I would have been working as a final year medical student. I got little sleep during this period, though on the plus side I did earn £12 a month. Not long afterwards, I graduated. I went back to South Africa for the first time several years later to see my mother who was ill, this being nine years after I had first left South Africa to become a doctor.

When I started work as a doctor in the Royal City of Dublin Hospital in 1958, my board and lodgings were free but I was only earning £16 a month. I had to rely on some money from my parents in South Africa in order to make two ends meet. After a few years, I was offered a very lucrative job in Canada. I was about to take this up when I met a man who was to have a major impact on my life. This was Dr Lawrence Godfery, who ran a hospital in Dublin. This hospital used to treat patients with tuberculosis, but tuberculosis had been eradicated by then (the early 1960s). Instead, the beds were filled with 600 geriatric/elderly infirm patients. There was little in the way of a geriatric service in Ireland at the time. Dr Godfery inspired me with his sincerity, his humility and his compassion.

In the early 1970s, Dr Godfery was diagnosed as having Multiple Sclerosis, a crippling disease of the nerves. Apart from my own father, I had never come across such a person as Dr Godfery. Around that time, I was wondering what to do – whether to go to Canada, back to South Africa or go to India. I asked my father for advice. My father told me – "You tell me you are doing work that is needed, and above all you like this man. So if he has the brain, but hasn't the power of his legs, then wheel him around." That's precisely what I did. For the last 20–30 years of his life, Dr Godfery was largely crippled due to Multiple Sclerosis. I still worked closely with him, as his Deputy, but I literally had to wheel him around the hospital. Dr Godfery in fact became a patient in the very hospital where we both worked. He died in 1993, being very disabled during the last few years of his life.

"Earmarked"

Around this time, a young Indian man, Tilak Rai Vij, had come from India to Northern Ireland. He had arrived in Londonderry in 1949. He was 17 years old when he came over, and he spoke good English – in fact, on the boat journey from Bombay he had acted as interpreter for his brother and his brother's wife who had accompanied him on the journey. Tilak Rai had been 'earmarked' by his family in India to be a doctor. Just as in those days it was customary for an Irish family to 'earmark' one of their sons to become a priest, so in Indian families it was common for one of the children to be 'earmarked' to become a doctor. Tilak Rai and his brothers were from a farming family in Northern India. While his brothers in Londonderry went into the clothing business, Tilak Rai decided to pursue an academic career. He initially studied at the Technical College in Londonderry, and he then went to the Royal College of Surgeons in Dublin to study medicine. He met up with Sumanth Jeawon, whose story is told above. Tilak Rai qualified in medicine a few years later, in 1958, at the same time as Sumanth Jeawon. It is ironic that in their later years (1980s/1990s), both of these doctors underwent major heart surgery for cardiac disease.

Other Colonial Students

Most of the Indian students in Dublin came from British colonies such as South Africa, Guyana, Trinidad, Jamaica, Barbados, Mauritius, East Africa, etc. They were usually the descendants of 'indentured labourers' who had been brought over from India by the British to work in these colonies. In the case of those from South Africa, their forefathers had originally been shipped by the British from India in 1860. Two boatloads of Indians, one of northern Indians and one of southern Indians, left Madras and arrived in South Africa at this time. Such labourers had to work for a period of five years, after which they were given the choice of returning to India or remaining in South Africa. For most Indian students in Dublin, their parents were able to afford their expenses for studying and living in Dublin, but a few students like Sumanth Jeawon had to struggle to make ends meet.

Dublin was an attractive place for overseas Indian students for several reasons. There was a strong catholic/missionary influence that prevailed in colleges like the National University of Ireland (that later become known as University College, Dublin). Since missionaries had a strong foothold in many British colonies such as India, this was a link that brought some Indian students to Dublin. Some colonies, such as Mauritius, did not have a university. The Prime Minister of Mauritius was a man of Indian origin, called Ram Ghulam. In the 1950s, he arranged for £30,000 to be donated to the Royal College of Surgeons in Dublin on the understanding that a certain number of capable, well qualified students from Mauritius could gain entrance to the College to study medicine. Since the Royal College of Surgeons was not state funded, and largely depended on students' fees for its income, it found such an arrangement to be beneficial. A few years later, a deputation of senior professors/officers from the College visited South Africa, and collected £1–2 million from the Indian community there on a similar basis. Funding sources such as these helped the College to build a new wing.

INDIAN ENTERTAINMENT: MOVIES, MUSIC AND CARD GAMES

> Going to watch an Indian movie in Northern Ireland was an interesting experience as a child. You would sit there, and there would inevitably be a sad part in the film. When you looked round, you could see white hankies out. Both Indian men and women would be wiping away tears! *[A young Indian boy in the 1950s]*

Life for the early Indian settlers was largely all work and no play, but as time went on they began to build up recreational activities in their spare time. Coming as most of them did from a strict Hindu background, most of the Indian men and women were teetotallers, and only a few smoked. In India, pubs were practically unheard of. One of the major recreations was, and still is, watching Hindi films. Their melodramatic stories and catchy songs often provided the ideal means of escape from the harsh realities of day-to-day living. Such films would be all the more welcome in Northern Ireland, since they would remind the Indian settlers of their mother country and of the family and friends that they had left behind.

Films

In Northern Ireland, an Indian film society was set up in Londonderry in the early 1950s, with Manohar Lal Chada as its first secretary. Suchet Singh was the first treasurer. The first films that they obtained were Hindi documentary films that were hired from the Indian embassy in London. A projector would be rented locally, and the film (usually 16 millimetres film projected onto a small screen) would be shown in the home of one of the Indians, usually the home belonging to Manohar Lal Chada. Snacks would also be served. After 1–2 years, the films grew so popular that it was decided to hire a cinema hall. In the 1950s, the Hindi film industry in India was beginning to take off. Movie films, rather than documentaries, were obtained by post from the Indian Film Society in London and would have a show on Sundays every month in cinemas that were hired for the afternoon. Cinema halls were usually closed on Sundays for the showing of western films.

Films were first shown in Londonderry in the 1950s at the Palace Cinema, Shipquay Street or at the City Cinema, William Street. The location later changed to a cinema in Maghera, and finally to a cinema in Draperstown. Compared to Londonderry, which was at the far west of Northern Ireland, Maghera and Draperstown were more centrally located. This meant that they would be more convenient for Indians who had to travel from different parts of the province. The cinema hall would be hired for a Sunday afternoon, and Indians would congregate at that place. This occasion also provided the opportunity for a social gathering. For Indian ladies, who were often indoors for much of the time and saw little of other Indian families, this was a particularly welcome break from the monotony and boredom of living in a strange country. For children, going to Hindi films was usually a required fact of life, one they had to take part in even though many of them had very little understanding of the story in the film. In the 1950s and early 1960s, films were usually black-and-white, and very rarely would they have English subtitles. After the film was over, groups of families would usually go to someone's house for an evening meal. It was only in the 1970s/1980s that the introduction of video recorders and the availability of Indian movies on video tape changed habits, with the result that no Indian films were subsequently shown in local cinemas. The 1990s also saw the introduction of an Asian satellite TV channel that regularly showed Indian movie films.

Although films were initially shown in Londonderry and in the west of the province, Belfast saw similar developments in the late 1960s. In 1966, the Asian Film Society was formed in Belfast. The Lido cinema on the Shore Road, Belfast was hired for one Sunday each month. After a year and a half, the Asian Film Society moved its venue to the Park Cinema in Oldpark Road, Belfast. It continued to meet there every Sunday till the end of 1969. Then a major development took place. Along with two other Indian businessmen, Ram Shukla and Paul Sharma, a Belfast businessman by the name of Raj Joshi, who was also secretary of the Asian Film Society, bought the Rex Cinema in Woodstock Road, Belfast. During the week, the cinema showed English films in the usual way. But on several Sundays a month, the film, the audience and the whole atmosphere became typically Indian. During a long interval half-way through the film, tea and snacks were consumed, and there was a chance for Indians to meet each other and to gossip. It was intended that the cinema might also function as an Indian community centre, providing an opportunity for children to attend classes on Indian language and culture, but this did not get off the ground to any significant extent. For eight years, the Rex Cinema mainly fulfilled its role as a cinema and as a meeting place for Indians. In 1980, the Indian Community Centre was opened in Clifton Street, north Belfast. This centre took over the social functions that the Rex Cinema provided. The introduction of Indian films on video cassettes had in fact meant that there was little need for a cinema that showed Indian films.

Indian films were generally of little interest to the local population, but one exception to this was a film called 'Aan' that was shown in the 1950s. The title 'Aan' means 'Pride'. It had English subtitles, and it was the first Hindi film to be shown in local cinemas. It contained the usual theme of melodramatic Hindi dialogue and songs, and it starred the famous Indian actor Dilip Kumar. This was also one of the first Indian films that showed a motor car in one of its scenes. The car itself had been borrowed from one of the Maharajas in India. In previous films, transport was usually of the horse-and-cart variety!

The India League

In the Irish Republic, a society was formed in the early 1950s that, amongst other things, sponsored the showing of Indian films. This was called the India League, which followed on from an earlier grouping called the *Indian* League. The Indian League had been set up 1–2 years earlier by an Indian family from South Africa, the Rastamjis. Mr Rastamji was an Indian businessman, of the Parsi sect, who lived in South Africa. He sent his wife and three children to Dublin so that his children could receive a good education. He was in fact a good friend of the Aga Khan, who had horse stables in Ireland. It was through the Aga Khan that Mr Rastamji secured links with colleges in Dublin.

Sumanth Jeawon, whose story was told earlier, was one of the key founders of the India League. He wanted to set up a society that was more broad-based than the Indian League, one that would cater for Indian students and that would also appeal to the local Irish population. He gave it the name India League. He would hire a hall and show films 3–4 times a year. Very occasionally, the India League was able to invite Indian artists to perform dance routines – e.g. a famous Indian dance troupe, called 'Ram Gopal and his troupe of Indian dancers' came in the 1950s. The India League also had a cricket team and a table-tennis team. Since many of its members were South African Indians, the India League was also used as a platform to make the local Irish population more aware of the political situation in South Africa. Subsequently, a

A DAY OUT IN DUBLIN. *A group of Indians from Northern Ireland on a day's outing in Dublin. The occasion was the celebration of Ireland becoming a republic in 1949. 1 – Ram Parshad Chada. 2 – Swaran Singh. 3 – Janki Das Chada. 4 – Manor Lal Chada. 5 – Lakshmi Narain Chada. 6 – Vachant Singh. 7 – Munsha Singh. 8 – Bawa Singh. 9 – Suchet Singh.*

strong anti-apartheid movement did start up in Dublin. One of its leaders was Khaled Ismail, who went back to South Africa in the early 1990s to become a member of the new multi-racial South African government.

Music

Many Indian families brought Indian records with them when they came from India. These were usually the '78-RPM' variety, and had the HMV (His Master's Voice) label. In the 1950s, records were produced in India especially for export to Indians living out of India. They were large in size, yellow in colour, and '33-RPM'. These records were plastic and unbreakable, to ensure their safe export. Their production was, however, stopped after a while, probably due to poor sales.

Other Pastimes

The other pastime enjoyed by Indian settlers was playing cards. Initially, the cards themselves were imported from India. The card games were usually fairly simple, consisting of Rummy, and they might involve money on a minor scale. During card games, there was a youthful spirit and a camaraderie amongst the young Indian settlers that resulted in a jovial atmosphere and an ideal form of relaxation. Card games would usually take place on Sundays, and would often stretch into the early hours of Monday morning. On one Monday morning, the child of an Indian businessman arrived late for school. His headmaster asked him to explain why he was late. He replied, 'My dad was playing cards!' The child must have slept in due to his father returning home after a late-night card game.

A few Indian settlers would gamble in other, more unique, situations – e.g. on one occasion in the early 1950s, two Indians in Northern Ireland (Paul Kapur and Paul Kher) had a race to see who could go the fastest around a seaside town, wearing a vest rather than a shirt and holding aloft a toy windmill! On another occasion, these two Indians also had a race to see who could be first to consume two bottles of milk and six pieces of Indian bread!

INDIAN CULTURE, RELIGION AND LEGACIES

> Every Sunday morning, like clockwork, my father would go into the office that kept his store of clothes and business items. It was the only secluded part of the house where he could get some peace. For about half an hour, he would read aloud from a holy book that he kept in this office. Not only did it remind him of his religion, but it also provided a means of solace and relaxation from the busy life he led during the week. It probably also gave him an inner strength with which to face the ups and downs of his new life in Ireland. *[A young Indian boy observing one of the first generation Indian immigrants]*

Practising religion had to take second place to earning a living for the early Indian settlers. If prayers were to be said, then they would have to be said in the home of a particular individual. When Indian ladies joined their husbands, they might set aside part of a room for pictures of Hindu gods/goddesses and for other holy items (*Plate 8, p. 95*). This area would then be used for prayers or other rituals. When a Hindu or Moslem priest was required, for religious ceremonies such as weddings or funerals, he would be brought over from Scotland or England. Very few Indians converted to Christianity prior to the 1960s, though in subsequent decades the increasing number of mixed marriages meant that some instances of conversion did take place. In the early 1950s, some Indian students in Dublin obtained permission from the local Salvation Army Hostel to allow Moslem students to use a room on

Fridays, the Moslem holy day, for reading the Koran, the Moslem holy book.

In Northern Ireland, the first formal Indian community association was set up in 1959. This was called the Indian Social Association. Meanwhile, in Belfast, an association was formed in the mid 1960s called the Belfast Indian Association. This was largely run by and for Indian students at Queen's University, Belfast though it did attract support from other Indians living in Belfast. Up till 1982, Indians who chose to set up cultural or religious activities had to hire a hall. A temple management committee was set up in November 1979, with the aim of raising funds to procure a temple building. The first president of that management committee was Mr Manohar Lal Chada, and the first secretary was Mr Raghu Nath Sabharwal.

An Indian temple building (*Plate 9, p. 96*) was formally acquired in 1982, with the consecration ceremony taking place on May 16, 1982. The Indian Community Centre, as it was called, was formed out of a former church in Clifton Street, north Belfast. It has two large halls, and 18 rooms. The building was bought for £35,000. An initial deposit of £3000 was needed fairly urgently to ensure the purchase of the building, and this was made from six donations of £500 each by local Indians. Subsequently nine prominent local Indians spearheaded a fund-raising effort to find the remaining £32,000. This involved visits to the Irish Republic, London, Birmingham, Liverpool, Manchester and Glasgow.

The consecration ceremony was attended by Mr M Varajadarajan, Minister of Supply at the Indian High Commission in London, and the Lord Mayor of Belfast, Alderman John Carson and his wife. A 44-page souvenir booklet, written in both Hindi and English, and printed in India, was produced to commemorate the event. In addition to cash, many local Indians donated deities or 'murtis' (i.e. statues representing Hindu gods and goddesses) and also other religious items, often in memory of a loved one. In a number of these cases, the 'murtis' were donated in memory of parents in India who had passed away (*Plates 10–16, p. 96–99*). It is said that 'absence makes the heart grow fonder', and this applied all the more to Indian settlers in Ireland when they thought of loved ones in India, such as parents, who had helped them come to Ireland in the first place.

The temple itself comprises two halls, one on the lower floor and one on the upper floor. The temple has a small flat which houses the resident priest. The first priest was Mr K D Shastri, known as Shastriji. He was the temple priest from 1985 to 1990. Before him, the duties of a priest were occasionally performed by Mr R P Shukla, who did this in a part-time capacity when the need arose. The Belfast City Council has generously helped in providing financial and other support for cultural and religious activities in the centre. More recently, in 1996, the temple was successful in receiving a grant of over £300,000 from the Charities Lottery Board. This has enabled major renovation in the temple. As part of this renovation, specialist artisans have been brought over from India to carry out skilled artistic and masonry work.

The consumption of meat or alcohol is banned from the temple building. The building is available for use by the local community, e.g. for playing badminton in one of the halls.

The Hare Krishna movement also has a presence in both Northern Ireland and the Irish Republic (*see Appendix 1 and Plates 17–21, p. 100–102*).

The Belfast Islamic Centre, which opened in 1986, provided a religious forum for those from the Indian subcontinent who practised the Islamic faith, and also for Moslems from other parts of the world (*Plate 27, p. 106*). Prior to 1992–3, they would bring over a Moslem priest or 'malvi' from England, but after that time they were able to secure a resident malvi who lives in Belfast. In 1994, the Islamic Centre had around 1200 members from the Indian subcontinent on its books. They hold Sunday School activities, and cater for the religious and social needs of Moslems.

There are estimated to be around 6,000 Moslems in the Irish Republic, with a much smaller number, perhaps around 1,000, in Northern Ireland. Many of these will, of course, have originated from countries outside the Indian subcontinent, e.g. the Middle East. Ireland's largest mosque is located in Dublin, with smaller mosques in Cork, Galway, Limerick and Ballyhaunis (in County Mayo). In 1959, the Dublin Islamic Society was formed, and this has now become the Islamic Foundation of Ireland.

The first mosque in Ireland was established in Dublin in 1975. In 1983, the location of the mosque was moved to the site of a former Presbyterian church (*Plate 25, p. 105*). There are plans for a purpose-built new mosque in Dublin (*Plate 26, p. 105*).

In 1990, a Moslem National School was created, with the opening ceremony of the school being performed by President Mary Robinson. Most of the million pounds needed for the school building came from Islamic countries overseas. In 1993, there were 150 pupils at the school.

The Moslem community in Ballyhaunis, County Mayo, had its origins around a meat factory that was set up in 1974 by a local Moslem. At its peak, there were around 100 Moslems living or working in the community, though this number has now halved. The mosque in Ballyhaunis was the first purpose-built mosque in Ireland.

In Londonderry, Indians who belong to the Sikh religion have teamed up with other Sikhs and also Hindus in Northern Ireland to buy a former church Primary School and convert it into a Sikh temple or 'gurdwara' (*Plate 22, p. 103*). This gurdwara was bought in 1992 for £80,000 and it was refurbished at a cost of £130,000. Some financial assistance was also made available from a local urban development fund. The gurdwara opened in early 1995. It does not have a resident priest, and is open to worshippers twice a week.

The Irish Republic

In the Irish Republic, where the Sikh population is around 250 strong, the main focus of activity is around the Sikh temple that was established in Dublin in 1986, when an old theatre was taken over and refurbished (*Plates 23–24, p. 104*). Services of worship are held every Sunday, and attendance is often bolstered by Sikhs from Limerick, Cork and Waterford.

In the Irish Republic, two organisations have been formed in Dublin with the aim of promoting Indian cultural and Indo-Irish cooperation. One is the *Ireland-India Cultural Society* that was formed in 1976. It holds a number of cultural and social functions throughout the year, and includes members of the local Irish community who have a particular interest in India or who happen to have links with India. It is particularly concerned with promoting ties between India and Ireland, and some of its officers are from the local Irish community. Its membership is largely of professionals, though it does have members with other backgrounds. The other organisation is the *India Club*, which was formed in 1971. Its membership includes a significant number of Indian businessmen. It also holds social and cultural functions on occasions such as Diwali (Hindu festival of lights – equivalent to Christmas).

Those Indians living in the Irish Republic have also been able to keep their links with India with the help of the Indian embassy that has been established there since 1964.

Legacies

In a number of small ways, early Indian settlers have left some form of legacy behind. One of these was Tara Chand Vij, who was a keen draughts player. In his memory, an annual drafts trophy was set up by his son, Kamal. The trophy is called the TC Vij cup, and it is formally awarded each year by one of the Vij children.

REMEMBERING ONE OF THE VIJ BROTHERS. *This trophy was set up in memory of Tara Chand Vij, whose photograph is shown earlier (page 111), and who was a very keen draughts player. This trophy award for the best draughts player in the local Londonderry area was set up by his son Kamal in 1983.*

I myself set up a scheme in memory of my father, who died in April 1993. Most proceeds from my first book, published in 1988, were used to buy resources for the disabled in the community around Ballycastle, where my father lived and worked.

KEEPING IN TOUCH WITH THE MOTHER COUNTRY

We went back to India in July 1964 on a ship that took us from Liverpool to Bombay. This was my first trip to India, and I was then only a young girl of 15 years. Our grandparents said that they wanted to see me, my broth-

REMEMBERING A NORTH ANTRIM INDIAN – *Funds in memory of the first Indian in north Antrim, Dwarka Nath Kapur, were used to buy this piece of equipment for a visually impaired lady in the local area. The equipment scans text from a page, and displays it in large print on a TV screen. Pictured in this photograph are, from left to right, Mr Bill Tweed (of the local health authority), Mrs Martha Hill (the lady receiving the equipment), Mrs Margaret Craig (of the local health authority), Mr Jim Loughrey (of the local health authority), Mrs Phulan Rani Kapur (wife of Dwarka Nath Kapur), Dr Narinder Kapur (son of Dwarka Nath Kapur), and Mr Eamon McHale (of the local health authority).*

ers and my sisters, before they died. We went in the hottest and most uncomfortable time of the year in India – in July and August. We had to go at this time, because this was the time of the school holidays, and my parents did not want us to go at some other time and miss school. We went by ship because of all the bulky items that we took along with us. We were an attraction on the ship, since passengers got to know that seven Indian children, all born in Ireland, were going to India to see their grandparents for the first time. My grandparents had in fact given my parents strict instructions – 'Don't come back to India unless you bring your children with you'.

We took along with us a green Ford Zephyr car (my father was initially going to take over a Land Rover, but he found it too cramped). We also took along a cooker and a washing machine for my uncle in India. We went on a Scottish shipping line, the Anchor Line, and the journey took 20 days. There were eight of us on the boat – my mother and her seven children.

My father had flown to Bombay the day before our arrival, and he was there to meet us at the customs' hall in the port of Bombay.

We drove in the Ford Zephyr car from Bombay to our village of Talwan in northern India. We did not have a map – the only directions my father was given were the names of the main towns on the way from Bombay to Talwan. Travelling with seven children in a car on Indian roads, in the hottest time of the year, was no minor experience. It took us three days to make the journey by car. We travelled by day and rested at night. When we were driving around in the village of Talwan, I asked my father to stop the car and talk to someone I recognised – it so happened that I remembered him from the ship journey, as he was also on the boat that took us to India.

When we were in India, one of my uncles got married. The Ford Zephyr car was used at the wedding to carry the bride and groom. It was quite a novelty, and it was much admired by local Indians, since there were very few such foreign cars in India at that time. *[Charlotte Vij, a member of the Vij family who came to Ireland in the 1940s]*

An eight-year old girl, Sushma Prakash, died of a brain tumour in 1989 after a brave one year struggle. In her memory, her father – local Indian G.P. Dr N Jayaprakash – and his wife built a nursing home in the town of Antrim, Northern Ireland. This is called the Sushma Nursing Home, and it caters for the elderly and infirm in the local community.

SUSHMA PRAKASH (1981–1989).

SUSHMA NURSING HOME. *Built in 1990 in Antrim, Northern Ireland by a local Indian G.P. and his wife, in memory of their daughter.*

The Indians who came to Ireland always kept in close touch with their mother country. In the early days, they would even discuss amongst themselves how much money each was sending back home to their relatives who were usually not very well off. If one person was not sending enough, he would be advised by others to send a bit more. 'Luxury' items were also sent – one of the items sent to a close friend in India by an Indian businessman was a radio-cum-record player.

When a particular person went back to India, he would usually meet up with his own relatives and friends, and also the relatives and the friends of some of his fellow Indians in Northern Ireland. Before he left, he would be reminded not to tell those in India how much the Indians in Northern Ireland were earning! In India, some relatives and friends might get inflated ideas about how much their loved ones were earning in Ireland, and might therefore expect much more to be sent to them.

Some of those who were left behind in India would express a wish to join their relatives or friends in Ireland. One such Indian asked his uncle, who had been in Northern Ireland a few years, if he could join him. His uncle realised that his nephew would never be able to cope with the rigours of door-to-door selling and the rough and tumble of dealing with customers. He therefore tried to discourage his nephew, saying that since he could not ride a bike, he would find it difficult to work in Ireland, where many an Indian businessman would start off with a bike and suitcase. His nephew, not one to be easily daunted, promptly took lessons to learn to ride a bike. After several months practice, he wrote to his uncle asking if he could *now* come over to Ireland, since he had successfully learned how to ride a bike! On this occasion, his uncle had to be blunt, and tell his nephew that he could not cope with the rigours of business life in Ireland.

Other Indians were in fact reluctant to come over from India to Ireland, but were brought there by close family ties. In one case, a couple in India, who were childless apart from an adopted daughter, came to Ireland only after a relative there promised to give his son to be adopted by them.

Up to the 1960s, contacts with India would usually be by post, since long-distance phone calls were very difficult to make. In the early decades of settlement – 1920s, 1930s and 1940s – few Indians went back to India on a regular basis. If a trip was made, it was for a specific purpose, usually to get married or bring over one's family from India. The Second World War made it difficult for Indian settlers to go back to India, with the scarcity of ships and the dangers associated with travelling by boat. It is possible that some of those who came to Ireland in the late 1930s, and who had intended to stay for only a few years and then to return permanently to India, were obliged to stay in Northern Ireland during the early 1940s due to the war. They perhaps changed their minds about returning as a result of this. From the 1950s onwards, it became more popular to go back to visit relatives. Such visits would invariably involve taking lots of gifts. In the 1950s, and up to the early 1960s, this trip home was usually by sea, but after that time it was usually by air. The advent of regular commercial flights to India by aeroplane was a major contribution to the establishment of regular contacts between Indians in Ireland and their home country (*see Plate 28*). Up till recent times, goods from Britain were highly valued in India, even if the equivalent item was readily available in India. This was partly due to the superior quality and durability of British goods, but also of course because any item that was brought for a relative in India would be given free!

In 1940, one of the Indian settlers in Ireland was returning home to India for a short visit. His name was Faquir Chand Sehgal, and he came from a village in north-west India called Nakodar. World War II had broken out a year earlier. While his boat was going through the Mediterranean, it was struck by a German torpedo and was sunk. He was one of the many passengers who died as a result of this sinking.

Sikh Traditions

Family members, such as parents, who were left behind in India, were always keen to be reassured that their sons/daughters were behaving like 'good Indians', were keeping up with religious and social customs that they had been taught in India, and that they were not being 'corrupted' with western habits. This was all the more so when it came to individuals who practised the Sikh religion, which had strict rules about men wearing turbans and not shaving their beard. Relatives in India frequently asked for photographs to be sent back from those in Ireland as part of the reassurance that all was well there. However, this created a problem for one of the Sikh settlers in Northern Ireland. He had shaved off his beard and removed his turban, mainly as a result of the need to blend in with the local Irish, who were somewhat apprehensive about seeing someone in a turban. This Sikh therefore got hold of an old photograph of himself, one that showed him wearing a turban and beard, and a more recent photograph of his wife taken in Northern Ireland. He took these along to a local photographer. This photographer was then able to join the two together into a single photograph, which was then sent to relatives in India.

Another Sikh who was settled in Northern Ireland removed his turban, cut his hair and shaved off his beard after he came to Ireland from India in the early 1970s. When his parents, who were very orthodox Sikhs, found out that this had happened, they were extremely angry. A few years later, when someone from Ireland was visiting these parents of the Sikh gentleman who had shaved his hair, he told them that he had met his son in Ireland. They replied – 'Our son? He died some years ago'. They regarded him as having died from the time when he committed his act of shaving his hair/removing his turban.

Going Back By Land

One Indian (Mr R P Mehan) who went back to India for a holiday actually ventured the journey by land. This is his story.

> In April 1965, I took my Austin 60 car on an overland trip to India. After taking the car ferry to England, I took another ferry from Dover to

Ostend. I had in fact planned to go to India by myself, but I picked up one person from Liverpool, who was heading for Ludhiana in north-west India. When we were in the Turkish embassy in London getting visas, we met a second person who was also heading for India. So, I ended up taking two passengers with me.

I myself did all the driving, both to India and on the return journey. I got road maps from the Automobile Association. I drove to Germany, Austria, Yugoslavia, Bulgaria, Turkey, and then to Iran. When we arrived in Tehran, the capital of Iran, we went to the offices of a shipping company in the city and we found that the person in charge was a Sikh gentleman from the Punjab! He asked us where we were staying. We said that we had only just arrived. He suggested we stay in the local Sikh temple or 'gurdwara'. So we stayed there for a few days. It was a huge house that had been partly converted into a temple, but where around 100 Indian families were staying.

When we were in Iran and other countries, we were very aware that there were thieves about and that we had to be very careful with our goods. We were told that an American once came to Tehran, and stayed in the Gurdwara. He left his driver to sleep in the car, while he slept in the Gurdwara. When he came out in the morning, the driver was still asleep in the car but the four wheels had been stolen and replaced with bricks!

After Iran, we had planned to go to Afghanistan. However, around this time a war was taking place between India and Pakistan. The Pakistan government would not give us a visa to go through Pakistan, and we were advised that there might be some trouble on the way from Iran to India. So we decided instead to go to the port of Basra. Basra was in Iraq, but was very close to Iran. We found that a boat left there every week to go to India. From Basra, we took a boat to Bombay, and we were able to take our car with us on the boat.

The journey to India had been fairly uneventful, but a frightening incident did occur in India itself, around 200 miles from Bombay. Around midnight, a group of men, probably bandits, put drums across the road, intending to hold us up and rob us. We managed to get past them – it is possible that when they saw the aerial on the car they thought that it was an army vehicle and moved aside rather than open fire. We were very scared, but we managed to get out of the situation without any injury.

On the return trip from India in August 1965, we were again refused a visa by the Pakistan government to go through Pakistan. As companions, I had my brother and a distant relative. I took my car on the boat from Bombay to Basra. This time, however, I went through Iraq, Jordan, Syria and Turkey. This route was a less direct route than the direct Turkey-to-Iran route that I took on my original journey to India, but the roads were much better. On this return journey from India to Ireland, I covered ten countries in seven days.

On both journeys, I carried spare parts in the car in case of any break down. Fortunately, the car proved to be very reliable, and I only had a couple of punctures to worry about. I had bought it new, and by the time I had finished the round trip I had done 20,000 miles.

On one of the roads from Iraq to Jordan, we were told that the road had no garage for 200 miles and that it was therefore important to stock up with petrol, water, etc. I therefore decided to stock up at a garage in Iraq. My A60 car had a 10 gallon capacity. I asked for it to be to filled up to the brim. However, when I got the bill it was for 11 gallons. I went to the owner and told him that this was impossible. He gave me a refund for the extra cost – his staff had tried to cheat me out of a gallon of petrol by setting the indicator at one gallon before they started to fill the tank with petrol!

VIP VISITORS FROM INDIA

NEHRU'S SECOND VISIT TO IRELAND AS PRIME MINISTER, 1956. *This was Nehru's second visit to Ireland as Prime Minister of India. On this occasion, he came to receive an honorary degree from the National University of Ireland (which later became known as University College, Dublin). This was in 1956. He is shown with a group of Indians who had made a special trip from Northern Ireland to Dublin in order to see him.*
1 – Ram Prashad Chada. 2 – Vijay Lakshmi Chada. 3 – Kaushal Chada.
4 – Jawaharlal Nehru. 5 – Leila Chada. 6 – Manor Lal Chada.
7 – Des Raj Dhand. 8 – Kanta Chada. 9 – Janki Das Chada.
10 – Lakshmi Narain Chada.

NEHRU'S FIRST VISIT TO IRELAND AS PRIME MINISTER, 1949. *This was Nehru's first visit to Ireland as Prime Minister of the newly independent India. This was in 1949, two years after India's independence. He is shown at Dublin airport, being received by the Prime Minister, Eamon de Valera.*

When the Indian Prime Minister Jawaharlal Nehru visited Dublin in 1956 to receive an honorary degree, a group of us went down from Northern Ireland to see him. His sister, Vijay Lakshmi Pandit, who was an important figure in her own right, had also come with him. We happened to be staying at the same hotel as him. We saw him seated at a table, and introduced ourselves to him. We asked if we could have a photograph taken with him. He was a very pleasant man and he readily agreed. While we were assembling for this photograph, a number of students from Dublin who were also present in the hotel crowded around and tried to get in the front so that they would appear along side him in the photograph. Nehru realised this, and told them to go to the back since we had come down specially from Northern Ireland. The students of course did this, and the result was this photograph.

During Nehru's speech, a child in the audience began to cry, and Pandit Nehru's sister, Mrs Vijay Pandit, went over and comforted the child. Nehru addressed us in English. Nehru told the audience, many of whom were engineering and medical students, to think of occasionally going back to India, especially to the villages, and to help to raise the standards of those who were living there. He warned the Indians that if they went back, they should not expect the same level of equipment and facilities that they were used to in the west. He also told them to work hard in Ireland, to remember the colonies from where many of them had come, and to maintain cultural links with India. *[Johnnie Chada, who settled in Sligo in the west of Ireland]*

NEHRU'S SECOND VISIT TO IRELAND AS PRIME MINISTER, 1956. *Nehru is shown as he walks in procession as part of the ceremony to receive his honorary degree from the National University of Ireland. Eamon De Valera, the Prime Minister of Ireland, is walking behind Nehru.*

NEHRU'S SECOND VISIT TO IRELAND AS PRIME MINISTER, 1956. *Nehru is shown signing the formal documents relating to his honorary degree, with Eamon De Valera, the Prime Minister of Ireland, looking on.*

NEHRU'S SECOND VISIT TO IRELAND AS PRIME MINISTER, 1956. *Nehru is shown with a group of Irish school children who took part in an Indian art competition.*

NEHRU'S SECOND VISIT TO IRELAND AS PRIME MINISTER, 1956. *Nehru is shown presenting a prize to an Irish school girl who took part in an Indian art competition.*

While many Indian VIPs visited England after India gained Independence, only a few ventured over to Ireland. The few who did come usually had a specific purpose, and this was usually to attend an official function such as receiving an honorary degree. Krishna Menon, who spent much of his time in London in the 1930s and 1940s agitating for India's freedom, and who was the first Indian High Commissioner in London, obtained an honorary law degree from the King's Inn, Dublin. In later years, Dr Radhakrishnan and Dr V V Giri, both of whom were

FIRST VISIT BY INDIAN HIGH COMMISSIONER TO NORTHERN IRELAND. *The Indian High Commissioner, based in London, made this first visit to Northern Ireland in the mid-1960s. He is shown in the centre of the photograph with a group of local Indians, and with Eddie MacAteer on his left, the leader of the local Nationalist Party in Northern Ireland.*

FIRST VISIT BY INDIAN HIGH COMMISSIONER TO THE IRISH REPUBLIC. *The Indian High Commissioner, based in London, made this visit to Sligo, in the Irish Republic, in 1958. He is shown second from the right. 1 – R P Meahan. 2 – S P Mehan. 3 – P L Verma. 4 – Nand Lal Mehan. 5 – Bal Makand Mehan. 6 – D N Chada. 7 – B K Shah (High Commissioner). 8 – Jim Gannon (Mayor of Sligo).*

President of India, also came to Dublin to collect honorary degrees. When President Radhakrishnan came to Dublin on a state visit in 1962, he was proudly shown by Eamon De Valera, the President of Ireland, an engraved sword that De Valera had received in 1919 in San Franscisco from the Hindustan Ghadr Party, a revolutionary freedom organisation based in India.

For those Indians who lived in Dublin in the 1950s and early 1960s, before an Indian embassy was established in 1964, they were 'looked after' by the Indian embassy in London. Consequently, there were occasional visits by embassy personnel or Indian dignitaries to Dublin to meet the Indians there and discuss any problems with them. During that period, there were visits to Dublin by Indians such as Krishna Menon, who was the first Indian High Commissioner in London.

TASTING WESTERN MEDICINE

> The National Health Service had not yet started. In the early 1940s, we would have to pay two shillings and six pence (twelve and a half pence in today's money) for a short consultation with a General Practitioner, and five shillings for a long consultation. *[One of the first generation Indian settlers]*

In the India that they had left behind, the settlers would have been accustomed to supplement formal medical treatments with remedies handed down over generations – 'old wives tales', etc. Most of these remedies would have been homeopathic treatments or ones based on the use of certain food items/plants/herbs, etc.

Going to the doctor or having hospital treatment in Ireland would only present problems to those Indians who were not so fluent in English. This tended to be the womenfolk, and so their husbands would often act as translators when explanations to medical staff or instructions from medical staff had to be given. This would be particularly valuable when ladies were giving birth to babies in hospital. Needless to say, the food in the hospital was not very attractive to Indians, not only because of the meat dishes but also because the vegetables tended to have a boiled, spice-less nature that was very different to the curried food that the settlers had been accustomed to in India.

Patterns of illness and health care have in recent decades been broadly similar for Indians as for the local Irish community. It is difficult to be certain if the tendency for Asians to suffer diseases such as heart disease, diabetes, etc. has been reflected in a higher incidence of such ailments compared to that of the local Irish population. Similarly, the rarity of illnesses such as multiple sclerosis amongst Indians in Ireland, compared to its relatively high incidence amongst the local population, is superficially apparent, but formal statistics do not exist in this respect.

The pattern of health care for children and adults is broadly similar for those of Indian origin as it is for the Irish. In the case of elderly Indians, there is however a significant difference. This is shown by the extreme reluctance of Indian families to allow their loved one to enter a nursing home or old people's home, if that person can at all be looked after at home. It is customary in Indian society for parents, as they get older, to live with one of the sons, and this is regarded as a form of obligation on the children. While the custom may not be so rigidly followed in Indian communities that are settled in western countries, there is still a strong tendency to look after parents within a family setting for as long as possible. One of the oldest Indians, Hans Raj Treon, lived till the age of 89 years. He was in good health until he died. He came to Northern Ireland in 1963. He was able to speak both Urdu and English, and at the age of 60 years he learned to read Hindi.

RACIAL DISCRIMINATION

My Indian student friend and I answered an 'ad' for board & lodging in Belgrave Square, Dublin. We were then accepted over the phone for board and lodging. When we were unpacking, my friend came to me and said – "We have to get out of here, because they don't take non-Europeans. The person whom we spoke to was the maid, but the landlady wants us out." "I don't believe you," I said, "I'll go and speak to her." I went down to see her. "I'm from South Africa, and quite frankly I'm staggered by this", I said, I recounted the history of the two freedom movements in Ireland and South Africa. But she wasn't going to budge. She said she did not harbour any feelings of racial discrimination, but that she thought that it might not be good for business and the other tenants might object. As if to prove the point that she was not racially prejudiced, she pointed out that she had one Indian lodger in her house (he was an anglicised Indian who sounded very polished). She said that we could remain for the night, but the next morning we would have to leave. In the morning, we left and I found somewhere else. That is how I got to know my first Irish family, the O'Hallions, with whom I stayed for a while.

While I was living with an Indian family, I was studying along with an Irish lodger. There were some children disturbing us – they would tie a piece of

> thread to the knocker of the door, make the door knock from a distance, and then run away. My Irish friend caught one of these children. The father of this boy reported us to the police, thinking that it was me who had chased and caught the boy. We all went to the police station. The police soon realised that it was not me who had been involved in the incident so they charged the poor Irish fellow. The case went to court, and I found that the police superintendent had rallied a lot of the neighbours who started giving evidence against my Irish friend. However, the young boy himself made an amazing statement in court, one that he was probably groomed to make. He pointed to me and said – "The black man told me to go down on my bended knees and said that in Africa, where he had come from, they used to boil white people and eat them." Eventually, the case was settled out of court. *[Sumanth Jeawon, when he was a medical student in Dublin]*

In both Northern Ireland and the Irish Republic, the Indian community integrated well with the local population. On the one hand, the Indian settlers found the Irish to be very friendly. On the other hand, the Irish population also took a liking to the pleasant, sincere and hard-working nature of the Indians with whom they mixed as neighbours or with whom they did business. In a sense, the Irish and Indians felt close to each other, in that they had both suffered discrimination and hardship at the hands of the English. Indeed, it was not unknown for English landlords in the 1930s and 1940s to have signs outside their accommodation that read – "NO BLACKS, NO IRISH, NO DOGS" (Heaven help an Indian from Ireland who knocked on a landlord's door with a dog on a lead!). As Partha Mitter points out in his book *Art & Nationalism in Colonial India 1850–1922* (Cambridge University Press, 1994), 19th century cartoons in English magazines often portrayed both the Irish and Indians as apes, with the English portrayed as lions.

An example of lack of racial awareness dates from the beginning of the 20th century, and took place in London rather than Ireland. A lady, with her child, stopped a Sikh medical student (who was later to be the father of one of the early Indian settlers in Ireland). The lady asked the Sikh student for directions, which the student duly gave. The child then turned to his mother and said, in an astonished tone, "Mummy, it speaks!"

By and large, Northern Ireland has been outstanding in the excellent relations that have existed between the coloured and the white populations. Any racial discrimination has been acknowledged by most Indians to be much less than what has occurred in England. Nevertheless, human nature being what it is, some discrimination has undoubtedly taken place. It is very difficult to know the extent and pattern of such discrimination. Discrimination on purely racial grounds is often difficult to prove in specific instances, and relatively few racial episodes actually get reported.

Racial discrimination is something that is often difficult to prove. It is quite possible that in a number of cases simple jealousy occurred on the part of some of the local Irish population, in view of the rapid success by Indian businessmen, who worked such long hours and who provided such a good and relatively innovative service to their customers.

One instance, which occurred in the Irish Republic in the 1940s, may well have been a by-product of such jealousy, or may even have reflected some degree of racial discrimination. Charlie Verma was an Indian businessman who had successfully built up a retail clothing business. One of his sources for goods was a local factory, *Fruit of the Loom*, that was run by an Irishman, Mr W B McCarter. This was a particularly useful source of goods for Charlie Verma, especially during World War II when there were shortages of items, including some clothes. Some Irish wholesalers from Dublin came to Mr McCarter, objecting to the fact that he sold goods to Charlie Verma. Presumably, they had received complaints from local Irish businessmen who had felt that their own business was suffering from the competition. The Dublin wholesalers wanted Mr McCarter to stop selling goods to Charlie Verma, and threatened that if he did not do so they would stop buying goods from his factory. However, Mr McCarter was a man of principle. He steadfastly refused to give in to their request. He told them that he did not care if they stopped dealing with him. He liked Charlie Verma, and he would continue to do business with him. If they wished to take their own business elsewhere, they could do so. When Charlie Verma went back to India for a few years in 1947, Mr McCarter gave him £40 as a leaving present, such was the admiration and friendship he had for him.

Two Incidents

Let us look at two examples where there was more direct indication that racial sensitivities were perhaps not as good as they could have been.

On January 11, 1994 one of the local radio stations (Downtown Radio, also called Cool FM) was broadcasting its regular music/chat programme in the evening. The disc jockey was Gene Wilson, born in Coventry. During the programme, he made a number of 'jokes', including telling Indians in Bradford to go home if they didn't like it there and making jibes about monsoons in England while playing Doris Day singing 'The Black Hills of Dakota'.

The *Belfast Telegraph* carried a news feature the following day, along the following lines –

> Downtown Radio's head of programming, John Rosborough, said today: "I've listened to the tape – and I didn't like what I heard. I'll be speaking to Gene about this." The show has an average of 10,000 listeners. Many were shocked by the remarks.. One said: "I rang the station immediately to complain but was told the producer wasn't available." "It was disgusting to have to listen to that sort of abuse on the radio." But Mr Rosborough added: "If you listen to Gene's show regularly, you'll know it's a zany show." "He's originally from Coventry and he was making the point that, when he wants to cheer himself up, he goes back to Coventry." "The 'Black Hills of Dakota' wouldn't be a normal choice of record for the show but that just shows you he was being zany." "But anything that could be taken as racist is not acceptable at Cool. I haven't seen him yet but I'll be speaking to him." Sunita Sharma, spokeswoman for Northern Ireland's 1,000-strong Indian community, said: "This is terrible, disgusting." "I'm originally from England, I've only been here 10 years, and I always thought racism was worse over there." "But it disgusts me that you can say this on the radio here and get away with it. I've never heard of anything like this before." Mr Wilson was not available for comment.

As mentioned earlier, racial discrimination was much more prevalent in England than in Northern Ireland, and a very small number of British soldiers from England brought some racial intolerance over with them when they had a tour of duty in Northern Ireland in the 1970s/1980s. In Londonderry, a few Indian businessmen had cause to complain to army headquarters about what they regarded as provocation by some British soldiers. In such instances, the local police inevitably took the side of the Indian businessman.

On one occasion, an army check-point was in place in Londonderry. A young Indian businessman came up to the check-point in his van. He was told by the soldiers that he could walk beyond the check-point, but that he could not take his van. However, the Indian saw other vehicles being let through. The Indian then got his father to come along in the van. They were still not allowed through by the soldiers. The Indian men then got one of their Irish friends to take over the driver's seat and try to get through, while they were sitting in the back. This time, the van was let through. The elder Indian businessman immediately went to the Police Station. The sergeant was very sympathetic, and indicated that such matters were not under his control. They brought the soldier concerned to the police station. When he came in, he almost had a fight with the younger of the two Indians, and they had to be pulled apart.

Government And Race Relations

The Race Relations Act in Great Britain does not apply to Northern Ireland, and neither is there any equivalent legislation in The Irish Republic. However, there are plans to introduce similar legislation to Northern Ireland at some stage in the future. It is ironic that one of the members of parliament for Northern Ireland was Enoch Powell, who held the seat for South Down from 1974 to 1987. He had long been an advocate of strict control of immigration of coloured citizens to Great Britain, although there did not appear to have been any major change in race relations in South Down or other parts of Northern Ireland during his tenure as Member of Parliament.

In 1993, the Social Democratic and Labour Party (SDLP) in Northern Ireland brought out a document that was a position statement with respect to race relations in Northern Ireland. It was drawn up by Paul Gupta, ethnic minority liaison officer for the SDLP. The document called for race relations legislation to be enacted in Northern Ireland.

In 1992/1993, the Central Community Relations Unit in Northern Ireland launched a public consultation exercise on race relations in Northern Ireland. The consultation document set out a number of options for future legislation. A total of 55 responses were received to the document, and most of these supported the idea of legislation. In April 1995, the Secretary of State for Northern Ireland, Sir Patrick Mayhew, announced that legislation on race relations would be introduced into Northern Ireland and that this would broadly follow the lines of the Race Relations Act of 1976 that applied in the rest of the United Kingdom.

In December, 1995, the Minister for Equality and Law Reform in the Irish Republic, Mr Mervyn Taylor, launched an anti-racism and equality education pack for use with youth groups, schools and community groups. The President of Ireland, Mary Robinson, wrote an Introduction for the education pack.

Racial Discrimination In Reverse!

It should not be forgotten that discrimination is a multi-edged sword. Those Indians who had spent most of their life in Ireland, and who then went back to India, invariably found themselves having difficulty in adjusting to life in India and relating to people in India. On one occasion in 1964, a 15 year old girl from Londonderry went back with her family to their home village. She would invariably have looked different in her dress, hair-style and appearance compared to local Indian girls. On one occasion, while she was out walking in the village, two men who shared a bicycle, screamed at her in Punjabi – "Get back to where you came from!" She felt rooted to the spot, and could not even think what to say. It helped make up her mind that her home was very much in Northern Ireland rather than India.

LAYING THE DEAD TO REST

FIRST RECORDED FUNERAL OF AN INDIAN SETTLER TO IRELAND. *Keher Singh probably came to Northern Ireland in the 1930s. He died in 1940, and this photograph shows a group of Indians present at his cremation, which was in an open field on the outskirts of Londonderry. 1 – Ujagar Singh. 2 – Suchet Singh. 3 – R P Chada. 4 – F C Sumra. 5 – Dalip Singh. 6 – Manor Lal Chada. 7 – Mohabait Rai Vij. 8 – Bawa Singh. 9 – Janki Das Chada. 10 – Banarsi Das Chada. 11 – Bhagat Rai Kindria. 12 – G L Sumra. 13 – Roshan Lal Mehan. 14 – Baj Nath. 15 – Morari Lal. 16 – Munsha Singh. 17 – Pyare Lal Abroal. 18 – Kharaiti Ram.*

The Londonderry Journal, its edition of Friday morning, January 3, 1941 recorded the death of an Indian settler who had died in Londonderry itself. It was on a page that also had a number of items relating to World War II. The news piece about the funeral was as follows (with the original spellings preserved) –

> *LONDONDERRY HINDOO'S FUNERAL CREATES A UNIQUE PROBLEM*
>
> *Ministry Consent to Cremation*
>
> A unique difficulty has arisen in connection with the funeral of a Hindoo who has died in a Londonderry hospital.
>
> He was one of a number of Indians who reside in the city and who carry on business as peddlers, selling various articles from door to door.
>
> When arrangements were made for the funeral, it was found that the deceased's Hindoo comrades stated that this would have to take place according to their rites. These stipulate that the body must be cremated on a funeral pyre, and a portion of the ashes then sent home to India, to be put in the river Ganges.
>
> The only crematoriums, however, are in two cities across the Irish Sea.
>
> Cremation in the City of Londonderry would not be permitted by the Corporation authorities.
>
> The local Hindoos decided that a solution of their problem would probably be to take the body out to a country district, and have it cremated there in their presence as prescribed by their rites.
>
> Some of them approached Mr Patrick Maxwell, M.P., and the Ministry of Home Affairs were communicated with by 'phone, and the facts placed before them. The matter was pointed out to be urgent, the man having died on Monday.
>
> The position is believed to be without precedent in the Six Counties, if not Northern Ireland.
>
> *To be cremated today*
>
> Last evening the Ministry telephoned that they would agree to the cremation taking place as sought by the Londonderry Hindoos.
>
> It is learned that the cremating ceremony will take place today beside a river in a rural district some miles from Londonderry City.
>
> Members of the R.U.C. or possibly representatives of the Public Health Authority will be present.

The person who had died was Keher Singh, who died on Monday, December 30, 1940. Being a Hindu, the normal practice would have been for his body to have been cremated. Since there was at that time no crematorium in either Northern Ireland or the Irish Republic, the logical step would have been to transport the body by boat to Glasgow, where there was both a crematorium and also the availability of a priest to carry out the relevant religious ceremonies. There was a boat link between Londonderry and Glasgow, but because of the war most of the boats were in war service, and it was not possible to readily send bodies to Glasgow.

A few years later, another Indian settler known as Ved Paul or Yashpal died in 1942. He was cremated in an open space near Danamana marina, Londonderry. Shortly after this cremation, there was an outbreak of foot-and-mouth disease and some members of the local Irish community thought that it might have been related to the occurrence of the cremation on open ground.

After the war was over, it was possible to readily transport bodies to the crematorium in Glasgow. In 1947, Mr Banarsi Das Chada died. He was an Indian businessman based in Londonderry. His body was also transported to Glasgow by boat. The ashes were sent by post to Bhagwara, his home town in northern India. They were collected from the post office by a relative, and taken to the holy city of Hardawar, in northern India, where they were scattered in the river Ganges. The wife of Bal Makund Mehan, one of the first settlers in Northern Ireland, died in 1956. Her body was transported by boat from Londonderry for cremation in Glasgow.

The first crematorium in Northern Ireland was opened on the eastern outskirts of Belfast in September, 1961. It is known as the Roselawn Cemetery and Crematorium. The first Indian who was cremated there was in fact a member of the Indian embassy staff in Dublin, a Suraj Prakash Singh Malhotra. He was a 32 year old employee of the Indian Embassy in Dublin. He died on February 21, 1962, at St Luke's Hospital, Dublin, and he was cremated in Belfast two days later. The first crematorium in the Irish Republic opened in Dublin in 1982. In the early 1960s, an Indian student from South Africa died of acute pancreatitis in Dublin. His body was in fact flown back to South Africa for cremation.

It is the Moslem tradition to bury their dead, and they have usually reserved a plot in part of a Christian churchyard prior to their death. More recently, a group of Moslems in Belfast have selected a plot of land that will be reserved especially for them and for their relatives.

Rites

Certain religious rites have to be followed for both Hindu and Moslem funerals. These are performed for Hindus in Northern Ireland by the resident Hindu priest in Belfast. For Hindus in the Irish Republic, the services of this priest or of a priest from England are sought. It is traditionally the case that, after death, Hindus have their ashes taken to the holy Indian city of Hardwar in northern India. While this was commonly done in the 1950s and 1960s, in recent years there has been a trend for Indians to decree that their ashes are scattered in the sea around that part of Ireland where they lived.

Moslems try to ensure that their priest or 'malvi' is present to perform a ceremony at the graveside. The body is usually taken first to the person's home, and it is then transported to a local cemetery.

In any circumstance, death brings great sadness to family and friends of the person who has died. In such a close-knit community such as that of the Indians who settled in Ireland, the death of a member of the community was particularly keenly felt. To realise the close bonds that existed, one needs to remember the great camaraderie that existed amongst the small group of Indian men who settled in Northern Ireland. They shared happy times and sad times, they shared each others' joys and hardships as if they were their own. They readily gave each other money for things such as making a return trip to India, bringing a wife and children from India, buying a vehicle, etc. This closeness bred a sense of gratitude, a trust and a togetherness that is difficult to describe, but it was visible at the funeral of one of the first Indian settlers in Northern Ireland.

> I was standing there, a young man in my 20s, watching the procession of friends and relatives pay their last respects to the body as it lay in the coffin. Then, two men in their mid-50s came into the room. They looked at the coffin for a few seconds but it seemed like a few minutes, such was the intensity of their gaze, an intensity that displayed a sense of disbelief. They then embraced each other, and broke into a flood of tears. They cried, 'He is dead. He is dead.' The person who had died was the one who had summoned both of them over to Ireland, once he himself had initially got settled. He had helped them both establish their business. To one of them, he had given money so that he could bring his wife and children over to Northern Ireland from India. One of the two men, in his wreath, wrote the simple words, 'You will never know how much I loved you till I meet you again.' Ironically, and tragically, this very person was to die later the same year.
>
> Another man, this time a close relative of the dead person, and who had also been helped by him to settle down in Northern Ireland, had to be restrained as he broke down and tried to talk to the dead body with the words, 'I'll tell you the story of how we both came to this country.' *[The perspective of a young Indian in the 1970s, witnessing an Indian funeral scene for the first time]*

4: MAKING MONEY

GOING TO WORK ON FOOT AND BIKE

> I would have to walk, carrying a suitcase full of clothes. The clothes would usually be small, light items such as underwear, shirts, ties, etc. rather than large, heavy ones. Saturday would usually be confined to working in Londonderry, and the rest of the week would involve going by bus to neighbouring areas – Limavady, Dungiven, etc. I would leave at nine in the morning and come back at nine at night, often without a meal all day. I got my wares from a variety of sources, mainly Belfast and Glasgow. I would go to Belfast by bus and train. Going to Glasgow was an overnight journey by boat.
>
> On one occasion, I was carrying this suitcase of clothes when it snapped and broke. I had to find some way of mending it, and I did this by taking the string from my underpants and tying it around the case!
>
> I had a bike for four years, which I originally bought for 30 shillings. I would carry a case in the front and a parcel in the back. Initially, when using the bike, I would travel up to 50 miles a day. My suitcase would include things such as socks, jumpers, cardigans, ladies underwear, shirts, etc. In winter time, there was snow and ice to contend with, and all year round there was always the possibility of being drenched in the rain. It was therefore essential that the clothes were in a waterproof case, and that they did not get wet during trips to customers. *[The experiences of three first-generation Indian businessmen]*

From the 1930s to the 1950s, it was not uncommon for an Indian businessman to ride his bike for distances of 50 miles. In some cases, the bike would be carried onto the train, taken to another town, and then ridden there. In other cases, the bike would be tied on to the rack on the top of a bus – the Indian businessman would travel as a passenger, keeping his suitcase of clothes with him, and when he got to an area where he would find his customers, he took his bike off the rack and went on his way.

Riding a bike on lonely country roads, especially at night, had its own hazards and adventures. On one occasion, an Indian businessman was returning home around midnight after a hard day's work. He was trying to get to Letterkenny in County Donegal, and had been to some country areas selling goods to customers. He had been told a short-cut by one of his friends, and decided to take this. However, he found himself riding for miles and miles down a narrow country road, with no sight of a main road or a town. He eventually came across a pub, and he saw two young ladies at a water pump getting some water. He asked them for the directions to Letterkenny, but they got frightened and started to run away. Eventually, he was able to reason with them, indicating that he was lost. Then they told him the directions. After a while, he did find himself on the main road, and was able to make his way home.

Some of those Indian businessmen who lived in Londonderry in the 1930s and 1940s found themselves walking to places across the border in the Irish Republic like Letterkenny – one such Indian walked a total of 32 miles in one day. Usually, however, those who walked would combine this with using a bus as well. There was a reluctance amongst the Indians to use umbrellas (these would have been a little cumbersome, especially if two suitcases were being carried!), and in the many instances of inclement weather it was more convenient to simply wear a raincoat and a hat. Going into country areas, where many of the customers were farmers, also meant that one's shoes would invariably get very dirty. One Indian wife recounts how she would have three pairs of shoes for her husband, and how he would often end up wearing rubber 'over-shoes' or wellington boots to protect his feet against the dirt.

Setting up a business from scratch often meant going where new customers could be found, armed only with a suitcase full of clothes to sell. This type of work would frequently involve days away from home, sometimes going to new parts of the locality each day, staying in bed-and-breakfast if this was necessary. Around this time in the 1940s, one of the Indian businessmen in Northern Ireland had a 'shop' in St Johnson, a small village across the border in Donegal. On certain set days of the week, he would travel to the Irish Republic and the local people would come to buy clothes from the shop.

Going on bike had its own hazards, as the following tales by an Indian businessman indicate –

> I used to ride my bike quite fast, sometimes up to 30 miles per hour, and often with my hands in my pocket. I would even on occasions pass cars

> that were on the road, since in those days (1940s, 1950s) cars did not go very fast. Once, late at night, I was going quite fast on the bike and was approaching a railway crossing. I had a suitcase of clothes on the back of the bike. The gate would be across when a train was coming, and the gate-keeper would put a light out in the centre of the gate to signal that a train was due and that those approaching the gate should stop. This time, however, the gate-keeper – who happened to be one of my lady customers – had left the light at the side of the road rather than in the middle. It was only at the last minute that I realised the gate was across. My bike went straight into the gate with such force that the gate flew open and the front of my bike was bent. I managed to hold on to the bike, but it landed on the track. I could hear the train approaching. I quickly pulled the gate back, and dragged my bike from the track. The train rushed by shortly after. The gate-keeper came out, hearing all the commotion. I had to give her a telling-off for not putting the light on the middle of the gate. My bike was at first completely out of action, and I had to use brute force to straighten it out such that it could be wheeled home.
>
> On another occasion, the snow was very deep and the roads were very icy. I went out on my bike as usual, even though some of my Indian friends stayed at home. As I went out, I found that I was the only one on a bike. One Irishman shouted at me – 'Johnny get back inside, otherwise you'll be killed.' I nevertheless completed my day's work. On the way back home, my bike must have skidded 3–4 times. On one occasion, it was a very steep slope and I came off the bike when it skidded. The road was so icy that I literally had to crawl up on my hands and knees to get hold of the bike. Further on, I was cycling in the snow when a car pulled out in front. I realised that I could not brake, since I would definitely skid. I therefore put my foot into the snow, and used my foot as a brake to slow down my pace. Luckily, I managed to avoid colliding into the car.

In the 1940s and 1950s, winters were harsher than in more recent years. From November to February, there would frequently be heavy falls of snow, with the snow lying for a week or more. In those years, snow ploughs and gritting lorries were few and far between. During particularly severe spells of weather, the Indian businessmen would be forced to stay at home, and they would pass the time playing cards! On one occasion, an Indian businessman who did venture out was caught up in a blizzard and had to stay the night at the home of one of his customers.

GETTING A CAR

> I bought a second-hand car, a Ford 10, for £16. I shared the car with an Indian friend. A local Irishman taught me how to drive.
>
> When I bought my first car in the 1940s, it had one door missing! *[Two of the first Indian businessmen to own a car]*

In view of the small number of cars on the roads, and the freedom that this gave to drivers to drive as they wanted, there was the temptation for Indian businessmen to have a race on their way to wholesale clothing centres in Belfast from towns further north. One car would overtake, and then slow down to let the other car overtake, etc. On one occasion, when one Indian businessman overtook another Indian businessman this resulted in a stone coming off the road and breaking his windscreen. After this incident, that practice stopped!

GETTING A CAR. *One of the early Indian settlers to Northern Ireland, Bal Makund Mehan, with his Austin 8 car. This photograph was probably taken in the 1940s/early 1950s.*

At the end of a year in business, and often less than this, the Indian businessman would have earned enough money to move up from a bike to a van or a car. Mohabbat Rai Vij, based in Londonderry, was the first Indian to buy a vehicle in Northern Ireland, this being a car that he bought in the early 1930s. Banarsi Das Chada was the second Indian to buy a car. When he bought a car, he himself could not drive it, and he had to wait for his brother (Manohar Lal Chada) to come over from India in 1934 and teach him how to drive the car. This car, which was bought second-hand, was a twelve horse-power Singer car.

A few weeks after they bought the car, the dynamo stopped working, and the lights in the car went out. The Chada brothers were in their

Singer car, and Mohabbat Rai Vij was in his own car in front. The Chada brothers reckoned that if they kept close behind Mohabbat Rai Vij in his car, they could manage to get back safely to their base in Londonderry. They were approaching Sion Mills, a town close to Londonderry in Northern Ireland. When they were going round a bend, they crashed the Singer car into a wall. The car was a write-off. Fortunately, no-one was injured. They reported the incident to the police, and they were fined for careless driving. At the court hearing in Strabane, a town near the border, the solicitor defending the Indian who was driving the car said – "Although this is a coloured man, he has a white heart, since he immediately reported the matter to the police, even though no-one was hurt and no other car was involved." As a result, the fine was a relatively light one.

This accident was in fact a blessing in disguise – the Singer had been rather big and expensive to run. The Chada brothers replaced this with an Austin 7 (7 standing for seven horsepower). This car did 52 miles to the gallon of petrol. It had a soft top, a perspex-type screen, and a handle to start the car. The handle was a substitute for the ignition switch – it was pushed into the bottom of the engine underneath the front of the car and rotated vigorously. The car had no automatic wipers – there was a wiper on the screen, but this had to be moved manually. It had no heater. The car also had no electric 'blinkers' as indicators, but an arrow that came out from the side of the car. The arrow was operated by a manual lever-type switch inside the car. In 1939, shortly before the outbreak of World War II, the two Chada brothers bought a van. During the war years, they in fact had two vans and a car.

On one occasion in the early 1950s, an Indian businessman was driving his van in the north-west part of Northern Ireland when a cow strayed across the road. The cow was killed, and the van was a write-off, but he fortunately escaped injury.

Although many Indians moved from going around on foot to travelling by bike and then by van, some missed out on the bike. Harry Bedi, who came in 1951 from the village of Phillaur in northern India, could not ride a bike when he came to Ireland. Someone in his village had been killed while riding his bike, and his father therefore forbade him from riding a bike. After six months in Ireland, Harry Bedi bought a second hand van for £250, purchasing this from the Indian (Tara Chand Vij) who had helped him to come over from India to Ireland. He learned to drive the van in two hours, having been taught by a local Irishman in Londonderry.

Usually a van rather than a car was the first purchase for Indian businessmen. A larger number and variety of clothes could be carried in a van, and since the businessman's family would not be with him when he was out selling clothes, there was little need for seats for passengers. In any case, if passengers had to be carried, they could always sit on blankets or make-shift seats in the back of the van!

By 1939, Ram Partap Gupta was able to buy a car, a Morris Minor that he purchased second hand for £10. For the Indian businessman who came in the 1950s, it was almost essential to get a car since most other businessmen had cars. Therefore, in order to run an efficient and competitive business, he had to have a vehicle of sorts. Those who arrived in Northern Ireland from India had little in the way of money, since it was virtually impossible to obtain foreign currency such as pounds in India. One newly-arrived settler bought a van from another Indian settler and paid for it by asking his relative in India to pay money to a relative of the seller.

In other cases, it was the pure generosity of those Indians already established in business that was critical. When Chaman Lal Treon arrived in Northern Ireland in the early 1950s, he found a van had already been bought for him by Sat Pal Kapur so that he could readily get his business off the ground.

Even up to the early 1950s, relatively few people had cars and so the roads were rather empty. Mr A S Anand, who lived in Portrush on the northern coast of Northern Ireland, bought his first car in 1955, and at that time there were only four cars in the town.

Scrapes

> I had arrived in Northern Ireland a few weeks earlier, and I was told by my friend to learn to drive a car by practising on my own on the deserted beach of a small seaside town on the north coast. After a lot of practice, I made my way to a town about 40 miles away to rendezvous with my friend. I found myself in a cul-de-sac, and I realised that my friend hadn't taught me how to get the car into reverse gear! I therefore had to get the help of a stranger to tell me how to put the car into reverse!
>
> On one occasion, in the 1960s, when I was driving on the beach, I got stuck. The tide was coming in, and there was danger of the van being swept out to sea. I quickly called an Irish friend, and I paid him a few pounds to pull me out. *[The experiences of two first-generation Indian businessmen in Northern Ireland]*

Another Indian businessman described the following incident that happened around 1959 –

> It was late at night, with snow and ice on the road. My car skidded right into the ditch and turned on its side. I had just visited a customer who was a farmer. He had given me eggs in part exchange for the clothes that I had given him. The eggs in the car came right over me, and broke over my clothes. I managed to walk to the farmer's house. The farmer got his tractor, and got me out of the ditch. He then towed me to my home. I eventually arrived home at three o'clock in the morning. Naturally, my wife was waiting up, worried sick. After this incident, I always carried a bag of sand and a shovel in the car, in case I ever got stuck in snow or ice and had to get myself out.

Learning to drive was an experience in itself. It was only in the late 1950s that formal driving tests became compulsory. Prior to then, it was a matter of trial and error or getting a friend to teach you how to drive. A driving license itself was simply obtained by completing an application form. Consequently, many Indian ladies obtained such licenses in the 1950s, even though none of them even sat behind the driving wheel of a car! Northern Ireland was in fact behind the rest of Great Britain in its decision to introduce a compulsory driving test before one could get a license. This resulted in a number of people from England and Scotland, including Indian friends and relatives of those living in Northern Ireland, coming over to Northern Ireland to get a driving license, and then going back to their home town to drive, without having to do a driving test!

Cars and vans from the 1950s and earlier decades did not have the comforts that we take for granted in the cars of today. Many did not have automatic windscreen wipers, or any wipers at all. Thus, during rain or snow, the screen might have to be periodically cleaned manually by the driver. With the more severe winters of that period, it was not unusual for the tyres of cars and vans to be fitted with chains. Indicators might not be available in the car or perhaps would not work satisfactorily, and so drivers had to be expert in using hand signals.

After a hard day's work, driving home at night had its own hazards. One Indian businessman, in the 1950s, fell asleep at the wheel of his car. He had little sleep the night before, having been up late entertaining an Indian who had recently arrived from India. Losing out on this sleep, together with a hard day's work the next day, meant that he dozed off as he was going around a corner in his van. The van turned over on its side, but fortunately he was not hurt.

To Indians who were driving vans and cars in wintry weather, this was a new experience, since driving a car in the snow was unheard of in those parts of India from which they had come. The customers of the Indian businessmen would, therefore, be invaluable in terms of giving advice – as in one case, where an Indian businessman, who had never seen snow before, could not get ice off his windscreen and he was advised by his customer to remove the ice with salt.

On another occasion, the night was a very stormy one – it was in fact the same night on January 31, 1953 that the ferry between Northern Ireland and Scotland capsized with the loss of many lives. An Indian businessman was about six miles from his home. He was visiting some customers, and it was late in the evening. The clutch in his car had broken outside the customer's house. The car was full of a stock of new clothes, and it also contained some money. Without any hesitation, the customer arranged for the Indian businessman to be driven back to his home, and for the son of the customer to fix the car the next day and to deliver it back to the businessman.

LEARNING THE LANGUAGE

> A few Indian businessmen were lodging in a house, when the landlady had to go to hospital for a while. Her name was Mrs Miller, though she ended up being called Mrs Malla. Some of the Indians visited her in hospital, but one Indian businessman – whose English was quite limited – was unable to get there to see her. When she came back home, he wanted to offer his sympathies in view of her illness and to apologise for not having visited her in hospital. He said to her – "Malla, you the hospital, me not the hospital. You the sick, me the very sorry. You come back again, me still very sorry." One of the other Indians, whose English was much better, was there and he joked with Mrs Miller. "You see what he says – 'You've come back and he's still very sorry'." She replied that she knew full well what he meant, and that she did not take it at all badly! *[A story recounted by one of the Indian businessmen who settled in Northern Ireland in the 1940s]*

For Indian settlers who planned to set up business in Northern Ireland, it was all the more essential to acquire a fluency in English so that they could communicate to their potential customers. Key phrases that were learned by Indian settlers (often on the boat journey to Britain) were 'Me cheap', 'You good', 'You lucky'. One helpful Indian, who himself knew only a little English, tried to teach another who knew even less. He tried to teach the word 'understand', but instead taught the word 'Hindustan' (this is Hindi for India, since it literally means 'land of the

Hindus'). "You Hindustan, Me Hindustan" ("You understand, Me Understand"), are the words he would valiantly try to say during classes with his student!

A number of Indians used ingenious ways to try to communicate with their customers. One of the Indians who came in the 1930s, Bal Makand Mehan, knew how to speak and write Urdu (a language similar to Hindi, and taught in Indian schools around that period). During his first few months working in Ireland, he would write on the back of his hand the words 'Buy Something?', but these word sounds would be written in Urdu as he did not know how to write English. Thus, when he met a customer at the door, he would look at the back of his hand and remember the word sounds he had to say.

Most Indian men who came to Ireland could speak English fairly fluently, since British rule in India meant that English was taught in most schools and was commonly used in public life. However, a few individuals had to learn English from scratch. It is interesting that those who had to learn English in this way subsequently developed a strong Irish accent, while those who knew English fluently when they first arrived in Northern Ireland retained the accent that they had in India.

One Indian settler, who knew very little English when he came to Ireland, decided that the best way to learn was to see an English film in the local cinemas every night (or 'picture halls' as they were then called). There were two cinemas in the town where he was based. Each cinema would show a film for two successive nights, and the film would then be changed for another different film. By going to one cinema hall, and then the following evening to the other one, and then back to the first one, it was possible to see a different film every night of the week. This is what the enterprising Indian settler did. And so he picked up fluency in English in no time!

One unfortunate Indian settler, during his first few months in Northern Ireland, came to a house to see if he could find a customer for his clothes. He knew little English, but wanted to be friendly to the couple who came to the door. It was a particularly nasty weather, with strong winds, and he remarked on the bad weather to the lady. Unfortunately, he included some Hindi words with some English words, and the sum total of his utterances were in fact similar to some local swear words. The lady's husband took particular offence at this, and 'roughed up' the poor Indian traveller!

In spite of such experiences, most Irish folk were able to understand the pigeon English that they occasionally encountered from the travelling Indian salesmen. Although most of the local Irish population did not know how to speak an Indian language, one or two had in fact served in India, perhaps in the British Army, and they were thus familiar with some Indian phrases. On one occasion, this worked against a couple of Indian businessmen. One went to a house to sell some goods. A lady answered the door. The Indian businessman pleaded, to the point of insistence, that she buy something from him, but the lady refused. Her husband was standing near by her. As the Indian businessman gave up and left in despair, he swore at her in Hindi, fully confident that she did not know what the words would have meant. But her husband, who had served in India, *did* know what these words meant. He therefore took it upon himself to slap the Indian around the face!

Another Indian businessman with very limited fluency in English found himself trying in vain to explain to a lady customer that he was trying to sell her some corsets. He used all sorts of gesticulations, but to no avail. He finally thought he found the name for them, calling them 'belly binders'!

GETTING A SUPPLY OF GOODS

My name is Ram Swarup Sharma. My first warehouse account was with a clothing wholesaler, Dixon Mason & Co, in Bedford Street. The manager of the store was a Mr Herbert, to whom I had been introduced. Mr Herbert used to be Lieutenant General in the Army, serving in the Middle East. He gave me £25 credit. Thus, I could buy up to £25 worth of goods each week. I then repaid him whatever I could, when I had the money. This was usually daily. A number of Indians were helped by his firm, and so this firm seemed a logical one to approach.

After a year in Belfast, I brought my wife over to Northern Ireland. Before she came, therefore, I started to save for a house (I was living with a Moslem businessman called Jamal Dean at the time). I therefore bought less goods from the warehouse. Mr Herbert, who was very observant, in spite of having to cater for 10 staff in his warehouse, asked me what was wrong, since I was not buying many goods from him. He brought me into his office. I explained that I was saving to buy a house for my family. Mr Herbert insisted that if I ever needed help I should only ask. I was quite taken aback at this. I thought that perhaps this was just an off-hand remark, and so I ignored it.

After my family came, my wife suggested that I should go to Mr Herbert for the help I needed for buying my house. I had saved up £150 as a deposit

> to buy a house, and I needed a further amount in the form of a bank loan. However, no bank was prepared to give me a loan just like that, and I needed a letter of introduction in order to get the loan. On one occasion, Mr Herbert sensed that something was amiss, and asked me – 'What's troubling you?' I explained my situation. Mr Herbert told me that he had promised me help six months ago, and asked me why had I not taken it up. He immediately gave me a letter of credit. I recall that I was so shocked at this act of generosity that everything went blank in front of my eyes and I started crying!

Mr Herbert had in fact helped a number of Indian businessmen set up their trade, and was affectionately regarded by many Indian settlers in Northern Ireland.

In the earlier years (1930s, 1940s), goods were generally bought by post, or less frequently in person, from Glasgow or London. In the case of purchases from London, a few Indians had a specific agent in London, Mr Gulam Mohammed, who was based there. He would be sent an order from the Indians in Northern Ireland for particular items, together with a sum of money. He would be asked to procure certain clothing items from wholesale firms in London, and he would go around various firms getting the best deals that he could find. Having done this, he would post the goods to Northern Ireland. This arrangement worked well, and it obviously required an element of trust on both sides, since it involved both sides keeping an account of what goods had been ordered, how much money had been sent, etc.

In later years, when wholesale firms began to get established in Belfast, that city became the source of goods for the Indian businessmen. One of the first tasks for an Indian businessman was to establish contacts with particular wholesale clothing firms, and to gain their trust such that he could open a credit account with the firm. For those who did not already have contacts who could introduce or 'sponsor' them to the director of the wholesale firm, this was no easy task. The sponsor who introduced someone was considered to be held responsible for that person. If that person got into debt with the warehouse or refused to pay an account, the sponsor might be held responsible for the unpaid bill. Sometimes this understanding might get out of hand –

> Mr Herbert of Dixon Mason & Co was owed some money by an Indian businessman, who happened to be a relative of Bagwan Das Dhand. Another Indian businessman suggested to Mr Herbert that he write to Mr Dhand, since Mr Dhand generally paid up 'bad' accounts held by Indian businessmen. Mr Dhand had in fact paid off some other debts that this particular businessman had owed to others. Mr Herbert wrote a letter to Mr Dhand – 'This person owes me some money. Can you kindly pay up.'

When Mr Dhand received the letter, he was understandably furious. He did not even have an account with Dixon Mason & Co. He went to see Mr Herbert.
"Do you know me?" he asked.
"No," said Mr Herbert. "I've never seen you before."
"How then do you explain this letter? Did I introduce this businessman to you? Did I give a guarantee for the person's debts? How can I be held responsible for his debts?"
Mr Herbert trembled when he was faced with this error. He immediately apologised and agreed that he should never have sent the letter. Mr Dhand was impressed by the apology, and he accepted that Mr Herbert was a fine person who had made a mistake on this occasion.

SELLING GOODS TO THE LOCALS

An Indian businessman had sold cushion covers to a lady. She was paying for the items by a small, weekly repayment. When he came to her house, he repeatedly didn't find her at home. One day, he finally found her in. He tried to explain to her – "Missus, me came to your house, you opened the door, you let me in, me not came in on my own [indicating that it was she who wanted his goods in the first place]. You opened the case and you got 'crookshutter' ('crookshutter' was the name of a town in India, but it was the nearest that the fledgling Indian businessman knew to the word 'cushion cover'). Me came for money, 'tu lukgieye' [this is Hindi for 'you went hiding'], me came again for money, 'tu feir luckgieye' [Hindi for 'you went hiding again']. Me not get money, me go to police." The threat to go to the police persuaded the reluctant customer to start making regular payments for what she owed the businessman!

On another occasion, a young child – seeing the Indian businessman for the first time visit his home to sell goods – asked him if he was a red Indian and what dress he wore. The Indian businessman replied that he wore head gear, with feathers sticking out of the top! *[Two stories told by first-generation Indian businessmen, the first relating to Northern Ireland, and the second relating to the Irish Republic]*

Gaining the trust of customers, and thence their business, was the greatest challenge facing the Indian businessmen who started off in the clothing trade for the first time, whether it was in the 1920s or 1950s. Fortunately, the Indians who started selling clothes around that time had a number of things in their favour.

Firstly, the Irish to whom they were selling goods were generally very friendly and trusting. Some Irish men and women felt a sense of affinity with people from India since they were nationals who had been under the same imperial, colonial power. After India became independent in 1947, the local Irish tended to give the Indian businessmen more respect. Many of the Irish, especially those in rural areas and the poorer folk (many of whom tended to be Roman Catholics), were simple in their life-style and God-fearing, just like the Indians themselves. Even if they did not want to buy an item of clothing on a particular day, some customers would still invite the Indian to come in for a cup of tea. They would always be ready to give the Indian businessman friendly advice, even if it was tongue-in-cheek. One wise old lady advised a young Indian businessman, who had been in Northern Ireland a few years, to remember *three* things and he would be successful – 'Don't get involved with local women. Don't get involved with local politics. Don't go out without a raincoat!'

A second factor that helped Indian businessmen was that they provided the convenience of coming out to the homes of customers. Most customers, especially those in the country-side, did not have ready transport such as cars with which to travel to towns to do their shopping.

Thirdly, the Indian businessmen offered customers credit facilities. Customers did not have to pay for the goods in full when they received them. Payment could be delayed, with regular, small payments over a period of time. No interest was charged on the original cost of the goods.

Fourthly, especially during World War II and in the ten years or so afterwards, there was rationing/shortage of clothes. This meant that a salesman who could provide certain clothing materials easily was well received. During the war years, there was in fact more money in circulation – American soldiers were stationed in Northern Ireland, and they provided purchasing power. In addition, many factories were involved in the war-effort, and those who worked in such factories also had some purchasing power.

Fifthly, the enterprising, hard-working nature of the average Indian businessman – regardless of any physical or psychological hardships that he may have suffered – meant that he was more likely to be successful than some of his local Irish counterparts. In some cases, during rationing, the businessman would arrange to collect clothes coupons from his regular customers, and he would redeem these in the warehouses in Glasgow. Sometimes customers gave sugar instead of money for goods that they received, or if they did not take sugar in their tea they would save it for the Indians. Most Indians were accustomed to taking sugar with their tea when they were living in India – very sweet tea, usually boiled with milk and a few spices in a pan, still is a delicacy in India.

Routine

After a number of years, most Indian businessmen would have built up a customer base of 300–500 people. Particular days of the week would be set aside for going to particular parts of the locality. Usually, one day was kept free for sorting out goods and orders and going to wholesalers in Belfast. Most of those who were in the clothing retail trade kept a store/shop at home where their stock of drapery items were kept. Customers would come to this store in the evenings, while during the day the businessman would usually be out in the countryside meeting his customers. Customers might also come on Sundays, as this also was a day when Indian businessmen would be sure to be at home. The bulk of his business would be in small towns or hamlets in the countryside, though one day would often be kept for customers who lived in the town in which the businessman lived. Having a customer-base of several hundred people meant keeping accurate records of what had been sold to each customer, how much each customer was paying weekly, how much remained outstanding, and which new orders had to be processed.

The system that was developed was a simple but very efficient one. Each customer had a note book, often a 'little red book', in which was kept an account of the goods he/she had bought, how much he/she had paid per week, and the amount that was still outstanding. The Indian businessman had a set of much larger books, one book for each locality. This book would contain the sales record relating to each customer in that locality. The book therefore provided a check for the records that were kept in the 'little red book' by each customer. A further small note-book was usually kept by the Indian businessman, and this contained the orders for clothes that had been made by each customer. In order for a business of this type to be run efficiently, it was not only necessary for the system to be operated well, but it required the businessman himself to have an encyclopaedic knowledge of his customers, the goods that he kept in stock, the orders that had been made by customers, fashion trends that would affect his business, etc. Many professions require a good memory, and this was certainly one of them.

Going around new roads, new avenues, new estates and knocking on doors to sell clothes was a tough and arduous task. While some people would agree to buy an item, a few would refuse. Any one day might therefore be mingled with success and happiness on the one hand, and failure and despondency on the other. By and large, success and happiness were more in evidence than failure and despondency, since the Irish people themselves were friendly. In addition, they knew that they were being offered a valuable service by the door-to-door salesmen. Over the years, Indian businessmen would build up trusting and close relationships with their customers. If the customer fell on hard times, payments would be deferred or even cancelled altogether. In a few cases, Indian businessmen even helped poor customers pay their bills. The customers themselves were equally trusting of the businessmen – on the allotted day that a businessman was due to come, a key would be left in the front door to let the businessman in. If the customer could not be at home, her account book and money would be left on a table in the living room. A standing joke amongst the local Irish in parts of Northern Ireland was that, if one of them was seen wearing a new piece of clothing such as a new hat, the others would ask – "Has the darkie been around, then?"

Customers who were particularly loyal and friendly would 'spread the word', and help to gain further customers for the Indian businessman. In one instance, a customer living near Dublin, who ran a little farm, suggested to the Indian businessman that he should invest in pigs. She indicated that if he bought the pigs and paid for the feed, she would keep them and look after them. Later, the pigs could then be sold for profit. The Indian duly bought some pigs and paid her to feed them. Unfortunately, a few of the pigs fell ill, and the price of pigs also went down. As a result, the businessman lost all his investment!

Sikh Traders

Those Indian men who closely adhered to the Sikh religion wore turbans as part of the religion. The turban was worn to cover the hair that was in fact never cut, and such Indians also wore beards. Many Sikhs did in fact cut their hair, shave off their beards, and stop wearing turbans just before they came to Ireland. They realised that if they were dealing with the public in their homes on a regular basis, many Irish folk might well be scared off by the sight of seeing someone wear such a head-dress. Trying to persuade a Sikh to get rid of his turban and to shave off his beard was no easy task. One of the Indian businessmen used a clever ploy to persuade one of his fellow businessmen, who was a devout Sikh, to do this. This Sikh had just arrived a few weeks earlier from India. The Indian businessman told the Sikh to come with him on his business calls in the countryside, so that he could see what it was like selling goods to the locals. When they got to a particular house, the

Indian businessman left the young Sikh sitting in the car, while he himself went in to the house to talk to the customer. He knew this customer particularly well. He told her to go to the car, to pretend to collect an item of clothing from inside the car, to briefly look at the Sikh gentleman sitting in the car, and to then run back screaming to the house, with her hands in the air. She dutifully did this. When the Indian businessman came back, he told his Sikh friend – "Look, you frightened this young lady to death. You'll really have to remove your hair if you want to get on with the locals and persuade them to buy your goods." His friend was persuaded by the event, and agreed to do this!

One group of Sikhs who kept their turbans were a group called the Bhartedas. Some of those that initially came to Ireland travelled around different towns, akin to latter-day 'gypsies'. They would read palms, tell fortunes, etc. In later years, however, most of them resorted to the clothing trade, and they were typically seen trading in market fairs that were held in towns or the countryside. A second subgroup of Sikhs who often kept their turbans were doctors and similar professionals. They would tend to encounter less surprise from their colleagues/patients than would door-to-door salesmen. In addition, their income was not dependent on how they appeared to others.

Moving To The High Street

During the early years (1930s–1960s), the vast majority of Indian businessmen in Northern Ireland carried out a door-to-door trade, and very few owned shops in the High Street. There were, however, a few early ventures along these lines. One of the first High Street shops was a shoe shop in Londonderry called Corner Boot Stores. It was opened in 1943 by the Chada brothers in Waterloo Street, Londonderry. Later, in the 1950s, the Sumra brothers and the Vij brothers opened several clothing/textile shops in Londonderry.

In addition to carrying out retail clothing business, a number of Indian businessman opened warehouses through which they sold wholesale goods to retailers. The first Indian-owned warehouse was opened in Belfast in 1964 by the Tohani brothers, who had originated from Allahabad in northern India. One of these brothers, Sat Pal Tohani, had initially come to Glasgow in 1958. He worked there as a bus conductor and bus driver. On a holiday to Ireland, he was encouraged by one of his friends to set up business there. He initially started a retail clothing business, before opening his warehouse in Belfast in 1964. This warehouse sold a wide range of goods, from clothes to household linen.

AN INDIAN SEEN THROUGH THE EYES OF A LOCAL

MRS MARTHA HILL, IN LATER YEARS. *One of the first members of the local community to become a customer of the Indian businessmen.*

My father and mother were from Ballycastle, a small seaside town in the north of Northern Ireland. My parents had emigrated to Scotland, as did many from Northern Ireland, since there was more chance of employment there. My father worked in Glasgow docks.

I was born in Scotland, the eldest of nine children, but I came back on holidays to Ballycastle, since my grandmother lived there. I worked as a machinist in Glasgow. In 1946, on one of those visits to Northern Ireland, when I was a young lady of 19 years old, I met my husband-to-be. Since he lived in Ballycastle, and I lived in Glasgow, over a period of three years we only saw each other for six weeks before we got married in 1949 in Glasgow.

We moved to Ballycastle in 1950. At that time, my husband was in the Royal Air Force, usually based in England. I was alone at home with my baby son, a couple of years old. Coming from a big family of nine children, one that was very close-knit, I felt this loneliness all the more. I would often take my son to the seaside, from where you could see the Scottish coastline (the Mull of Kintyre), and I would often sit there looking across, wondering what my mummy and daddy were doing at the time, and wishing that I could walk across the sea to Scotland!

One day, in 1952, an Indian gentleman knocked on the door, with a suitcase full of clothes. He had a van that was parked outside. He told me that he had recently arrived from India, and that he was planning to settle down in Ballycastle. He came into the house, and started talking to me about the goods he had for sale. My little son was standing beside me, and kept interrupting the Indian businessman by repeating words that he was saying, since he could not understand what the man was saying. I was about to smack him when the Indian gentleman pleaded with me not to, as he quite understood that it might appear bewildering for the little boy to see and hear an Indian.

The kindness and friendliness shown by the Indian businessman was all the important to me because of my situation. I was really a stranger in Ballycastle, since I had lived most of my life in Glasgow, and I knew very few of the neighbours. Since the Indian gentleman too was far away from his home country of India, he could sympathise with my feelings of being away from my own family in Scotland.

The Royal Air Force allowance given to my husband was very small, and I only had the barest of furniture – a table and a few chairs downstairs, and a cot and bed upstairs. The easy payment system that was offered by the Indian businessman was all the more welcome because of the little money that I had. He trusted me to pay back for the goods over time, and this helped to give me confidence.

The Indian businessman had a number of items in his suitcase, and the first thing I bought off him was a blanket. My daughter, who now has a family of her own, probably still has that blanket, over 40 years later! I was initially a bit reluctant to buy the blanket, and get into a credit arrangement, since I had been brought up in a strict household that discouraged mixing with strangers and having any sort of money dealings with them. However, this Indian businessman put me at ease and promised to help me out any time I was in need. It was important that we kept our sense of dignity in such situations, and he helped us feel that way. He even told me to call him any time in the evening, or on Sundays, if I suddenly needed new clothes in a hurry.

In later years, when my children were born, he did in fact help me out with clothes for the christening of the children. I had seven children in all. I might need sets of new clothes in a rush. It might be for Xmas, Easter, going back to school, a funeral/wedding, or a church service such as Holy Communion. He would provide the clothes, and I could pay him back in instalments whenever I could afford it. At that time, my husband had left the Royal Air Force and was working in the local forestry commission, earning just £6 a week, and so we could never afford new clothes in one single payment. My husband unfortunately spent a lot of money on drink, and that meant that there was even less money available for things such as clothes.

I usually paid the Indian businessman every Saturday when he would do his calls in this area. On one occasion, things were particularly tight and I did not have any money to pay him. I was quite embarrassed, and decided to go into the back garden to hang my washing around the time that he was due to come. I hoped that he might not see me, and therefore I could avoid payment for that week. My little son was with me at the time, playing around in the house. He would instinctively know that each Saturday this Indian would be coming, and my son would be out there to meet him. As was the case for many other customers, we generally left our front door unlocked or with the key in the door on the days that the Indian businessman was due to come. We would trust his honesty to come in – sometimes money would be left on a table, along with the repayment book, and the Indian businessman would simply take the money and go out again. When the Indian businessman came on this occasion, and could not find me at home, he called out my name. My son immediately told him that I was in the back garden and took him there by the hand! I explained that I could not pay on this occasion – he immediately told me not to worry, and that I could pay at some other time when I could afford it.

He would come every Saturday, and whenever he came he always inquired after my children, asking how they were getting on. He would end up knowing a lot about our family, and we would therefore tend to see him as a family friend rather than a businessman. When in later years, I developed problems with my eyes and had to go into hospital for an eye operation, he reassured me, since he himself had undergone a similar eye operation.

On one occasion, when my daughter was due to go to Canada to stay with a Canadian family and work as a nanny, he brought along a set of Irish linen for her to take along as a present to give to the family – he knew that we could not afford this ourselves. He made the same gift when one of my other daughters went to the United States of America.

On another occasion, my daughter had to take one of her children fairly suddenly to hospital. Because we were not well off, the children never slept in pyjamas, simply in their undergarments, but we would need a pair of pyjamas for the hospital stay. When my daughter went to collect the pyjamas, the Indian businessman also gave her, as a gift, a dressing gown and a pair of slippers so that her son could also have these to wear in hospital. The little boy felt so proud, since he had never worn a dressing gown or bedroom slippers before in his life! It was gestures such as these that endeared the Indian businessman to our hearts. *[This is the story told by Mrs Martha Hill]*

INDIAN CAFÉS, RESTAURANTS AND BARS

Indian settlers, by and large, did not venture into any other businesses other than the clothing business. However, they were by nature an enterprising people, and if a potentially lucrative opportunity arose they would try it. Thus, in the late 1930s, an Indian settled in Londonderry, who already had a retail clothing business, bought a bar in Londonderry. He kept it for a few years, hiring a barman to run the business, but he did not keep it after that period.

It was not till the 1950s that Indian cafes and restaurants started to appear. In Dublin, the first Indian restaurant was run by a Mohammed Butt, originally from East Africa, who opened one called the Golden Orient in the early 1950s. In the 1950s, Nand Lal Abroal – an Indian who came to Northern Ireland in 1936 – opened a grocery shop on the Shankill Road in Belfast. This shop remained open for 20 years. In 1957, a coffee shop was opened in the Shankill Road, Belfast by Mr R S Sharma. In 1964, there is a record of a Mr D D Sharma having a fish and chip shop in the Old Lodge Road, Belfast.

These were probably the first Indian cafés to be opened in Northern Ireland, though it is not clear if they served Indian food as such. The first Indian restaurant as such to open in Northern Ireland was the Ajanta restaurant, which was opened in Belfast in 1968. It was opened by Diljit Rana, whose story is described elsewhere in the book (page 202–204).

5: BOMBS AND BULLETS

EXPLOSIONS AND GUNFIRE

The vast majority of Indians settled in Northern Ireland have been unaffected by the troubles. They have never taken sides in the conflict between the two communities in Northern Ireland. In most cases, their work as businessmen or professionals has usually not been affected in a major way by the troubles. However, it is impossible for them to have escaped the effects of the troubles completely, and there have sadly been a number of incidents involving loss of life, loss of business and damage to property.

Casualties In Uniform

There have been several deaths of Indian or Pakistani personnel who were employed by the British Army. In one incident which occurred on September 5, 1981, three British soldiers were lured from a hotel in Lisburn to a flat in Belfast by female members of the IRA. Lying in wait for them in this flat were IRA gunmen, who killed the soldiers. One of the soldiers was a young 20 year old Sikh, by the name of Sohan Virdee, who had grown up in England.

A 45 year-old Pakistani, Noorbaz Khan, who was working as a civilian lorry driver for the British Army in Londonderry, was shot dead by the IRA on June 26, 1973 as he drove a lorry from Bligh's Lane British Army base in Creggan, Londonderry. It is reported that he sent back money to Pakistan to support poorer family member and relatives who lived there, and that over 20 people depended on this 'income' from Great Britain.

A further fatality occurred amongst those Indians who have over the centuries worked for the British Army as 'tea boys', i.e. provided the army with refreshments in field settings. One of them was killed by the IRA, allegedly because he was carrying out intelligence work on behalf of the British Army. His name was Mohammed Khalid, an 18 year old man, who was found shot in his car on April 22, 1974, near Crossmaglen, County Armagh.

A further, tragic incident that involved someone of Indian origin occurred in Germany in the 1980s. During that time, the IRA waged a campaign against British soldiers based in Germany, partly because they were such easy targets there. On October 26, 1989, a serving RAF officer, Mahesh Kumar Ismalia, 34 years old, was off-duty, filling his car at a petrol station in Wildenrath, Germany. His six month-old daughter, Niurati, was in the back seat of the car. The IRA sprayed the car with bullets, killing both father and daughter.

Businesses In Flames

Some businesses run by Indians, especially in Belfast and Londonderry, have been damaged or destroyed as part of the terrorist campaign. One of the first stores to be destroyed was Sumra House, a clothing store in Londonderry that was owned by the Sumra brothers – one of the first Indian settlers in Londonderry, who came there in the 1930s and 1940s. A bomb was left in the shop, with a warning for all to leave at once. The bomb exploded, causing complete destruction of the store. The store was rebuilt several years later.

The first Indian-owned wholesale clothing warehouse, a three-storey building located in Belfast and run by the Tohani family, was blown up by terrorists on April 5, 1977. The staff, including the wife of the owner of the warehouse, were made to lie on the floor by two gunmen, who planted three bombs, one of which was attached to a petrol can. They first rifled the till, and then placed one of the bombs near the telephone. The owner was just returning to the store as the staff were fleeing from the premises. It took four fire crews to tackle the blaze. The building was completely destroyed, but fortunately no-one was injured. The attack was described by two members of staff in the following report that appeared in the *Belfast Telegraph* newspaper of the same day –

> Someone rang the bell and I pushed the buzzer and told him to push the door. A man with a girl came in. I shut the door behind him and he told us to lie on the floor. He then opened the door again and let another man in. This man was carrying the bomb which was in a plastic bag that smelt of petrol. He planted the bomb while the other robbed the till, jumping over

DESTRUCTION OF A STORE IN LONDONDERRY.
This large clothing store was owned by the Sumra family, one of the first Indian settlers to come to Northern Ireland. It shows the store before and after it was bombed by the IRA.

> the counter to reach it. He told me to unlock the till, but I said it was open. There was a man standing outside all the time. The other two then shouted that we had five minutes left to get out, and they ran out.

Ironically, the same Indian family who owned this warehouse also owned a textile factory in Warrenpoint (a town on the border with the Irish Republic), and this factory had also been blown up by terrorists three months before.

A clothing shop owned by the Vij brothers in Butcher Street, Londonderry for many years was next to a bar that was bombed in the late 1970s. The structure of the shop was therefore affected, and the Vij brothers had to move to a shop in Abercorn Road. One Saturday afternoon, the IRA left a bomb in that shop. It is reported that the IRA had intended to plant the bomb in a shoe repair shop elsewhere, but that shop was closed, and they had to put the bomb somewhere. They therefore left it in the Vij brothers' clothing shop in Abercorn Road. Tara Chand Vij coolly and calmly took the bomb out and it exploded in the middle of the road without causing major injury or damage.

Hotels in Northern Ireland were particularly susceptible to attack by bombers, who regarded them as high profile economic targets which, if destroyed, would affect business confidence and the tourist industry. Mr Diljit Rana, whose story is described later (page 202–204), owned the Plaza Hotel in Belfast from the early 1990s onwards. His hotel was bombed six times directly or indirectly (by a bomb in the vicinity of the hotel), but his motto was that he never closed. His hotel also received hundreds of hoax bomb calls. On one occasion, on June 6, 1992, his hotel was damaged by a bomb that was placed in the hotel itself. As a result of that explosion, a fire hydrant burst, causing flood damage, in addition to that caused by the bomb. Later that day, the bombers struck again. They had left a bomb, and given a warning that it was in the hotel. Mr Rana and a policeman scoured the hotel, and they eventually found it in a container underneath a cushion. The bomb had failed to go off. It seems that the bombers had in fact come back to the building after the first explosion in order to plant the other bomb.

Close Encounters

Individual Indian businessmen have encountered 'risky' situations, where they fortunately escaped injury.

> I was going out once to deliver some goods near Omagh. It was the 1970s. When I reached the outside of the town, near the border, it was late at

> night and there was heavy snowfall. They were building a bridge in the area. There was only one-way traffic on the bridge, with traffic lights. When the light showed green, I moved on. When I was half-way, another car came from the other side. I stopped, got out of my car, and told the other driver – 'Look, since the light was green, you should have waited on the other side. This is my right of way!' He then took a gun out and said – 'In this part of the country, this has the right of way.' So I had to reverse all the way back, even though I had a trailer full of goods attached to the back of my car, and reversing with the trailer was quite awkward in the snow.

Once, an Indian businessman in Belfast encountered a customer who refused to pay for his goods. The businessman became angry with him, but the customer brought out a gun and threatened him. The businessman challenged the customer to try and shoot him. He then bravely took hold of his gun with his hand. The Indian businessman reported him to the police, and he had his gun confiscated. On another occasion, an Indian businessman in Londonderry went to collect an outstanding debt from a customer, and was attacked and beaten with a stick.

Intimidation and protection rackets have been an unfortunate feature of some parts of Northern Ireland during the troubles, and Indian businessmen have not been immune to such unpleasantness. Those businessmen who had premises close to loyalist/nationalist areas were particularly susceptible to blackmail. On one occasion, a café owner had been regularly visited by a terrorist group. They demanded monthly payments of £8 towards a 'prisoners fund', and this was given. However, after a while, they suddenly raised their payment demand ten fold to £80 per month. The Indian café owner protested that he could not afford this. A few weeks later, his café was burned down.

In Londonderry, a few occasions did arise whereby Indian businessmen were robbed when they went into an area that was known for its paramilitary activities. It should be mentioned at the outset that, in general, when Indians went into any areas for work they were treated well and were respected for the service that they provided. There was an unwritten code amongst organisations like the IRA that such businessmen were not to be attacked, since they performed a worthwhile service to the local community and were completely impartial to the situation in Northern Ireland. However, some of the younger elements who were members of other, less disciplined groups did not have any such inhibitions.

One day in the late 1970s, an Indian businessman, Tara Chand Vij, was robbed in the Bogside. He was attacked from behind, and he was hit over the head with a gun. He bled from the wound, but he otherwise suffered no major injury. To avoid being robbed in similar situations, Tara Chand Vij would keep money in his shoes. When he came home, he would then empty out his shoes. He had been advised by other Indians to stop going into dangerous areas, but he firmly believed that he had immunity from such attacks and he continued his normal business regardless of the dangers.

On one occasion in the 1970s, an Indian businessman was robbed of some money by paramilitaries. He then went to his customers in the local community where the robbery took place, and they were able to promptly ensure that the money was returned to him.

In another incident, a Mercedes car owned by a member of the Indian community in Londonderry was hijacked by paramilitaries. It was a new car, with 'personalised' number plates. The car was then abandoned by them and it had to be blown up by the army in case it contained a bomb.

On a further occasion, an Indian gentleman – who lived in a small town in Northern Ireland that was staunchly Protestant – found himself the victim of abuse, with bricks thrown at his house. He went along to an Indian friend and asked him if he could suggest a painter. "Why a painter?", asked his friend. The gentleman explained that he had decided to paint 'loyalist' slogans on the outside walls of his house, slogans such as a Union Jack, a crown, 'God Save The Queen', etc. and see if this prevented further attacks on his house. This did the trick! He no longer had any trouble from those who had previously taunted him.

A small number of Indian families left Northern Ireland as a direct result of their businesses being adversely affected by the troubles. Although it is difficult to be sure of precise figures, this number is probably around six. Many more families and individuals did of course move to England or Scotland for purely business, educational or family reasons. Most of those who moved to Great Britain retained their links with Northern Ireland. When the Hindu temple in Belfast was being established, many such families residing in England gave generously towards the appeal for funds.

Indian Doctors At The Front-Line

Many Indian doctors and other health care workers have been directly or indirectly involved in looking after casualties of the years of violence.

Mr Panesar's experiences as a surgeon are described elsewhere in the book (page 205–207). During 1974–75, the author himself carried out research on missile injuries to the brain while working at the Royal Victoria Hospital, Belfast. On a few occasions, Indian doctors got caught up in an incident and had to offer first aid. One Indian doctor was at home in a small sea-side town one Sunday morning, when a bomb went off without warning outside a chapel. This was in the early 1970s. It had been intended to go off while church-goers were coming out of the chapel, but it had gone off prematurely. A few people, however, were around at the time, and were injured. When he heard the bomb go off, the Indian doctor went to see how he could help, and travelled with some of the injured to the local hospital. Fortunately, there were no fatalities as a result of this incident.

On a second occasion, this time in 1993, the same Indian doctor was sitting in his parked car on the outskirts of Belfast. He was waiting in the car for his daughter to come out of a house. It was late in the evening. Suddenly, a car came towards him, veered onto the pavement in front of him and came to a halt. Two men jumped out of the car before it came to a halt. A neighbour came out and started screaming. When the Indian doctor went to the car, he found a man slumped over the steering wheel of the car, shot in the head. He was bleeding profusely. The doctor applied first aid, trying to stop the bleeding, till the ambulance came. The neighbours were surprisingly calm, even though there was a fear that there may be a bomb left in the car. The car, which was a taxi, had apparently been hijacked some time before. The taxi driver, a Catholic, had been forced to drive to a Protestant area, where the crime was committed. Fortunately, he survived the shooting, although he is likely to have been left severely disabled.

International Hopes For Peace

When the IRA declared a cease-fire on August 31, 1994, the Indian embassy in Eire, the Republic of Ireland, passed on the message of the Indian government to the Irish Prime Minister. Mr Lal Dingliana, the acting ambassador in Dublin, said that the message from the Indian parliament that was conveyed to the Irish Government was that Delhi "hoped for permanent renunciation of the violence."

Mother Teresa of Calcutta (who in 1928 spent a couple of months with the Sisters of Loreto in Dublin) visited the Corrymeela Centre, near Ballycastle, in the first week of July 1981. This centre was established a

MOTHER TERESA IN DUBLIN, 1993. *Mother Teresa with the President of Ireland, Mary Robinson.*

number of years earlier as a haven for reconciliation, to provide an environment where young people of varying traditions could meet in an atmosphere of peace and tranquillity. In June 1993, Mother Teresa visited Dublin, and on this occasion she was given 'freedom of the city'.

Another indirect link between India, Northern Ireland and the troubles has arisen from the Gandhi Foundation. This was formed in 1983, following the interest in the life and teachings of Gandhi by the film

'Gandhi'. The president of the Gandhi Foundation is Lord Richard Attenborough, and its chairman is Lord Ennals, former Labour cabinet minister. The foundation has offices in Kingsley Hall Community Centre in East London, where Gandhi stayed in 1931. Its aims are to spread the knowledge and ideas of Gandhi throughout Great Britain. It holds lectures and courses with this aim in mind, and it publishes a regular newsletter.

In 1988, the Northern Ireland Project was set up by the Gandhi Foundation following a summer school of the Foundation that was held in July 1988 in Oxfordshire. 'The Northern Ireland Project', led by Peter Cadogan helped to generate informed discussion amongst members of the Gandhi Foundation about the situation in Northern Ireland, and has tried to apply Gandhian principles to ideas about resolving differences between communities in Northern Ireland.

The last Viceroy of India and its first Governor-General after independence, Lord Louis Mountbatten, visited Ireland every year, staying in his holiday home on the west coast of Ireland. He would go fishing on his boat, along with family and friends. Many years earlier, as the last Viceroy, he had supervised the partition of India, an event that was associated with an estimated million dead or injured. On August 27, 1979, his small fishing boat was blown up in Mullaghmore Harbour in County Sligo, the Irish Republic. He was killed, along with members of his family and a young child who was a family friend. One of the members of the IRA gang was subsequently convicted for the crime. It is worth noting that, after his murder, official flags in New Delhi were lowered to half mast as a mark of sorrow and respect for Lord Mountbatten.

An interesting side-line to the troubles is the conversion of a former IRA man to the Hare Krishna faith. Martin Blake, 34 years old, who grew up in west Belfast, served time for IRA membership when he was 19 years old. Three years later, his brother was shot dead by loyalist gunmen. His grief over this event turned him totally away from violence and led him to convert to the Hare Krishna faith. He has adopted the name Uddhva Dasa, and lives with his wife Helen, who was born a middle-class Protestant in the Malone Road area of Belfast. The couple and their three children are members of a County Wicklow commune of Hare Krishna followers that includes six other families. They are strict observers of four main Hare Krishna tenets – only having sex for procreation; not drinking alcohol, tea or coffee; not gambling; and not eating meat. Martin wears a traditional dhoti, a white skirt-like garment and loose tunic that is worn by married Hare Krishna men (unmarried men wear an orange robe). His wife, Helen, wears a sari.

A MOTHER AND HER UNBORN BABY: INNOCENT VICTIMS

One of the first, and perhaps most tragic, incidents that involved an Indian settler occurred on October 5, 1974 in Greenhaw Road, Londonderry – a 'Republican' area of Londonderry. Asha Chopra, a 24 year old Indian housewife (*Plate 29, p. 193*), had come to Londonderry in the 1960s with her husband Pralad. Her husband was the nephew of one of the Vij brothers who came to Londonderry in the 1940s and 1950s. Her husband had come over to Northern Ireland in 1964. He initially stayed for a couple of months to look after his uncle's business while his uncle was in India, but he liked it so much in Northern Ireland that he stayed on. In 1964, he went to India to find a bride, and Asha was that bride.

Asha came from a village called Pugwara in northern India. She was four months pregnant with her third child. She was in her car, which had been stopped near some traffic lights due to a hoax bomb scare that had been set up by the IRA as a trap to lure policemen to an ambush. They had taken over a nearby house to set up the ambush. A shot rang out, presumably intended to kill a policeman, and it struck Asha Chopra in the head. She was rushed to hospital, but she died a few hours later. Asha in fact lived across the road, quite close to the shops, but she had decided to take the car to go shopping that Saturday afternoon. Her two young children were also in the car at the time. They witnessed their mother being murdered, but they themselves were unhurt. Her son still lives in Northern Ireland, but her daughter returned to India. Her husband also returned to India, and remarried some years later.

It is ironic that only a few days before Asha was murdered, an elderly Indian man who lived nearby, a Mr Nagra, also died an horrific death. This was the result of being run over by a train at Bellarena station in Londonderry. His funeral had taken place the day before Asha was killed. Asha had gone to the funeral on the Friday afternoon. It is reported that later that day she had spoken to her husband about her impending death. She said to her husband things like –

> "Make sure your second wife is good to my children."

> He replied –

> "Don't be silly. You are not going to die, and I'm never going to get married again."

A week after the murder, Asha's uncle went to meet some of the local IRA commanders in Londonderry. He asked them why they had carried out the killing. They apologised for the murder, and said that it was unintentional – they had simply killed the wrong person.

Although the IRA publicly blamed the army for the killing, the bullet was reported to have come from an armalite rifle, a type of rifle used by the IRA. In 1978, one of the members of the gang who carried out the killing was convicted of the crime. He was sentenced to 15 years in prison. This person was reported to have been 17 years old at the time of the killing. A further irony surrounding this tragedy is that the house in Londonderry where the young IRA man had lived once belonged to a close relative of Asha Chopra. Asha and her husband had in fact lived in this house for a short time after they came from India.

The day after her murder, a Roman Catholic priest in Londonderry, Father Anthony Mulvey, spoke out strongly against the murder. He noted –

> In Londonderry, we like to think that we welcome all strangers as God's children but yesterday one such stranger, a coloured woman, was killed in this parish. God forgive us all if anyone should think less of the tragedy because she was a stranger and a coloured person. She was a mother driving her children home and was diverted by a policeman who thought there was a bomb nearby and she was shot. This was murder. There was intent to kill and she was killed. It could well have been one of yourselves.

Asha Chopra's death appears to have been the only one associated with the troubles that involved Indian civilians who had come to settle in Northern Ireland.

AIR INDIA DISASTER

Public tragedies in Northern Ireland have been dominated by the 'Troubles' that took place between 1969 and 1994. However, it is worth noting a terrorist event involving Indians that occurred near the coast of Ireland. This was the bombing of an Air India jumbo jet en route from Canada to India via London. Police believe the bomb was in a suitcase that had been transferred to the Air India plane in Toronto from a Canadian Pacific Airlines flight that originated in Vancouver.

The flight was Air India 182 from Toronto to Bombay, with stops in Montreal and London. The pilot of the plane was Captain Hanse Singh Narendra. The plane, called *Emperor Kanishka*, contained 307 passengers and 22 crew. Most of the passengers were Canadians of Indian origin who were travelling to visit families in India. The plane crashed into the sea on the morning of Sunday June 23, 1985, as the result of being blown up by a bomb. It fell into the sea a few hundred miles off the south-west coast of Ireland, with debris being scattered over a ten mile area. All 329 people on board died as a result of that disaster. 131 of the bodies that could be retrieved were brought to south-west Ireland. One of the first vessels to arrive at the scene of the disaster was the Irish warship, *Le Aisling*. The ship's crew recovered 38 bodies from the sea. They braved shark-infested waters to retrieve bodies out of the sea. The crew had to lower an inflatable boat into the water, and the three crewmen in the boat had to enter the water to lift the bodies so that they could be hoisted up to the warship, *Le Aisling*.

A coroner's inquest was held in Cork on September 17, 1985. This was mainly for the identification of the bodies, their injuries and some comments on the possible cause of the plane coming down. The presiding coroner was Mr Cornelius Riordan. One of the doctors who gave evidence at the hearing was Professor Cuimin Doyle, head of the Histopathology Department at Cork Hospital. He reported that most of the bodies had suffered severe fractures and other injuries, as if the bodies had been thrown clear of the aircraft at a high altitude. This type of injury is known as a 'flail injury', where the body rotates wildly, just like a leaf flutters and spins as it floats to the ground from a height. However, Professor Doyle also observed that one of the lady passengers, who was five months pregnant with a baby boy, had probably been alive (though probably unconscious) when she hit the water, the cause of death in her case being drowning.

One of those on the ill-fated plane was Dr Y Nayudamma, a former Director-General of the Council of Scientific and Industrial Research in India. At the time of the plane crash, he was vice-chancellor of Jawaharlal Nehru University in New Delhi. His wife was a surgeon, based in Madras in southern India. When she heard that her husband had died on the crashed plane, she committed suicide, burning herself to death in a way that mirrored the ancient Indian tradition of *suttee*, whereby a widow throws herself on the funeral pyre of her husband in the event of his death.

The resident Hindu priest in Belfast went down to the Irish Republic to help with the last rites for victims who had been found in the sea. A memorial to those who lost their lives has been erected in a field near the town of Ahakista in South West Ireland, this being the closest town to the point where the bodies were brought back. The field was kindly donated by a local farmer, and each year there is a pilgrimage to this site by a number of relatives of those who died (*Plate 30, p. 194*). The pilgrimage is usually accompanied by a few Indians who are resident in Dublin, including a member of the Indian embassy staff.

In spite of the fact that thousands of fragments of the plane, including its flight recorder, have been brought up from the ocean floor, no one has yet been convicted for the Air-India bombing. However, the Canadian police have strong reason to suspect Sikh extremists, who may have carried out the bombing in revenge for Operation Bluestar, when the Indian government sent in troops to flush out militants from the Golden Temple in Amritsar in 1984. According to newspaper reports, a Vancouver-based Sikh activist, Talwinder Singh Parmar, founder of the separatist Babbar Khalsa sect, had been their prime suspect in the Air-India bombing. Parmar was killed in 1992 after a shoot-out with the Indian police. In the mid 1990s, Canadian police offered a reward (one million Canadian dollars) for further information about the bombing of the Air India jet, and they have also released sketches of two suspects they would like to interview.

A HORRIFIC CAR CRASH

It is an established fact, one that is perhaps well publicised within Northern Ireland but not so much outside Northern Ireland, that more people have been killed and injured on its roads than in the 'troubles'. A number of Indians and others from the Indian subcontinent have been injured or killed in road traffic accidents, but one particular accident in 1995 stood out for the grief it brought, grief that was shared by much of the local Irish community (*Plates 31–32, p. 195*).

Harminder Sandhu, a businessman from Londonderry, had promised to treat his two daughters (Prabjhot, aged five years and Amanjot, aged two years) and his brother's daughter (Harjot, aged five years) to a day out at Belfast zoo. On Friday August 18, 1995, he made good his promise. The children apparently did everything together, and had 'pet names' – Sweet Flower, Pussy Cat and Little Monkey. They had recently moved into a new house, where they lived with their parents and grandparents.

On their way home from the zoo, at four o'clock in the afternoon, Harminder Sandhu's maroon Volvo estate car was in a head-on collision with a lorry. Harminder and the three little girls all died instantly. Two teams of firemen, and a specialist unit equipped with cutting gear, worked at the scene of the accident for almost two hours to free the bodies from the wreckage. The driver of the 32-ton lorry was unhurt but in a state of shock. One witness remarked – "The car was in bits – it was all over the road".

The wife of Harminder Sandhu was in fact pregnant at the time of the loss of her husband, though she did not realise it at the time, believing that the pregnancy symptoms were brought on by the stress of the tragedy. She later gave birth to a baby girl, whom she called Harkiran (which means 'ray of light from God'). In a newspaper report, she indicated her mixed feelings at the birth –

> I felt so sad and lonely. I wanted to tell Harminder but he was not there....It's very much a new beginning for us all. I lost my husband, daughters and niece but Harminder's parents lost their son and all their grandchildren. I wanted something which reflected Harminder's name....I hope she grows up to look just like her father.

(Plate 29) ASHA CHOPRA. *She was shot dead by the IRA in an ambush in Londonderry that was meant to kill a policeman.*

(Plate 30) AIR–INDIA CRASH OFF THE COAST OF SOUTH-WEST IRELAND, 1985. *A memorial that was built in a field near the south-west coast of Ireland. It was near this spot that many of the bodies were brought from the sea. The part of the field was donated for the memorial by a local Irish farmer.*

(Plate 31) CAR ACCIDENT IN NORTHERN IRELAND THAT KILLED FOUR MEMBERS OF AN INDIAN FAMILY, 1995.
Wreckage from the Volvo car in which the family was travelling.

(Plate 32) CAR ACCIDENT IN NORTHERN IRELAND THAT KILLED FOUR MEMBERS OF AN INDIAN FAMILY, 1995.
The three children who died in the accident – Harjot and her cousins Prabjhot and Amanjot at a family birthday celebration. In the background is Harminder Sandhu, father of two of the children.

(Plate 33) HINDU WEDDING IN NORTHERN IRELAND.
The wedding took place in Coleraine, Northern Ireland, in April 1996. Sonia Ghaie, whose father came to Northern Ireland in the early 1960's, married Rajesh Thapar in a traditional Hindu ceremony. The top-right photograph shows Rajesh sitting on a horse as he begins his journey to the bride's house, where the wedding ceremony will take place. The bottom two photographs show part of the Hindu ceremony, where the bride and groom are carrying out instructions from the priest.

(Plate 34) FUNDS FOR EARTHQUAKE VICTIMS, 1994. *Mr L M Singhvi, Indian High Commissioner to Britain (in garlands) receives a cheque for over £10,000 from Mr D Rana (to his right). This was part of the money raised in Northern Ireland to help relief efforts for the Indian earthquake that occurred in September 1993 and left around 10,000 dead. The Indian Community Centre, Belfast, raised a further £7000.*

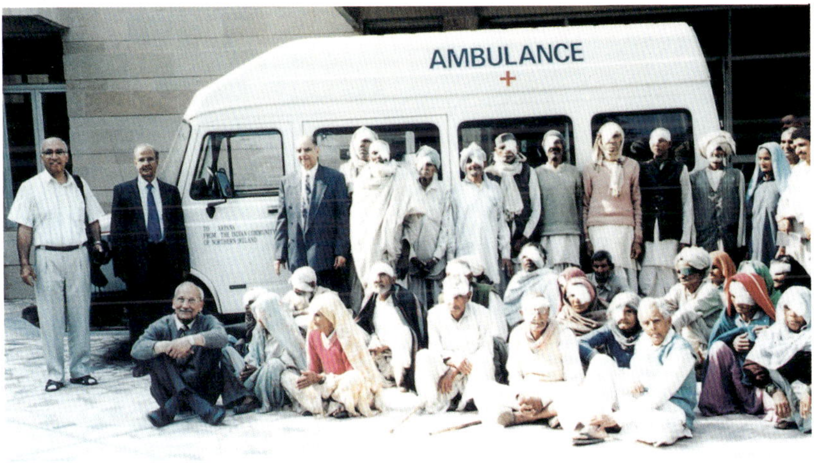

(Plate 35) DONATION OF AN AMBULANCE BY INDIANS IN NORTHERN IRELAND. *This ambulance was bought and equipped in Northern Ireland, with the help of the local Indian community, and then shipped to the Arpana hospital complex in northern India. On the far left is one of the Irish Indians who helped raise funds to buy the ambulance, Dr Davinder Kapur. To his left is Dr J K Mehta, Chairman of the Arpana Charities Trust. The next person on his left is Mr A S Anand, from Northern Ireland, who has also helped to raise funds for health care projects in India.*

6: ROMANCE AND SUCCESS

ROMANTIC ENCOUNTERS

> I was in Rome giving a talk at a conference in the late 1970s. The Indian ambassador had invited me and a few other Indians at the conference to go to an Indian concert that was being given by Ravi Shankar, the famous Indian sitar player. At the concert, someone who knew that I was from Dublin mentioned to me that there was an Irish lady at the concert who was very keen on Indian music. I was introduced to her. She was studying business management in Galway and was in Italy on a holiday. We had a whirlwind romance that took us to Naples and Capri. We got married in Ireland shortly afterwards, and we now have three children. *[Dr Sumanth Jeawon, an Indian doctor in Dublin]*

Although it is still more common for the children of Indian settlers to marry Indians, the number of 'mixed marriages' – i.e. marriages with members of the local Irish community – has steadily increased over the years. While some of the marriages between children of Indian parents are still 'arranged', in that the introduction of the bride to the groom has been arranged by the respective parents or intermediaries, the tendency is for such marriages to be less frequent. In addition, it is also less common for the bride or groom to come from India – rather he/she may often have lived in Ireland or Great Britain for a considerable time.

Indian marriages are usually performed according to Hindu custom, since the majority of Indians are Hindus (*Plate 33, p. 196*). This involves a ceremony that is usually between 1–3 hours long, with a Hindu priest performing rituals around a fire that has been prepared on a specially constructed 'stage'.

Marriages in the Moslem community also have a priest or 'malvi'. Unlike the Hindu ceremony, there is no fire, and the ceremony itself is much shorter, usually lasting around 20 minutes. The bride and groom each say three times that they agree to take each other in matrimony.

In the case of 'mixed' marriages, there is usually some compromise in the traditions that are followed, with both a Christian and a Hindu/Moslem ceremony being performed at some time. It would appear that 'mixed' marriages have been more common in the Irish Republic than Northern Ireland, where Hindu traditions have tended to be more in-grained, perhaps due to the closer association with the rest of Great Britain, where there are stronger concentrations of Indian communities with strong Indian traditions.

In the 1940s, 1950s and the 1960s, romantic relationships between Indian gentlemen and local Irish ladies were frowned upon by the 'elders' amongst the Indian community. On one occasion, one of the Indian men had formed a relationship with a local Irish girl. His friends decided that they would get together and decide amongst each other on the future of this affair. The nine of them met one Sunday in a small seaside town in Northern Ireland, with the particular person in attendance. They discussed what was to be done about this relationship. They decided to have a vote, by secret ballot. Each one wrote down on a piece of paper whether they thought the affair should be allowed to continue and if the person should be allowed to marry the Irish girl. They voted eight to one that the affair must stop, and that the Indian gentleman in question should go to India and find an Indian bride. He accepted this judgement, and subsequently went to India and got married. The irony of this story is that this marriage in fact broke down after several years, and he returned to the Irish girl in question!

In a few cases, there was also pressure from the local Irish community when an Indian gentleman married an Irish lady. On one occasion, the father of the bride accompanied his daughter to the church for the wedding, but he refused to walk down the aisle with her, as is the custom. On another occasion, the bride's father was so angry with the mixed marriage that was to take place that he once threw stones at the van of the Indian businessman who was to marry his daughter.

Although a number of mixed marriages took place before 1960, most of these were held relatively discreetly in registry offices rather than in chapels or churches. One of the first mixed marriages to be held in a church was in March, 1963. This was between Harprashad Vij and his wife, who had been born and brought up as a Protestant in Londonderry. On the occasion of the church wedding, Harprashad Vij was simply asked by the minister if he believed in God. He replied 'yes', and the ceremony proceeded. There was no pressure on him to become a Christian.

'MIXED MARRIAGE', 1963. *A wedding between an Indian settler to Northern Ireland, Harprashad Vij, and a local Irish girl.*

One young lady in Northern Ireland, whose mother was a devout Roman Catholic and whose father was an Indian settler and born a Hindu, was born in Londonderry. She married a Sikh man in India, with the usual Hindu ceremony taking place. Her mother accompanied her to India on a second occasion so that a Roman Catholic ceremony also took place there.

Another story is that of Patricia and George Yathindran. This was described in the *Belfast Telegraph*, January 3, 1969 –

> They met when she was 22 and he was 24. They literally bumped into each other in a Belfast street, started talking and that, according to Patricia, was that. They started going out together, and eventually decided to get married. The decision came more as a shock to their families than a pleasant surprise. Says Patricia, "George's family were still in India, and so far away that really they couldn't do much about it. He explained to them that it was his life and he had a right to do as he pleased. My own family also objected strongly and in the end we took the only way out. We ran away." Happily, Patricia's family did eventually accept the situation after a few months and they were reunited.
>
> The couple now live in the Stranmillis area of Belfast with their four children, three boys and one girl whose ages range from 10 to 16.
>
> Racial prejudice, Patricia points out, is something they just don't come up

against. George, who works installing burglar alarm systems, is readily accepted in the community.

"In fact I would say that he has more friends around here than I have. We lived in Birmingham for a while, but neither of us liked it. It's completely different over there. People just weren't friendly."

Since they were married, neither George nor his wife have gone to visit his homeland.

"We did discuss it once but in the end decided against it. George doesn't consider himself an Indian any more, he's a Belfastman now."

"George's family come from Trivandrum in South India and as there are only about four other people from that part of India living in Northern Ireland we aren't really very close to the Indian community over here."

"The majority of Indian families living in the province came from North India. Probably because of that we don't really mix much with the Indian community. As well as that they speak a different language from the South Indians and George even has difficulty these days writing a letter to his family in his own language."

'FROM POSTMAN TO PLAZA'

My name is Diljit Rana. I was born in Punjab in 1938. I went to university in Punjab, and I worked there as a civil servant. Before the Immigration Act was passed in 1962, every Commonwealth citizen had a right of entry to Great Britain. After that act was introduced, a voucher scheme operated. You simply applied for an employment voucher, and when this was obtained, you were then eligible for entry to Britain. I did not apply for one, but as a practical joke my friend put my name down for one of the vouchers. He was in the travel business, and he filled in five applications in the names of five of his friends, without any of them knowing anything about it. My name was one of the names that he put down in his voucher application. Thus, I got a voucher without initially knowing anything about it.

In the village where I was living, a brother of one of my friends happened to be visiting around this time (December, 1962). He was living in England, in Coventry, and he suggested that I take up the voucher and go to England. Out of curiosity, therefore, I decided to go to England.

I first came to Britain in 1963. I had hoped that, in view of my university training, I would be able to get a similar white-collar job when I arrived in Britain. But that was not to be, and it was quite a rude awakening for me. I worked initially as a storeman in Leamington Spa in a foundry that made gas cookers. I then worked as a postman. In the mid 1960s, I came on a holiday to the Irish Republic and Northern Ireland. When in the north, I went to visit some friends in Northern Ireland, people from my village whom I knew about or who went to the same school as me, and who had gone from India to settle in Northern Ireland. I was rather disillusioned with my job prospects as an employee in England, and I was looking for business opportunities in order to become self-employed.

DILJIT RANA. *This photograph was taken in the early 1990s during his term as President of the Belfast Chamber of Trade and Commerce.*

Northern Ireland seemed an easier place to set up business if, like me, you had only a limited amount of capital, since there was less competition than on the mainland. I already knew a few people in Northern Ireland. My wife and I therefore moved to Belfast in 1966. I started off in the catering industry. I first of all opened a café, called Sam's Snack Bar, in Victoria Square, Belfast. After six months, I changed the name of the café to Quality Curry House. I had this café for three years, from 1966 to 1969. Although many restaurants in the late 1960s were closing down due to the beginning of troubles, I had three Indian restaurants in 1969 and 1970, the other two being called the Ajanta and the Ellora. In 1971, however, when civil disturbances were at their worst, two of my restaurants were destroyed within four weeks of each other.

I was rather naive about the technicalities of compensation at that time. I had bought one of the restaurants for £5000. Within four weeks, it had been damaged due to a bomb in the block of buildings, and the Belfast City Corporation – who were dealing with compensation payments in those days – offered me £300 compensation for the restaurant! It took two years for me to get full compensation through the courts.

I was out of business in 1971, not knowing what to do. It was a difficult time. I went to the United States of America in the summer of 1971, and I spent a few weeks there looking around for possible business opportunities. I also had a look at prospects in Dublin and Cork. But we had a young family, and it would have been very difficult to just get up and go, especially when what little money we had was invested in Northern Ireland and since we were waiting for the outcome of nine bomb damage claims. I still thought that Belfast was a nice place, so in the 1970s, when other people didn't have much confidence, I still kept investing here and there – refurbishing and buying old properties. We just struggled on. From 1975 to 1981 I had retail and ladies fashion wholesale businesses, at the same time keeping my business in minor properties around Belfast. I kept up a positive attitude and a firm belief that things will change.

In 1985, I bought a site in Belfast when the general feeling in the city was one of uncertainty. Later, I built the Plaza Hotel on that site, and this hotel opened in 1990. I am currently proprietor of that hotel and also of the Renshaws Hotel in Belfast. In 1992–1993, I was President of the Belfast Chamber of Trade and Commerce. I am a Director of Belfast Community Radio, Justice of the Peace and a member of the board of governors of Lagan College. I was part of the British industry delegation that visited India in 1994, using Concorde as a means of getting around. One of the main TV channels in India made a short film about business links between Britain and India. The film included the story of my own business activities in Northern Ireland. In June 1996, I was awarded the MBE in the Queen's Birthday Honours list. This was for services to industry and the community.

Similar stories can be found in the Irish Republic. Mr Mahendra Lal ('Michael') Sharma came from the Punjab to Northern Ireland in 1955, having gained a degree in Maths and Physics when in India. He first came to Buncrana in 1955. In 1967, he built his first factory in Castlefin, in County Donegal. This factory made fashion clothes. By 1995, he had three modern clothing factories, all of these being near the border in the Irish Republic. He named his company, Nena Models, after one of his daughters. In total, he employs around 600 people in these factories. His factories supply clothes to many of the 'household name' retailers in Britain.

After a spell in the retail clothing business, many Indian businessmen expanded into the manufacture of clothing or into its wholesale distribution. Two of the first factories to be built by an Indian businessman were a knitwear factory that was set up by Jamal Dean in the 1940s in Belfast, and a shirt factory that was built by Nazam-Ul-Dean. Subsequently, other factories were set up in Londonderry, Belfast and other towns. One factory, Knitcraft Ltd, was set up in Letterkenny (the Irish Republic) in the 1970s, and was partly run by an Indian businessman from Londonderry (Northern Ireland). Thus, the Indian business community has helped to bring employment to many parts of Northern Ireland, strengthening their contribution to the local economy.

In the case of wholesale clothing distributors, one of the most successful of these has been the Ghaie family, based in Coleraine in the county of Londonderry in Northern Ireland. Mr Ratan Ghaie came originally from Phagwara in the Punjab. He initially came in 1962 to study engineering in London, but circumstances brought him to the town of Moy in County Tyrone, Northern Ireland, where he was involved in retail clothing. He eventually opened his wholesale clothing operation in 1976 in Coleraine, and this has flourished since that time.

INDIANS AS HEALERS

Kanwar Panesar grew up and went to school in Kenya, and his parents originally emigrated there from India. There was no medical school in Kenya at that time (the late 1950s), and so his parents sent him to Amritsar in northern India to study medicine. After graduating as a doctor, he came to England. He first of all worked in several hospitals in London. He also sat a number of post-graduate exams and obtained his qualification as a surgeon. In 1975, he came to Northern Ireland, since a hospital surgical job had come up there. He worked for a couple of years as a senior registrar in Belfast and Craigavon, and in 1977 he was appointed as consultant surgeon at the Altnagelvin Hospital, Londonderry. He was probably the first Sikh consultant to be appointed to a hospital post in Northern Ireland.

He came to Londonderry at the height of the troubles. Many of his friends in England were surprised and worried that he had chosen to take up a post in Northern Ireland. However, he soon realised that he had made the right decision, as he found the people of Londonderry to be very friendly and supportive, both at work and in the city itself. In addition, the schools were of a very high standard. When his children went to prep school, they were the first children in the history of the school to wear turbans. He was the chairman of the Parent-Teachers Association at the time. He went along to a gathering of the children and told them about turbans and their significance in the Sikh religion. Both of his sons attended Foyle Grammar School, Londonderry and were subsequently able to progress well in their academic studies and career. The elder son is a practising barrister in London, and the younger one is at university in London.

He was one of the consultant surgeons in post at Altnagelvin Hospital during some of the most horrific incidents during the troubles. These included the Claudy bombing, the bombing at the Drop-in-Well pub at Ballykelly, and the shooting at the bar in Greysteel – in all of these, there was considerable injury and loss of life.

Despite the horrific nature of the disasters, Mr Panesar and his colleagues managed to cope effectively, using recognized techniques of disaster and wound management that had been evolved over the years. When a disaster occurred, hospital staff always rushed to help, often arriving in hospital before the casualties, since they would have heard the news on the TV or radio. When a large number of casualties came in, they had to be classified into one of three groups – the walking wounded, those who could be saved and required urgent treatment, and those not requiring urgent treatment. Mr Panesar and his colleagues would usually have two surgical teams in the operating theatre, and one surgical team would be looking after the walking wounded. They would also have staff who were assigned to dealing with queries from the security forces and from the press. Most injuries were dealt with at Altnagelvin, except a few cases of severe head injury, who would be flown by helicopter to Belfast, or patients with severe burns – these patients would, after a while, be sent to a specialist burns unit in a hospital outside Belfast.

He has always had pleasant relations with the whole community. On one occasion, during the hunger strikes of the 1980s, there was a large demonstration near a Catholic area of Londonderry. He had to make a home visit to a patient in the area. At one point, he was stopped by the crowd from going into the area where the patient lived. One of the organizers recognized him. He came over to the car, and called out to the crowd – 'It's Mr Panesar, let him through', and he was allowed immediate passage through the parade and also on returning.

Mr Panesar has had a very rewarding career as a surgeon in Londonderry. One of his specialities is stomach cancer, and he has obtained success rates for long-term survival after surgery that are comparable to the best in the world. He set up one of the first units to develop and practise the new technique of 'key-hole surgery'. In 1994 he was awarded the distinction of a fellowship ('Ad-Endum') from the Royal College of Surgeons of Dublin.

Mr Panesar is president of the Northern Ireland Sikh Association, and he has been responsible for the establishment of the first Sikh temple ('gurdwara') in Londonderry.

Dr A Siddiqui, consultant psychiatrist based at Gransha psychiatric hospital, Londonderry was born in India and arrived in Londonderry in 1974. He is a former president and trustee of the Islamic Centre in Belfast, and has served as president of the Northern Ireland Division of the Overseas Doctors Association, as honorary secretary of the North West and Londonderry Division of the British Medical Association, and has been a member of the BMA's Northern Ireland Council. In February 1996, he noted that there were, at any one time, between 50–75 practising Moslems in Londonderry, with around 20 living permanently in the city. He found that it had been difficult to get 'halal' meat, but that local butchers had come to the rescue and such meat had been imported from New Zealand. He made a plea for Londonderry City Council to consider having cemetery provision for the Moslem community and help in establishing a community centre for those of the Moslem faith. He also encouraged the local education and library board to make appropriate reading materials available in local libraries.

Many Indians who grew up in Ireland went into health-related professions, ranging from medicine to nursing, physiotherapy and clinical psychology. Many more Indians came to Ireland either to study medicine – as in the case of many students who came to the Royal College of Surgeons in Dublin – or, more commonly, to gain post-graduate experience and qualifications before returning to India or moving abroad, often to North America. Many of those who returned to India have now become professors in their own medical speciality. At the time of writing this book (1996), in Northern Ireland there are around 20 consultants of Indian origin and around 40 General Practitioners of Indian origin. There are of course many junior staff from the Indian subcontinent who spend a temporary period in hospitals in Northern Ireland as part of a short-term contract, or who work in the medical school at Queen's University, Belfast, as part of a short-term research fellowship.

Two of the first Indians to graduate in medicine from an Irish medical school were Dr Sumanth Jeawon, whose story is related in Chapter 2, and Tilak Rai Vij who came to Northern Ireland in the 1940s, and enrolled in the Royal College of Surgeons in the early 1950s. Their stories are told on pages 122–127. One of the first Indian dentists in Northern Ireland was Mr Jovinder Singh Jassal. He qualified from Bombay University, and practised in Belfast from 1960, working in the school dental service for 32 years.

INDIANS AS UNIVERSITY SCHOLARS

In common with their counterparts in Great Britain, Indian school children in Ireland have tended to excel in scholastic work. This was partly due to the encouragement they received from their parents, whose own cultural heritage in India often emphasised scholastic success, and partly because they might have less inclination to engage in social activities with their Irish neighbours, due to differing interests and cultural values. Academic success extended beyond school or university, and a number have gone on to study in Oxford and Cambridge. Those who excelled tended to do so in science subjects such as computer programming, mathematics, physics, chemistry, etc. rather than arts/language based subjects. This may have been because the natural disadvantage in language that they suffered may have tended to discourage them from arts-based subjects, and also because there seemed to be greater immediate prospects of jobs from science-based subjects.

One of the first Indians to hold a university chair in Ireland, north or south, was Professor Gyan Sham Singh, Professor of Italian at Queen's University, Belfast. He was born in Jaipur, in the western state of Rajastan, and he travelled to Italy in 1957. In 1965, he joined the staff of Queen's University, Belfast as university lecturer, and in 1970 he was appointed as Professor of Italian. He remained in that post till his retirement in 1992.

Other senior university staff in Northern Ireland, who are of Indian/Pakistani origin, include Dr Narain of the Law Department of Queen's University, Belfast, Dr Vani Varooha of the Economics Department of the University of Ulster and Dr K Hussain of the Engineering Department of the University of Ulster. The current (1997) Professor of Anaesthesia at Queens University, Belfast is Professor R K Mirakhur, who is originally from Srinagar, Kashmir, in northern India. He was appointed as consultant anaesthetist at the Royal Victoria Hospital, Belfast in 1980, and he became professor in 1996.

INDIANS IN OTHER PROFESSIONS

Entry into the world of western media and arts has been less prominent amongst Indians, partly because their own cultural background would have contrasted so strongly with western ideas and there would consequently not have been a lot of encouragement from relatives or friends in the Indian community. However, a few Indians have recently ventured into the world of media and arts, and are beginning to make a success of it.

One Indian girl who was born in Northern Ireland, Sabina Dhand, moved with her parents to Manchester when she was nine years old, and later went into a career as an Asian pop singer. She has made a number of radio and TV appearances, and has been signed on by Fruitcake Music, a Manchester-based music company that is managed by Bushra Ahmed, who is also marketing director of Joe Bloggs, the famous clothing company. Sabina has been successful in UK Asian Pop awards, though her own music style is relatively unique and not in the tradi-tional Asian mould. She has therefore had mixed experiences in her career, as she once recounted –

> I think the bhangra scene is great, but what I do isn't Asian at all, and so some people find it too modern for their tastes. I remember one London restaurant I went to. It was a really upmarket Indian place, and I was supposed to perform in front of a traditional, well-to-do Asian audience. When I arrived in my western gear, the owners looked at me with such distaste. They were very rude, and I almost didn't go on. But when I did, the initial hostility of the audience disappeared and they were all clapping for more. It was only then that the owner was all smiles, telling me how good I was, and then he couldn't do enough for us.

In addition to success and achievements in their respective professions, Indians in Ireland have also made significant contributions to charitable work both in Ireland and, more particularly, for their home country of India. In the case of Ireland, one of the first Indian settlers – Mr Manohar Lal Chada – has been an active member of his local Lions Club, and in 1993 he was awarded the Melvin Jones Fellowship Award, one of the highest honours bestowed by the Lions Club organisation, for 25 years service to the Lions Club.

DR MOOSAJEE BHAMJEE. *Dr Bhamjee, of Indian origin but brought up in South Africa, qualified as a doctor in Dublin and went on to become Ireland's first non-white member of parliament.*

Politics

Relatively few Indians who settled in Ireland, North or South, chose to go into politics, but there were notable exceptions to this in later years. One of the most well-known figures in politics who originated from India has been the Member of Parliament for Clare, a county in south-west Ireland, representing the Labour party. His name is Dr Moosajee Bhamjee, and he is a psychiatrist by profession. He was Ireland's first non-white Member of Parliament. It is reported that during his election campaign to become a Member of Parliament, one of his slogans was –

You've tried the cowboys, now try the Indians!

Dr Bhamjee was a Moslem Indian who had grown up in South Africa. In South Africa, his family was not very well off. He came to Dublin on a scholarship to study medicine. He later trained to be a psychiatrist, and was appointed to a consultant post in Ennis, County Clare. He married a local Irish lady. He became well known not only for his work, but also for his medical talk show on local radio, where he would cover everything from teenage worries to depression in dairy farmers at the loss of their cows! His views were liberal ones, especially in areas such as divorce, contraception and abortion.

Dr Bhamjee was nominated to stand for the Labour Party in a seat that was once held by Eamon De Valera, the legendary Prime Minister of Ireland. De Valera's statue still stands in the town of Ennis. Dr Bhamjee in fact agreed to stand as candidate by chance – no one else seemed to want to go forward! He was popular with the local people not only because of his radio talk show, but also because he was a keen soccer fan and helped promote the game locally, especially amongst school children. He set up a junior soccer league, and soon it had five teams. He was very friendly and down to earth. His success at the polls was due to his personality, together with the fact that many children encouraged their parents to vote for him because of his links with soccer. When his winning vote was announced, he remarked –

> It's a day when I, a psychiatrist, am nervous!

Dr Bhamjee's first-ever trip 'home' to India came after he had risen to public notice in Ireland, when the Indian Embassy invited him to visit India. He wrote about his reactions to this visit to India in the 'Irishman's Diary' column in the *Irish Times*, 3 May, 1994. This resulted in a response from Mr Joe Fernandez in the *Irish Times*, 9 May, 1994.

A law lecturer at Queen's University, Belfast, Dr Narain, stood as an independent candidate for Member of Parliament in one of the general elections held in Northern Ireland in the 1970s, but he was unsuccessful in that attempt to become an MP.

Professor Kader Asmal was chairman of the Irish Anti-Apartheid Movement while he lived in Ireland. When Nelson Mandela came to power in South Africa in the early 1990s, Professor Asmal was appointed Minister of Water Affairs and set out to achieve clean water for all South Africans as part of the Reconstruction and Development Programme.

MODERN TIES WITH MOTHER INDIA

Ties with India and Pakistan are maintained by many of those settled in Ireland, especially the older members of the community. The nature of the ties have, however, changed somewhat. There are of course regular trips to meet relatives. By the nature of things, these are fewer than before, since many first generation relatives have passed away.

One of the major sources of bonding is that related to charitable activities. At the level of individual families, this has of course continued ever since the first Indian set foot on Irish soil. For many, one of the main reasons for travelling to Britain was to earn money, most of which would be sent back to India to try and improve the lot of the settler's relatives back in India. More general charitable activities have also been carried out by settlers from India. These are probably too many to mention in detail.

At times of natural disaster in India, the Indian community has usually given generously to the relief efforts, and in this they have also had the

MONEY FOR FAMINE RELIEF, 1965. *Mr J N Mehta, Indian High Commissioner to Britain (on right) receives £1001 from Mr A S Anand, President of the Northern Ireland Indian Social Association.*

support of the local Irish community. For example, in 1965 £1001 was raised for famine relief by the Indian community in Northern Ireland. At the time of the Indian earthquake in September 1993, over seventeen thousand pounds was raised by the local Indian community in Northern Ireland (*Plate 34, p. 197*).

Over many years, Dwarka Nath Kapur, from Ballycastle in north Antrim, raised money for an organization (SAKET), based in Chandigarh in northern India, that provided treatment and rehabilitation for the physically handicapped. In 1994, Dr Davinder Kapur, a General Practitioner in the town of Antrim, Northern Ireland raised funds that enabled an ambulance and surgical instruments to be sent to a charitable organization called Arpana, that is based around a hospital complex 100 miles north of New Delhi (*Plate 35, p. 197*).

Mr Harry Bedi, who came to Northern Ireland in 1951 and who married a local Irish girl, 'adopted' three children in 1994. They had become orphaned as a result of a terrorist killing in Punjab, and he has sent regular amounts of money that enable their education and upkeep in India.

In 1966, the father of one of the several Vij brothers who had settled in Londonderry decided to build a girls' High School in Talwan, where none existed. He put in a significant amount of his own money, and he also enlisted the help of his sons. His sons raised a lot of money in Northern Ireland, and they sent it to India to help build the school. After a few years, the school was eventually built. Sadly, the elderly gentleman who had started the project was murdered before he could see the fruits of his hard work.

Commercial And Industrial Links

Commercial and industrial links have been forged with India, and these date from the linen and jute factories that flourished in Belfast in the 19th and first part of the 20th centuries. In more recent times, firms such as Harland and Wolff, Shorts, etc. have had contacts with India as part of their normal commercial business. For example, an aircraft carrier that was being bought by India from Great Britain in the 1960s was commissioned by Harland and Wolff. An Indian crew came over to Belfast to be trained in the use of the ship and to formally take it over. The ship, called the *Vikrant*, was docked in Belfast bay for several weeks, and was open to the public to visit. A number of Indian crew jumped ship during their stay in Belfast, and a further number came back sometime later to settle in Belfast. A number of them married ladies from the local Irish community.

There have been links between the two jute industries in Northern Ireland and India. Mackie International, a jute machine company based in Belfast, established in 1955 a subsidiary company in India – the *Lagan Jute Machinery Company*. It employed 400 people. The managing director of that company was Robyn Hall, who came from Belfast. He spent part of his time based in Calcutta, covering other far east operations, and part of his time at Mackie headquarters in Belfast. The name ‘Lagan’ was not, as it may at first seem, derived from the river Lagan that flows through Belfast. Robyn Hall and a colleague happened to see the word ‘lagan’ on a bill-board poster in Calcutta that was advertising a film. They inquired as to what the word meant, and were told that it meant the tying of the bride and groom to each other during a Hindu wedding ceremony. They therefore decided to choose the word ‘lagan’ for their company in Calcutta. The factory flourished throughout the 1950s and 1960s. It was nationalised by the Indian government in 1973. Mackie International has recently bought it back, at minimal cost.

Robyn Hall played a key part in the industrial development of India, being the only non-Indian on one of the Industrial Councils of the Indian government. He therefore had dealings with a number of Indian leaders. These included the Trade Secretary at the time (late 1950s, early 1960s), Mr Lal Bahadur Shastri (who was later to become Prime Minister of India) and also Mr Jawaharlal Nehru, the first Prime Minister of India.

The Belfast firm of Mackies trained many engineers from the Indian subcontinent, and those who were trained took pride in their training. On one occasion, Robyn Hall was greeted in India by a former Mackie trainee, who showed him his card – it said, after the name of the individual, *B.Sc. (trained at Mackies)*!

At the present time, 40% of the world's jute production is said to take place in West Bengal in India. Jute has recently come more into favour, due to the fact that it is bio-degradable, thus posing less in the way of environmental pollution. It is used for making bags to store crops, for making the backing to carpets and in garment manufacture.

In more recent times, the first trade mission to India that was specifically from Northern Ireland made an 11-day visit in January–February 1996. There were nine members of the trade mission, and it was led by Mr John Wright, vice-president of the Northern Ireland Chamber of Commerce at the time. The trade mission included representatives from print & packaging, plastics, building construction, construction equipment, concrete products, textiles, heavy engineering and automotive industries. The trade mission visited New Delhi, Bombay and Calcutta, and their aim was to explore sales opportunities and also joint manufacturing possibilities.

In the case of the Irish Republic, in November 1995 the Minister for Trade and Industry, Mr Enda Kenny, led a 22-member trade delegation to India. The delegation included businessmen with interests in aerospace, electronics, energy, education, telecommunications and financial services. It is reported that for the years 1994–5 India exported to Ireland trade worth almost $US35 million, while it imported from Ireland trade worth almost $US20 million.

A different sort of delegation, but none the less important, was one that set out from Belfast in the spring of 1993. It was the first Irish expedition to Mount Everest, and it was led by Dawson Stelfox, an architect from Belfast. He and the seven other members of his team went to the summit of Everest by the notorious North Ridge. Stelfox reached the summit on May 27, 1993.

The major national sport in India, cricket, is popular in Northern Ireland, and this has resulted in a number of activities and connections that have indirectly helped to maintain Indian traditions. For a number of years, cricketers have come from India to play in local league teams during the summer season. This would have provided them with an opportunity to earn some money, and their presence would often be valued by the local Irish team. One such player was Raman Lamba, who once played in the Indian first class team. He has played for around eight years for North Down first eleven during the summer season. During the winter, while playing in India, he is Captain of the New Delhi team. His connection with Ireland is all the stronger since he is married to a local Irish girl!

Another player was Alf Masood, who was born in Lahore and played under 19's cricket for Pakistan, later becoming a naturalised Irish citizen and playing for Ireland and a number of Leinster league clubs.

In late 1994, the Northern Ireland Indian Gymkana Cricket Club was formed. It consisted of Indians who have settled in Northern Ireland, and it had its first competitive season in 1995.

For the generation who have been born in Ireland, going to India is almost like going to a foreign country. The climate, language, food, customs, standard of living, etc. are all so different to those they have been accustomed to in Northern Ireland. If the second-generation do go back to India, it is often in the company of their parents or simply for a holiday. It is very rare for a second-generation Indian, one who was born in Ireland, to return to India and settle there. The identification of the younger generation with Ireland rather than with India is shown by a recent incident where a young child of three years went to India with his mother. After a while there, he told his mother he wanted to go back home (i.e. to Ireland). When asked why, he replied – "Because all the other children here are black." Thus, he was not even aware of his own skin colour and could only identify with a culture where others were of a fair skin.

SECOND AND THIRD GENERATION INDIANS

While the 1950s and 1960s were the times when many Indian settlers, both in Northern Ireland and the Irish Republic, were getting their foothold and establishing themselves in the working communities, the

1970s and subsequent decades saw many Indians flourish on the foundations that they had built. In a sense, most of the stories of Indian settlers are success stories – the majority of them came from the Indian subcontinent with at the most only a few pounds in their pocket. They came to a country that differed in language, climate, culture, food habits and religion from the one that they had left, and yet they 'made it'. This was to a level at which they could afford a reasonable standard of living, usually own their own house, and readily provide for their children's needs.

Numbers

I have tried to obtain an independent estimate of the number of Indians in Northern Ireland by documenting the number of names of Indian origin in the Northern Ireland telephone directory. If one leaves out shop/business addresses, in the 1993 directory there were 201 such names. If one adds 2% to allow for ex-directory names, 2% for cases where a lady of Indian origin married someone from the local Irish community, and a further 2% for names that may have been inadvertently missed out, this then gives a total of 213 families. Assuming that there are approximately five members per household, this then would give a figure of 1065 people of Indian origin. Allowing for some limitations in using such a formula, it is remarkably similar to other figures that are generally adopted to indicate the numbers that are living in Northern Ireland.

Some research carried out by Martin Marger in the 1980s and reported in *New Community* (January 1989; 15: 203–210) estimated that there were 1200 of Indian origin in Northern Ireland.

It is interesting to compare the numbers of Indians with settlers from other parts of the world. In an article in the *Belfast Telegraph* of January 27, 1994, the following statistics – provided by the Multicultural Resource Centre in Belfast – were produced on the estimated population of various ethnic groups in Northern Ireland:

Chinese – 7,000
Travellers – 1,200
Indians – 1,000
Jews – 500
Pakistanis – 500
Vietnamese – 300
Iranians – 150
Italians – 150

A recent survey carried out in 1996 by the Centre for the Study of Conflict, University of Ulster, and documented by Greg Irwin, research fellow in the centre, found that there were 1050 Indians and 641 Pakistanis. It is worth noting that there are a number of individuals who, before 1947 (when India and Pakistan became separate countries) would have been classified as Indians, but who would now consider themselves as Pakistanis. When projecting an estimate to later years, growth in population has to be balanced against some emigration of Indians to Great Britain, and so the increase in future numbers may perhaps only be in the order of 10–20 people per year. The 1996 report by the Centre for the Study of Conflict put the number of Chinese to be between 3125 –5125, and the number of Travellers to be 1366.

'Illegal immigration' into Northern Ireland is very rare compared to mainland Britain, though a few cases have occasionally hit the headlines. One such case was that of Mr Harjinder Singh Bharaj, who worked as an engineer in India and who came to Northern Ireland in 1991 to study catering at Castlereagh College near Belfast at this own expense. He was arrested in August 1992 while helping out in a take-away restaurant in Belfast, since his temporary work permit had then expired. *The Sunday Life* newspaper, a local paper in Northern Ireland, took up his case and reported that for 32 days he was locked up in prison along with alleged child molesters and subjected to strip searches on a regular basis. He was released from prison on £12,000 bail. The local MP also took up his case, but to no avail and in November 1993 he was deported back to India.

Tinker, Tailor, Soldier, Sailor

While many of the Indians remain in the businesses that they or their fathers ran for the past few decades, many second and third generation Indians are also in a variety of other posts, ranging from the professions such as teaching and medicine, to industrial and catering fields. Many of those who have remained in business have branched out into property, wholesale business, etc. At the time of the field research for this book (1994–1996), there were around twenty Indian restaurants in Northern Ireland, with a further twenty 'take-away' cafés. It is worth noting that an increasing number of 'Indian' restaurants are in fact owned and staffed by Bangladeshis, a trend that is well developed in England. In his survey described above, Martin Marger estimated that the number of Indian restaurants and take-aways represented around 2.3% of the total number of restaurants in Northern Ireland, compared to the much

Sunblinds for hire

A hairdresser ready for work

A travel agent

A teacher with his pupils

A doctor examines a patient

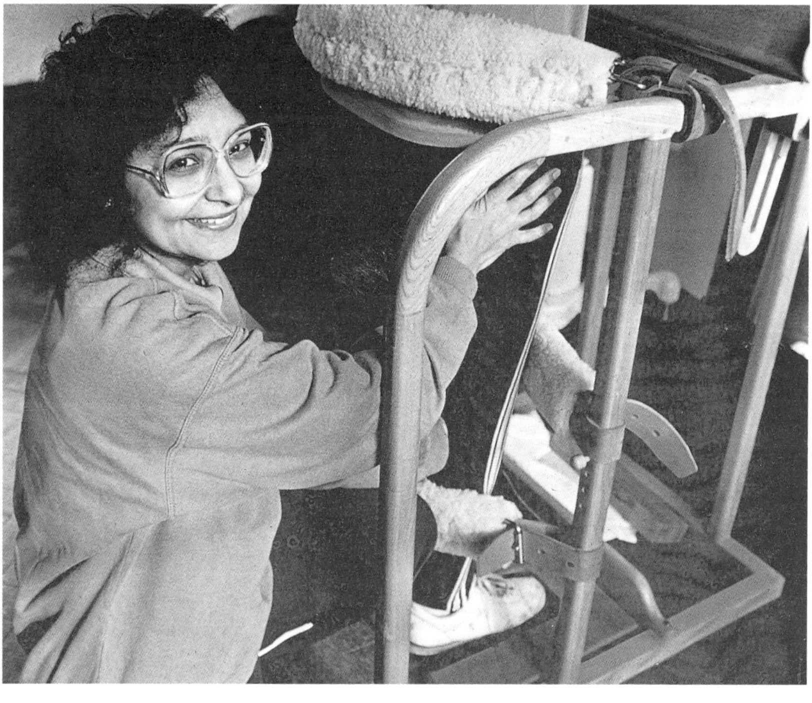

A physiotherapist at work

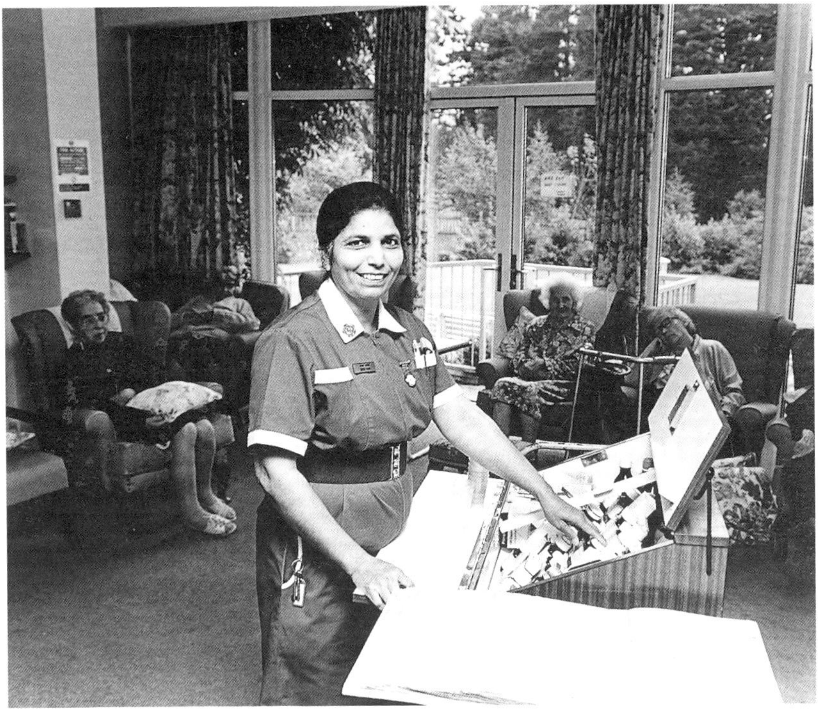

A nurse with her medicine trolley

An electrical engineer outside a power station

Clothes for sale

What's cooking?

larger number of Chinese restaurants – almost 18% of the total number of restaurants.

Very few Indians have entered unskilled/manual jobs, and the limited number of such jobs available – in view of the high unemployment rate in Northern Ireland – has meant that very few Indians have ventured to Northern Ireland from the rest of the United Kingdom to work in such jobs. To this extent, the business/professional mix of Indians who live in Northern Ireland is more similar to that found in North America than that found in England, where a sizeable number would be in factory work or similar fields.

Current Generation

The current generation of young Indians in Northern Ireland were invariably born in Northern Ireland and received their education there. Many have little fluency in Indian languages, and some have never set foot in India! A significant number will have chosen to enter into professions, with the rest in business ventures – these may in some cases be clothing businesses 'inherited' from their parents, but in other cases they will be quite different business ventures – e.g. dry cleaning, property, restaurant business, etc. Their sense of allegiance will tend to be to Northern Ireland first, and then India or Britain. Nevertheless, they still stand out in the local community due to the colour of their skin and some customs that they may continue to practise.

Most young Indians will not be vegetarians, as would have been their parents in many instances, and there would also be many fewer teetotallers compared to their parents' generation. Because they feel part of the local community, and have less cultural or family allegiance to India than their parents, they will tend to feel all the more aggrieved if they encounter racial discrimination or prejudice due to the colour of their skin. It is likely that in future years their children in turn will become more assimilated in the local community, there will be more instances of inter-marriage with the local community, and ties with India will inevitably become weaker. Indian culture is nevertheless a powerful force, and the advent of Asian television channels on cable/satellite TV has helped to keep this force alive. In addition, there will always be some instances of young Indian men going to India to seek a bride, one who will have inevitably been steeped in Indian culture. Therefore, some element of Indian traditions and values may be present for several generations to come amongst those of Indian origin in Northern Ireland.

The 1996 report by the Centre for the Study of Conflict found that the Indian community compared more favourably in terms of social profile than other major ethnic groups – there were higher rates of home ownership, more were better qualified, fewer were unemployed, and more were in the highest occupational classes. It is possible, therefore, that in future years these Indians may come to represent a second type of 'Irish Raj', perhaps a mirror image of the Irish Raj that was present in India several hundred years ago, but one that is much more benevolent and much more integrated into the local community!

APPENDIX 1

THE HINDU RELIGION IN IRELAND

Hindu Religion

Hinduism is the oldest living religion, with roots going back over 3,500 years to a time when a wave of migration brought the Aryan people down from the northwest into the Indus valley, and subsequently into the Ganges River plains and across India.

In practice, it involves a complex system of beliefs and institutions, based upon the ancient scriptures known as the Vedas, and finding expression in an immensely rich kaleidoscope of mythology and the worship of a multitude of deities.

While Hinduism may lay claim to millions of gods, in actual practice there are certain favourite gods that have become the focus of worship for the various Hindu sects. Three of the most important form a supreme trinity or triad, consisting of Brahma the Creator, Vishnu the Preserver, and Shiva the Destroyer. These three, however, like the other 330 million or so deities revered by Hindus, are aspects or manifestations of the one supreme Reality which is sought and worshipped. In this respect Hindus will reject the description of their religious practice as polytheistic, laying claim to an ultimately monotheistic faith in the final unity of the Divine Being. For the Hindu, the vast number of recognised deities, being part of the one supreme Reality, can therefore be used to represent that reality. Similarly, Hindus will repudiate the charge of idolatry in their worship; few, if any, could be said to worship the image, the material object itself. Beyond the form of the image (whether male or female, human or

FOOTNOTE: From Ryan, M (1996) *Another Ireland.* Belfast: Stranmillis College.

animal, or a combination of both) is the all-pervasive Brahman or Supreme Being. A common Indian tradition involves throwing away statues each new year to ensure that devotees remember that the statue is disposable – though not all Hindu groups observe this custom.

In accordance with its philosophy of the universality of truth and the recognition of many paths to God, Hinduism is extraordinarily receptive and inclusive in its attitude towards other faiths and traditions. The Christian festival of Christmas is often celebrated enthusiastically by the Hindu communities in the West, for example, and it is by no means unknown for Hindus to incorporate aspects of festivals associated with other world religions into their own traditional celebrations.

Hindus see life as a self-repeating cycle of events in which the manner in which one lives in this present existence will determine the quality of one's existence in a subsequent reincarnation, and by the law of Karma, this process will continue inexorably through many lives until one's spiritual destiny is ultimately worked out in the achievement of *moksha*, which means liberation or release from the grinding wheel of rebirths and successive existences. One can obtain liberation through many means, including devotion or selfless service, yoga exercises and meditation and one can choose any of these means according to one's ability, temperament, environment, and physical, mental and spiritual growth. Lord Krishna describes this freedom of faith and practice beautifully in the Bhagavadgita (the most famous and popular of Hindu scriptures):

> However men approach me
> Even so do I welcome them
> For the path men take
> From every side is mine.

For the devout Hindu the whole cosmos is one big family, and the supreme darma (ethic) is that of disinterested love and non-violence.

In another verse from the Gita, Sri Krishna sums up the entire art of living in one simple practical suggestion:

> To understand how to behave towards others,
> all we have to do is to understand
> that what gives us pain,
> gives others pain also.

Hindus in the Irish Republic meet mainly in each other's homes for religious observances. There are no temples and no recognised priesthood in the South (apart from the Hare Krishna Centre, which is described later in this chapter), and a priest has sometimes to be brought from Belfast for cremation funerals. But domestic worship is a strong tradition within Hinduism, and many homes have shrines where religious rituals are performed and all necessary observances carried out.

Different Hindus will select different gods for special attention in their worship. A shrine to Krishna, for example, might have many pictures of other gods and saintly figures, including those we associate with other traditions (e.g. Jesus, Muhammad, Mary, etc), as for Hindus the gods are not exclusive (nor indeed jealous) of each other.

Hindu Dress

There are no 'special' Hindu clothes, though many Hindu women favour the *sari*, the traditional garb of women. Saris are made from a single piece of cotton or silk measuring between 110 and 140 cm wide and five to eight metres in length. They are made in a great variety of bright colours, and are worn in different ways in different regions of India. The sari is usually pleated in the front, tucked into the petticoat to form a skirt, and then thrown over one shoulder. Sometimes a Hindu woman will cover her head with the sari. Usually a *choli* (a blouse or bodice) is worn under the top of the sari. A Hindu wife will often have a line of bright vermilion colour in the parting of her hair to show that she is married and that her husband is still alive. The small dot often seen on the forehead (called *tikka* or *bindi*) used to be the sign that a woman was married, but nowadays it is worn just as a decoration. Jewellery is also very popular, and many women have their noses pierced and wear a small ring or jewel in them.

The Northern Ireland Hindu Cultural Centre (*Mandal*) and Temple (*Mandir*) were established in 1979 following acquisition of premises formerly owned by the Methodist Church at Carlisle Circus in Belfast, and officially opened by his Excellency Dr. JP Singh, the High Commissioner of India, on 24th August, 1980.

The centre is administered and controlled by a committee of twenty trustees elected annually by the community, and is presided over by the full-time priest in residence at the Centre, Pandit Sharma.

The Centre is open every day from 9 a.m. to 12 noon, and from 5 p.m. to 8 p.m., with Temple services, normally lasting half-an-hour, at 10 a.m.

and 7 p.m. daily. There is no specially holy day in the week, but more extended acts of worship take place on Tuesday and Sunday afternoons, and at full moon.

The common terms used by Hindus for the worship of the gods are *arti* (praise) and *puja* (prayer) – though the terms are almost interchangeable. In place of sacrifices, these rituals take the form of offering gifts before images and symbols, with incense burning and chanting, and acts of reverence such as pressing the palms of the hands together in an attitude of worship. Normally, worship is led by the priest, but in Hinduism any responsible man can conduct worship and carry out other priestly duties. Although Hindus worship many gods and goddesses, most temples are dedicated to the service of a particular deity. The Belfast Temple is named after Lakshmi, the goddess of prosperity and wife of the great god Vishnu. She is a renowned beauty, sometimes depicted with four arms, holding a lotus.

As well as the services of worship, a range of cultural, social and educational activities take place at the Belfast Centre, including Hindi language classes for children during the summer months, Indian music classes and drama sessions. Dancing is a major feature of many occasions at the Centre. Hindus believe that dancing is the most beautiful of all the arts, and through it the stories and legends of the gods are re-enacted. The dancing and musicianship at the Belfast Temple is of a very high standard, adding great colour and excitement to festive occasions.

Visitors to the Belfast Centre will receive a warm and friendly reception whether attending one of the weekly gatherings or annual festive occasions, or at other convenient times, by arrangement with: Mrs Sharma, Secretary, The Indian Community Centre, 86 Clifton Street, Belfast 13 – telephone (01232) 249746. The Community's President is Mr TR Puri – telephone (01232) 628730.

School groups are always welcome, and the only convention to be observed on visits, apart from a general attitude of respectfulness, is that shoes must be removed before entering the Shrine Room. This practice is important to Hindus both because this area is considered to be holy ground, and also for reasons of hygiene. Sunday evening is usually a very good time to meet people and have things explained.

Externally, the building has little of ethnic interest, since the structure remains essentially that of a Christian Church. The social and recreational accommodation too is very much what one would expect to find within a Christian church complex: foyer, main hall, committee room, office, kitchen and store, on the ground floor; stage and auditorium, and some small rooms, upstairs. There is a small library off the main hall on the ground floor, with literature both in Hindi and English. The large kitchen can provide meals for several hundred people.

The Mandir, or Shrine Room, where prayers and rituals take place, is located to the right of the foyer, near the entrance to the main hall. Within, a kaleidoscopic wealth of colour and configurations dazzle the eye, as one surveys the phalanx of shrines arranged in order along the main wall of the sanctuary [*Plate 11, p. 97*].

Moving from left to right, the gods represented here [Plates 12–16, p. 97–99] are:

1. Hanuman, the monkey god, prominent in the Ramayana, which tells how he built a bridge from India to Sri Lanka by which Lord Rama crossed to rescue Sita from the demon King Ravana. His 'monkey face' reminds Hindus that one does not need to be beautiful to be a true servant of God.
2. Durga, the goddess of power or energy, whose eight arms symbolise the eight essential aspects of true life and religion – health, knowledge, planning, husbandry, reputation, unity, sincerity, compassion. Durga rides a lion, representing the need to keep the evil in human nature under control by the power of God. The crowns on and suspended above her head also symbolise the divine power.
3. Vishnu, the Preserver, whose four arms signify single-mindedness, true riches, good intentions, and liberation. In three of his hands he holds, respectively, a wheel (symbolising the universe), a shell which can be blown (symbolising spiritual awakening), and a weapon (symbolising that all power is from God and should be used only for good). His fourth hand is raised in blessing.
4. Lakshmi, wife of Vishnu, and goddess of good management and prosperity.
5. Lord Krishna, one of the most popular gods, and narrator of the Bhagavadgita (the most celebrated of the Hindu scriptures). It is believed that Krishna indwells every living thing. He carries a flute symbolising his desire to bring good cheer and encouragement to those who are oppressed by evil.
6. Radha, Lord Krishna's favourite consort. The Krishna – Radha love relationship is the theme of many devotional songs, symbolising divine – human love. The stories of Krishna's many love affairs are regarded by Hindus as parables illustrating the love between God and human souls.
7. Lord Sai Baba, an Indian guru born in 1926, who has established a Centre for religious teaching and spiritual living in South India, and

> regarded as worthy of a place among the gods. He is described as 'the father (Baba) and mother (Sai) of us all'. His simple clothing represents humility and love to all.

Set apart from the array of deities already described, in a special corner of the sanctuary, is the shrine of Lord Shiva, one of the greatest of the Hindu deities, who forms the triad with Brahma and Vishnu. He is known as the Destroyer, the counterpart of Vishnu, the Preserver, and is often depicted performing the Tandava, or 'world-shattering dance'. In this shrine, Shiva holds a ball, symbolising the world, and the image is set in the midst of a water fountain, representing the ubiquitous presence and peace of God.

The Temple shrines with their images are ceremonially washed with water and flowers by the priest twice every day.

Centrally placed above the main row of shrines is the great circular shield displaying at its centre the ancient symbol OM, the most sacred word in the Hindu faith, which signifies 'The Eternal' or 'The Ineffable'.

To the left of this central shield, another ancient Hindu symbol will be seen – the Swastika. This is considered to be a symbol of good fortune, and may represent the sun, or the wheel of Vishnu with the spokes bent. The limbs turn to the right, but when the Nazis adopted it as part of their insignia, they turned them to the left, which would be regarded by many authorities on symbolism as an evil omen.

Also centrally placed, at the base of the main row of shrines, is a small altar bearing a lamp with a continuously burning flame (*jyoti*) signifying the Divine Light, and a dish of simple offerings to the gods, of flowers and fruit.

Looking across the Shrine Room to the opposite wall, the visitor will see a striking array of prints of Hindu deities, overhung by a bell which is rung at the start of acts of worship to announce to the gods that worshippers are present, and to proclaim to the world that God's truth may be heard by all. A small platform for the priest and musicians leading the worship completes the furnishing of the sanctuary.

Major Hindu Festivals

Although the Hindu calendar is essentially lunar, some festivals are celebrated on the same date each year, whilst others are governed by the phases of the moon. The following are widely observed by Hindus annually, and are also the main festivals of Hindus in Ireland:

Lohri (January 13th) is a lighthearted occasion, reminiscent of Halloween, with coloured lights, bonfires, and feasting with nuts and fruit.

Shiva Ratri (February) is an all-night celebration in honour of Shiva, one of the greatest of the Hindu deities, regarded as constituting the triad with Brahma and Vishnu.

Holi (March) is the great springtime festival of Krishna, one of the most popular of Hindu gods; it is celebrated for five days with street dancing and processions, during which people throw red powder and coloured water over one another in a spirit of fun and rejoicing.

Baisakhi (April 13th) is the harvest festival, commonly observed throughout Northern India, and celebrated here with a typical vegetarian feast, music and dancing.

Rakhi (August) is otherwise known as Raksha Bandham; at this charming social function girls tie a silk thread on the wrist of a brother to protect him, while the brother promises to defend the girl, and gives her a special present.

Janamashtami (August) is a celebration of the birth of Lord Krishna at midnight when, as the clock strikes twelve, bells are rung, special prayers and hymns are recited, and the statue of the baby Krishna is placed in a flower-covered cradle.

Navaratri (October) is the festival in which nine days and nights are devoted to the worship of the many Hindu goddesses, especially Lakshmi, the goddess of riches and wife of Vishnu; Saraswati, the goddess of education and learning and the wife of Brahma; and Durga (or Parvati) who is the goddess of energy and power and the wife of Shiva.

Dussehra (October), immediately following Navaratri, is the day commemorating the rescue of Sita by Rama and the defeat of the evil demon Ravana, when this celebrated story is acted out in dance-drama.

Divali, or Diwali, or Dipawali (November) is the most festive time in the Indian calendar, when over a five-day period the festival of lights is celebrated with the lighting of many lamps (*divas*), exchange of cards and presents, and welcoming of the Hindu new year with fireworks, bonfires, dancing and feasting. The celebration also relates to Rama's victory over Ravana, and his safe return from exile to his capital, Ayodhya.

Hare Krishna – North and South

Hare Krishna, the popular name for the International Society for Krishna Consciousness (ISKCON), is part of an important and distinctive tradition of devotional faith, Gaudiya Vaishnavism, which began in the sixteenth century with the great saint Sri Chaitanya, but which participates in a much older movement possibly dating back thousands of years.

In 1965, as a representative of this essentially monotheistic tradition of Hinduism, His Divine Grace AC Bhaktivedanta Swami Prabhupada, on the order of his spiritual master, travelled from India at the age of seventy with the purpose of helping to re-establish spiritual principles in an increasingly atheistic and materialistic Western culture. Within the space of twelve years he established a worldwide confederation of over one hundred temples, schools and farm communities, and left more than seventy books on the culture, religion and philosophy of India, before his death in 1977.

Of the Indian gurus who came to the West during the sixties and seventies, Prabhupada was outstanding in that he refused to compromise the principles of the Vedic scriptures just to attract a following. He insisted that his disciples follow the four basic regulative principles of abstinence from meat-eating, illicit sex, intoxicants and gambling.

Vaishnavas (as Hare Krishna followers are more properly called) follow a spiritual process called 'bhakti-yoga' which aims at re-establishing one's forgotten, intimate relationship with God. 'Bhakti' is understood by Vaishnavas as being the essence of all bona fide monotheistic world religions, and they would see Christ and Muhammad as essentially teaching the same ideal of love of God.

Devotees became known as Hare Krishnas because of their frequent chanting of the Hare Krishna maha-mantra:

> 'Hare Krishna Hare Krishna, Krishna Krishna,
> Hare Hare, Hare Rama Hare Rama, Rama Rama.'

'Hare' means Lord and Krishna is the name of the god who is the particular focus of their worship.

The reason for the emphasis on chanting is to glorify God and to purify the heart of the material desires which prevent humans from understanding and truly loving him. The maha-mantra is a prayer and a meditative formula – a cry from the heart to God for protection from the miseries of the material world and for liberation of the spirit for the service of God.

Because the Hare Krishna movement came to the West during the sixties, there is a tendency in the minds of some to associate these groups with drug-taking, free love, and a 'hippy' lifestyle. In fact, their lifestyle is one of the most ordered and abstemious, and is often characterised by a genuine altruism, as demonstrated in the widespread 'Food for Life' programme which is dedicated to distributing food-aid to the needy. The food thus distributed is 'prashadam' (sanctified), and it is believed that the offering and partaking of it can help to make society more peaceful and prosperous.

A common practice in Hare Krishna communities is that of painting a leaf-pattern on the nose and forehead, representing a plant which is often offered by devotees to Lord Krishna; the lines imprinted in this process on the forehead represent the feet and toes of Krishna, suggesting symbolic bowing down at God's feet.

Wedding ceremonies in the Hare Krishna tradition [see plate 19] are extremely colourful and charming, and marked by homely but meaningful rituals and routines, with various symbolic actions, exchange of garlands and promises, rice-throwing, applause and good wishes to the happy couple. The atmosphere at these ceremonies is very relaxed and happy, with a delightful blend of informality with the traditional ritual observance (which at many points is comparable to the liturgy of a Christian wedding).

ISKCON has around a dozen Centres throughout the U.K. and Eire. Apart from a small community of about half-a-dozen Hare Krishna families who meet in each other's homes in Wicklow, there are three main ISKCON communities at present in Ireland – one in Dublin, and the other two in the North – as described below.

The Belfast Hare Krishna Temple, with its present address at Brooklands, 140 Upper Dunmurry Lane, Belfast BT17 0HE – telephone (01232) 620530, was first established in 1979, when two Hare Krishna devotees came from Dublin to Belfast to open a Centre originally in Agincourt Avenue. The President of the Temple is Padma-Malini Dasi.

Membership at the new Temple (opened in 1986) in Dunmurry is drawn from both Catholic and Protestant backgrounds, with two members presently from a background in Islam. Nearly all had stopped practising the religion of their birth before encountering ISKCON, but there are also some who have added Krishna consciousness to their original tradition and practice both together.

The community has developed slowly but steadily, and there are now about thirty members living in the two Northern Ireland temples with around a hundred congregational members in all. The husband and wife team who help lead the Dunmurry group, Shaunaka Rishi Das and Keshava Devi Dasi, report that the administration of the group 'has been a learning process over the years how to develop and maintain a community, and as most of the first members were very young, there have been the usual difficulties and mistakes; stability of the community has grown with the maturity of its members.'

Daily meetings at the Dunmurry Temple are held as follows:

4.30 a.m – Mangala aroti, incorporating the ceremony of deity worship; prayers to the spiritual master; congregational chanting (*kirtana*) of the holy names of God; worship of the sacred tulasi plant (*tulasi puja*); short reading from scripture.

7.00 a.m – Guru puja (worship of the spiritual master).

7.15 a.m. – Deity greeting and congregational chanting.

7.30 a.m. – Srimad Bhagavatam class (a talk and discussion on spiritual themes).

These sessions are attended by all residents of the Temple and by devotees who live nearby.

On Sundays at 3.30 p.m., there is a meeting attended by members of the congregation and by any members of the public who wish to come. This consists of chanting, a talk with open discussion of the philosophy of Krishna consciousness, deity worship, and a 'prasadam' feast of sanctified vegetarian food. The meeting ends at 6.30 p.m.

On Wednesdays between 6 p.m. and 7.30 p.m. there is a study group meeting for newer members who wish to deepen their knowledge of Krishna consciousness. This consists of chanting and a talk and discussion on the various scriptures, followed by a 'prasadam' meal.

There are also a couple of groups of congregational members who hold regular weekly or fortnightly meetings in their homes to discuss different aspects of their spiritual lives and for kirtana and prasadam.

The Belfast branch of the Hare Krishna 'Food for Life' programme has been formed recently to help distribute food to under-privileged people across the city. The community also offers courses on vegetarian cookery, meditation, and the study of the Vedic literature. A bi-monthly news-sheet, 'The Temple Times' is also produced. Occasionally, invitations are received to make presentations in schools and colleges.

The Dunmurry Temple is housed in a beautifully appointed villa, set amidst delightful gardens of trees and shrubs as well as a mini maze-hedge [see plate 17]. There is a well equipped kitchen and a very comfortably furnished lounge-reception room. The Shrine Room contains images of Radha-Krishna deities, and is decorated with pictures of Krishna and Lord Chaitanya, a sixteenth century Indian saint believed to be an incarnation of Krishna, very strongly opposed to the Caste system. Low tables and stools, rich hangings, incense burners, vases of flowers and a traditional 'throne' complete the furnishing of this elegant sanctuary. Rhythmic music on drum and bells accompanies the acts of worship [*Plate 18, p. 100*].

Hare Krishna Island, Inis Rath in Upper Lough Erne, County Fermanagh, is situated in the midst of one of Ireland's largest nature reserves. Following the principles of simple living and high thinking, the members of this rural asram are working towards a self-sufficient and ecologically harmonious situation with an emphasis on spiritual development.

As in the case of the Dunmurry community, the Hare Krishna devotees rise in the early hours to begin a morning of mantra meditation and bhakti yoga.

After the morning temple schedule there is breakfast, then a choice of activities ranging from cleaning and cooking to forestry work, building renovations and gardening. As a retreat Centre the island offers a perfectly conducive setting for study, introspection and meditation. As well as seminars and daily lectures and discussions, a twelve-week residential course of introduction to bhakti is available; students may enrol any time. Visitors are invited to come and stay for a day or two or longer, and are welcome to participate in different aspects of the community activities, or to choose to spend some time on their own. Overnight guests are asked to bring a sleeping bag, towel, etc. After three days guests are requested to contribute four hours work or £5.00 daily.

The Temple Room on Inis Rath has recently been renovated in traditional Vedic style with arches and rich decoration, as well as the many pictures and Radha-Krishna images, and a large silver and gold-plated altar.

Further information can be obtained by contacting: Giri, Hare Krishna Island, Derrylin, County Fermanagh, Northern Ireland, BT92 9EN – telephone (013657) 21512 (from U.K.) or (08 03657) 21512 (from Eire). To arrange picking up, boat crossing and accommodation visitors must phone the day before and on arrival in the nearest town – (Lisnaskea/Maguires Bridge/Ballyconnell). The name of the Temple President is Mani Das.

The Hare Krishna Cultural Centre, Dublin [*Plate 21, p. 102*], was first instituted in the mid nineteen-seventies, and became firmly established at its present premises in the city centre in 1982.

The Centre comprises a shop for the sale of artefacts and items of clothing, a Temple Room, and accommodation and facilities for the eight full-time members presently in residence. These members are from the United Kingdom, Ireland, the U.S.A., and Eastern Europe. The Temple President is a Scottish-born Krishnan, known as Giri Dhari Das. Whatever their social or national origin, Krishnan initiates are given a new spiritual Sanskrit name and strands of neck-beads to be worn throughout their lives.

As with the Northern ISKCON communities, each day begins here with a morning programme of religious observance:

4.30 a.m. – 5.00 a.m.	–	deity worship;
5.00 a.m. – 5.30 a.m.	–	readings and prayers;
5.30 a.m. – 7.30 a.m.	–	individual chanting using beads;
7.30 a.m. – 8.00 a.m.	–	worship of the spiritual master;
8.00 a.m. – 9.00 a.m.	–	Srimad Bhagavatam class (a talk with discussion).

Later in the day, members are often on the streets, chanting, distributing literature, and engaging in discussions with members of the public. Further meetings are sometimes held in the homes of congregational members. Bhagavadgita lectures for the public are given Monday to Friday at 6.30 p.m. Attendance varies from a few people to quite a sizeable gathering, depending on the occasion. Visits are sometimes made to colleges and other institutions for the purpose of giving talks.

Children of Hare Krishna followers go to special schools where learning how to advance in spiritual life and in knowledge of the scriptures is as much part of the curriculum as reading, writing and arithmetic.

As in the case of the Dunmurry community, an active 'Food for Life' programme is operated by the Dublin Hare Krishna Centre.

The centre-piece of the Temple Room in Dublin, with its arrangement of painted wooden arches and pillars, is the main shrine [Plate 21, p. 102] displaying prints of Lord Krishna and other deities – Sri Krishna Chaitanya, Prabhu Nityananda, Sri Advaita, Gadadhara, Sri Vasadi, Gaura, Bhakta, Vrinda – all associated in one way or another with Krishna. There are also photographs here of various gurus. Musical instruments for use in worship – drum, bells, sitar – are displayed beside the shrine.

Around the walls are scriptural texts and prints depicting different incarnations of Krishna. In one corner stands a symbolic 'throne' used solely to hold a framed portrait of His Divine Grace AC Bhaktivedanta Swami Prabhupada, who brought the tradition to the West. To one side of the throne are copies of the Bhagavadgita on shelves, while above hangs a banner displaying the famous Hare Krishna mantra in silver lettering.

Seating is in the form of low stools and mats scattered around the tiled floor, as well as a special floor-seat and a book-rest for use by speakers.

The address of the Hare Krishna Culture Centre in Dublin is: 56 Dame Street, Dublin 2 – telephone (003531) 6791306.

Hare Krishna Festivals.

Four main festivals are observed annually by Krishnans in each of the Irish communities, as follows:

1. ***Gaura-purnima*** takes place in March or April, and celebrates the birthday of Lord Chaitanya (believed to be an incarnation of Krishna) with fasting until moonrise, the performance of public chanting during the day, and in the evening the recital of stories and songs about Chaitanya with worship and feasting in the Temple.

2. ***Janmastami,*** in late summer (usually August) celebrates the nativity of Krishna, with fasting until midnight, when a special 'appearance of Krishna' ceremony takes place in the Temple, followed by a great feast. The day is spent in reading about the advent of Krishna, singing with musical accompaniment, and chanting.

3. ***Vyasa-puja,*** the day following Janmastami, celebrates the birthday of the founder guru, Srila Prabhupada, with fasting until midday and the performance of a special ceremony in which many flowers and garlands are offered to Prabhupada. Many devotees also prepare a written 'offering' or appreciation and some time is spent reading these out. There are also readings from the founder's biography. At midday, there is a communal feast.

4. ***Ratha-yatra,*** in the summer (usually July) is a major festival in Dublin, attended by devotees from all over Ireland, when the image of Lord Jagannatha (the Lord of the Universe) is pulled through the streets in a huge, colourful, wooden chariot. The festival involves feasting, dancing and chanting, and the assembled devotees join forces to help pull the cart. The deity at the centre of this celebration is not distinct from Lord Krishna, but represents one of Krishna's many incarnations. (The English word 'juggernaut' is derived from the name of this deity, because of the huge carts that are pulled along the roads in India at this festival).

A number of other, minor festivals are celebrated in the course of the year, to honour various gurus, with half-day fasts, congregational chanting, dancing, feasting and food distribution.

FURTHER READING

GENERAL BOOKS AND ARTICLES RELATING INDIA WITH IRELAND

Books

Cook, S. B. (1993). *Imperial affinities. Nineteenth century analogues and exchanges between India and Ireland*. New Delhi: Sage Publications.

Holmes, M. (Editor) (1997, in press). *Ireland and India*. Dublin: Trocaire.

Articles/Book Chapters

Devi, Ganesh (1992). India and Ireland: Literary Relations. In: J. McMinn (Ed), *The Internationalism of Irish Literature and Drama*. Colin Smythe.

BOOKS AND ARTICLES RELATING TO IRISH MEN AND WOMEN IN INDIA

Books

Davey, Cyril (1987). *Caring Comes First. The Leprosy Mission Story*. Basingstoke: Marshall Pickering.

Dick, Lois (1984). *Amy Carmichael: Let The Little Children Come*. Chicago: Moody Press.

Elliot, Elisabeth (1987). *A Chance to Die: The Life And Legacy Of Amy Carmichael*. Old Tappan, New Jersey: Fleming H Revell.

Grover V, Arora (1993). *Great Women of Modern India-1. Annie Besant*. New Delhi: Deep & Deep Publications.

Grover V, Arora (1993). *Great Women of Modern India-2. Sister Nivedita*. New Delhi: Deep & Deep Publications.

Hennessy, M. N. (1971). *The Rajah From Tipperary*. London: Sidgwick and Jackson.

Houghton, Frank (1953). *Amy Carmichael Of Dohnavur*. London: SPCK.

Murphy, Maureen (1995). *A Child Of Two Continents*. London: RSB Design.

O'Dwyer, M. (1925). *India As I Knew It*. Constable & Co Ltd: London.

Scoglund, Elisabeth (1994). *Amma: The Life And Words Of Amy Carmichael*. Grand Rapids: Baker Books.

Wilkinson, Margaret (1996). *At BBC Corner I Remember Amy Carmichael*. [This book – ISBN No. 0 948154 93 4 – is not widely available. It can be obtained (price £5.95 plus £1 for package and postage) from The Dohnavur Fellowship, 15 Elm Drive, Harrow, Middlesex, HA2 7BS].

Articles/Chapters

Bishop, Anthony (1969). An Irishwoman's account of the Indian mutiny. *Irish Sword*, IX, pages 38–46.

Cadell, Patrick (1950). Irish soldiers in India. *Irish Sword*, I, pages 76–79.

Cook, S. B. (1987). The Irish Raj: Social origins and careers of Irishmen in the Indian Civil Service, 1855–1914. *Journal of Social History*, 20: 507–529.

Fitzgerald, T. (1911). From Bombay to Salthill. *The Catholic Bulletin*, 1, pages 279–282.

Fraser, T. G. (1996). Ireland and India. In: K Jeffery (Ed), *An Irish Empire*. Manchester: Manchester University Press.

Murphy, L. D. (1925). Indian vignettes. *Irish Monthly*, LIII, pages 527–531.

Ruddock, George (1995). Amy Carmichael of Dohnavur (1867–1851). *Familia: Ulster Genealogical Review*, volume 11, pages 58–77. [At the time of writing this book, a list of minor corrections to the article could be obtained from the author – G Ruddock, 14 Carrickblacker Ave, Portadown, BT63 5BB, Northern Ireland].

Sharpe, Eric. (1996). The legacy of Amy Carmichael. *International Bulletin of Missionary Research*, July 1996, pages 121–124.

BOOKS AND ARTICLES RELATING TO INDIANS IN IRELAND

Fisher, M. (1996). Cork's Dean Mahomet. *Journal of the Cork Historical and Archaeological Society*, 101: 81–93.

Irwin, Greg (1996). *Ethnic Minorities In Northern Ireland*. Coleraine: University of Ulster, Centre for the Study of Conflict.

Mahomet, Dean. (1794). *Travels of Dean Mahomet. Volumes 1 and 2.* Published by Dean Mahomet. Printed by J Connor, Cork. *[A copy of this book is held in the British Library, British Museum, London. Ref. 1507/1395]*

Marger, M. N. (1989). Asians in the Northern Ireland Economy. *New Community*, volume 15, pages 203–210.

Ross, Alan. (1983). *Ranji. Prince of Cricketers*. London: Collins.

Ryan, M. (1996). *Another Ireland*. Belfast: Stranmillis College.

OTHER RELATED BOOKS AND ARTICLES

Books

Visram, R. (1987). *Indians in Britain*. London: Batsford.

ACKNOWLEDGEMENTS (REFERENCE MATERIALS)

The following sources have been especially useful in my research for this book, and I kindly acknowledge the help that they provided. I apologise to any individuals or organizations that I have left out, and I hope they may let me have relevant information that I can include in any subsequent printing of the book.

Rev. Maurice Ryan and Stranmillis College for permission to reproduce photographs and text from the book *Another Ireland* (1996).

Greg Irwin and the Centre for the Study of Conflict, University of Ulster.

Cook, S. B. (1993). *Imperial affinities. Nineteenth century analogues and exchanges between India and Ireland.* New Delhi: Sage Publications.

Cook, S. B. (1987). The Irish Raj: Social origins and careers of Irishmen in the Indian Civil Service, 1855–1914. *Journal of Social History*, 20: 507–529.

Fisher, M. (1996). Cork's Dean Mahomet. *Journal of the Cork Historical and Archaeological Society*, 101: 81–93.

Jiwa, S. (1986). *The Death of Air India flight 182*. London: Star Books.

Visram, R. (1987). *Indians in Britain*. London: Batsford.

Hennessy, M. N. (1971). *The Rajah from Tipperary*. London: Sidgwick and Jackson.

Devi, Ganesh (1992). India and Ireland: Literary Relations. In: J. McMinn (Ed), *The Internationalism of Irish Literature and Drama.* Colin Smythe.

Fraser, T. G. (1996). Ireland and India. In: K Jeffery (Ed), *Ireland and the Empire*. Manchester University Press.

Dutta, K. and Robinson, A. (1995). *Rabindranath Tagore*. London: Bloomsbury.

Grover, V, Arora. (1993). *Great Women of Modern India-1. Annie Besant*. New Delhi: Deep & Deep Publications.

Grover, V, Arora. (1993). *Great Women of Modern India-2. Sister Nivedita*. New Delhi: Deep & Deep Publications.

Gordon, L. A. (1990). *Brothers Against The Raj. Sarat & Subhas Chandra Bose*. New York: Columbia University Press.

Volumes of the Selected Writings of Mahatma Gandhi. Published by the *Publications Division of the Ministry of Information and Broadcasting, Government of India,* with the support of the *Navajivan Trust*.

Plus Northern Ireland, October issue, 1990.

The *Asian Age* newspaper.

Dr W Hart, University of Ulster.

Dr C K Munro, Londonderry.

Mrs George Duncan.

The Dohnavur Fellowship.

The Irish Presbyterian Church.

The Church Missionary Society.

The Irish Tourist Board and Ballynahinch Hotel.

Hulton Getty Picture Collection Limited.

Popperfoto Picture Library.

The Illustrated London News Picture Library.

The Belfast Telegraph Newspaper.

The Derry Journal Newspaper.

Ireland's Eye Magazine.

Public Records Office of Northern Ireland.

The British Library, London.

Centre for South Asian Studies, University of Cambridge.

Indian Institute Library, University of Oxford.

ACKNOWLEDGEMENTS (PICTURE MATERIALS & TEXT)

PICTURE MATERIALS

Sri Aurobindo © Asian Age
HRH The Maharaja Ranjitsinji © Ballynahinch Castle
Ballynahinch Castle © Ballynahinch Castle
Accident Scene © Belfast Telegraph
Imperial Airways Poster © British Airways Archives and Museum Collection
General George Thomas © By permission of The British Library (V18062)
Lady Dufferin © By permission of The British Library (Photo 2/1(4))
Amritsar Street © By permission of The British Library (566(4))
General Reginald Dyer © By permission of The British Library (V8014)
Area of Lahore known as Bhatti Gate © Concept Media Pte Ltd.
Amy Carmichael © The Dohnavur Fellowship Corporation
Preena © The Dohnavur Fellowship Corporation
Nehru arriving at Dublin Airport © G A Duncan
Nehru receiving an Honorary Degree at Iveagh House © G A Duncan
Nehru in procession © G A Duncan
Nehru with a group of children © G A Duncan
Nehru presenting a prize © G A Duncan
Sake Dean Mahomet © East Sussex County Library
Mahomet's Baths © East Sussex County Library
Hugh Boyd © Hulton Getty Picture Collection
Sir John Lawrence © Hulton Getty Picture Collection Ltd
Henry Lawrence © Hulton Getty Picture Collection Ltd
Lawrence Brothers © Hulton Getty Picture Collection Ltd
Sir Henry Lawrence at the siege of Lucknow © Hulton Getty Picture Collection Ltd

Annie Besant © Hulton Getty Picture Collection Ltd
Michael O'Dwyer © Hulton Getty Picture Collection Ltd
Mahatma Gandhi © Hulton Getty Picture Collection Ltd
Subhas Bose © Hulton Getty Picture Collection Ltd
Rabindra Nath Tagore © Hulton Getty Picture Collection Ltd
William Yeats © Hulton Getty Picture Collection Ltd
K S Ranjitsinji, Cricketer © Hulton Getty Picture Collection Ltd
Destruction of Lahore © The Illustrated London News
Crowds of Hindu and Sikh refugees at Lahore Station © The Illustrated London News
Hindus and Sikhs on a crowded lorry © The Illustrated London News
A column of Hindus and Sikhs leaving the Punjab © The Illustrated London News
Mother Teresa with Mary Robinson © Irish Times
Dr Bhamjee © Irish Times
Margaret and James Cousins © Dr C K Munroe
General Sir Eyre Coote © National Portrait Gallery
Lord Dufferin © National Portrait Gallery
Sarat Bose with Eamon de Valera © Netaji Research Bureau, Calcutta
Yella © Popperfoto/Reuters
Rev Dr WG Mulligan © Presbyterian Church in Ireland
John Nicholson © 'The Graham Mutiny Papers' PRONI (1980)
Dr James Graham © 'The Graham Mutiny Papers' PRONI (1980)
Romanies in their Original Homeland © Rex Features
Dublin Mosque © Revd. Michael Ryan
Elevation, New Islamic Centre, Dublin © Revd. Michael Ryan
Hare Krishna Centre, Dunmurry, Belfast © Revd. Michael Ryan
Shrine Room, Hare Krishna Centre, Belfast © Revd. Michael Ryan
Bridal Party, Hare Krishna Wedding, Belfast © Revd. Michael Ryan
Hare Krishna Cultural Centre, Dame Street, Dublin © Revd. Michael Ryan
Main Shrine, Hare Krishna Centre, Dublin © Revd. Michael Ryan
Sikh Gurdwara, Dublin © Revd. Michael Ryan
Sikh Shrine, Dublin Temple © Revd. Michael Ryan
Hanuman the Monkey God © Revd. Michael Ryan
Vishnu and his Consort, Lakshmi © Revd. Michael Ryan
Durga, Godess of Power © Revd. Michael Ryan
Lord Sai Baba © Revd. Michael Ryan
Lord Krishna and his Consort Radha © Revd. Michael Ryan

TEXT ITEMS

The Story of Patricia and George Yathindran, published on 3rd January 1969 © (Belfast) News Letter

A report on the bombing of a clothing warehouse in Belfast owned by the Tohani family, published on 5th April 1977 © Belfast Telegraph

A report referring to a Downtown Radio broadcast, published on 12th January 1994 © Belfast Telegraph

INDEX

Names of people are indicated in *italics.* Names of places are in CAPITALS. Page numbers of whole sections that cover a particular topic are in **bold**.